MY BROTHER'S KEEPER

My Brother's Keeper

Edited,
with an Introduction and Notes, by Richard Ellmann
Preface by T. S. Eliot

James Joyce's Early Years

by Stanislaus Joyce

NEW YORK · *The Viking Press* · MCMLVIII

PUBLISHED IN 1958 BY
THE VIKING PRESS, INC.
625 MADISON AVE., NEW YORK 22, N. Y.

LIBRARY OF CONGRESS CATALOG CARD NUMBER: 58-5403

PRINTED IN U.S.A. BY THE HADDON CRAFTSMEN
SCRANTON, PA.

The publishers' acknowledgments and thanks are due to Mrs. W. B. Yeats for permission to reprint letters by W. B. Yeats; to Mr. Sean MacBride for permission to reprint a letter by Maud Gonne; to Mr. Frank Archer for letters by William Archer, as well as the courtesy of the British Drama League in that connection; and to Mr. Diarmuid Russell for the letters by George W. Russell (AE).

Contents

Preface

by T. S. Eliot

CURIOSITY ABOUT THE PRIVATE life of a public man may be of three kinds: the useful, the harmless, and the impertinent. It is useful, when the subject is a statesman, if the study of his private life contributes towards the understanding of his public actions; it is useful, when the subject is a man of letters, if the study throws light upon his published works. The line between curiosity which is legitimate and that which is merely harmless and between that which is merely harmless and that which is vulgarly impertinent, can never be precisely drawn. In the case of a writer, the usefulness of biographical information, for increasing our understanding and making possible a keener enjoyment or a more critical valuation, will vary according to the type of which the writer is a representative, and the way in which he has exploited his own experience in his books. It is difficult to believe that greater knowledge about the private life of Shakespeare could much modify our judgment or enhance our enjoyment of his plays; no theory about the origin or mode of composition of the Homeric poems could alter our appreciation of them as poetry. With a writer like Goethe, on the other hand, our interest in the man is inseparable from our interest in the work; and we are impelled to supplement and correct what he tells us in various ways about himself, with information from outside sources; the more we know about the man, the better, we think, we may come to understand his poetry and his prose.

In the case of James Joyce we have a series of books, two of which at least are so autobiographical in appearance that further study of the man and his backgound seems not only suggested by our own inquisitiveness, but almost expected of us by the author himself. We want to know who are the originals of his characters, and what were the origins of his episodes, so that we may unravel the web of memory and invention and discover how far and in what ways the crude material has been transformed. Our interest extends, therefore, inevitably and justifiably, to Joyce's family, to his friends, and to every detail of the topography and the life of Dublin, the Dublin of his childhood, adolescence, and young manhood. What Joyce's brother Stanislaus has done for us is to make us acquainted with the family environment in which the two boys grew up, with details that no one else could have provided. We regret that he died leaving the story unfinished: we shall never have, from any other source, the account of the middle years in Trieste which Stanislaus could have given us. But we are fortunate to have so full an account of boyhood and youth in Dublin, by the man who was observing and studying his brother, sedulously, admiringly, and jealously, as no one else ever observed or studied him.

It would be a mistake, however, to classify this book as merely a unique piece of documentation on the early life of one of the great writers of the century. *My Brother's Keeper* is also a remarkable exposition of the relationship between a famous man and a brother of whose existence the world remained unaware. Stanislaus himself, in this book, becomes as interesting to us as James. The brothers are so much alike and yet so different! James Joyce was devoted to his father, and to his father's memory; the attitude of Stanislaus was very different, as instanced by his report of the terrible scene at their mother's death-bed. Where James, in political and religious matters, was indifferent or merely mocking, Stanislaus manifests a sometimes appalling violence. I have read the book twice, and find myself fascinated and repelled by the personality of this positive, courageous, bitter man who was a prey to such mixed emotions of affection, admiration, and antagonism—a struggle in the course of which, as Mr. Ellmann in his introduction points out, he saw his famous brother, at certain moments, with a startling lucidity of vision. I had thought that the book might be entitled *Memories of a Son and Brother*—with a difference. With another difference, *My Brother's Keeper* has a quality of candour which reminds me of Gosse's *Father and Son*. Possessed as he was by the subject of his memoir, Stanislaus Joyce, under the exasperation of this thorn in his flesh, became himself a writer, and the author of this one book which is worthy to occupy a permanent place on the bookshelf beside the works of his brother.

Introduction

by R<small>ICHARD</small> E<small>LLMANN</small>

T<small>O</small> <small>BE THE BROTHER OF A FA-</small>mous author confers its large duties as well as its small distinctions. Professor Stanislaus Joyce, who died in Trieste on June 16, 1955, at the age of seventy, bore his curious burden with nobility and discomfort. He was among the first to recognize James Joyce's genius, but he found his character 'very difficult' and his later work a waste. In spite of these reservations, he lived a life that was largely shaped for him by his brother's, he guarded truculently from others the right to criticize James, and at the time of his death he had written a substantial part of a memoir of their life together.

The book's title, *My Brother's Keeper*, summed up his painful service and his sense of bondage, and something else as well. When he referred to it himself, he would give the title and then add, smiling wryly, 'You know . . . Cain'. In part he wished to disarm the criticism he expected of his candour. Mainly he wished to put his case before an imagined tribunal, and sardonically presented himself as Cain because the evidence would show he was not. Yet he may also have felt his own role as helper to be a little ambiguous, confused, even, by a muted struggle for mastery over the creature who so mastered him. Like all his family, including his many sisters, Professor Joyce was capable of such great and sudden insights. It is not difficult to understand how genius cropped up in this household.

Although the title of *My Brother's Keeper* is only slightly applicable to the years described in this book, it has seemed too important to change. The memoir presents a picture of James Joyce's career and family life through his twenty-second year, with occasional glimpses of what was to come. The period when Professor Joyce did in fact keep his brother began a little later. If he had lived to finish his book, he would have told how in Trieste, from 1905 to 1915, he saved his brother from dubious friends, from dissipation, and from the greater danger of inertia. He would have made this claim as imperatively as possible (he does so in uncollected essays), because James never admitted either that he had been saved or that he needed saving. Yet there seems to be no reason to deny that James spent the ten years getting into scrapes and that Stanislaus spent the ten years getting him out of them.

Another claim Professor Joyce makes is even less contestable. Contrary to the fictional representation of the Joyce family life in *A Portrait of the Artist as a Young Man*, he demonstrates that his brother had an intelligent and sympathetic adherent in his own house. For if Stanislaus was later a keeper, he was always a disciple. Born December 17, 1884, he was nearly three years his brother's junior. He trailed him worshipfully. As a boy, he dutifully played truant with him. A few years later he began to serve as what James called in *Ulysses*, a little disparagingly, his 'whetstone'. James tried out his theories on Stanislaus, and Stanislaus made useful objections which helped clarify them. Then he began to note down his brother's clever remarks, and his own, in a diary, for he too had literary ambitions. In the diary, which often saw several rewritings, he tried a few experiments, as when, after reading Tolstoy's *Sebastopol Sketches*, he wrote down all the thoughts of a person going to sleep. James read what he wrote and patronizingly put it aside, but may have drawn from it one of several hints for the interior monologue. In later years, however, James preferred to attribute the discovery of the technique to the forgotten French writer Edouard Dujardin rather than to a member of his family.

Originally James intended to use Stanislaus prominently in his autobiographical novel. So in *Stephen Hero,* the trial run for *A Portrait of the Artist as a Young Man,* he depicts him as Stephen's brother Maurice, and speaks with chaffing affection of his 'sombre gravity' and 'his careful cleaning of his much worn clothes'. The two must have made a startling contrast as they walked through the streets of Drumcondra and Fairview, deep in talk or laughing, heads thrown back, in the unrestrained way of which both were unexpectedly capable; Stanislaus heavy-set, of medium height, muscular, James tall, thin, loose-jointed. In their manners too they were opposites, James unpredictable, Stanislaus as downright as a character in Ben Jonson. Stanislaus followed James's intellectual lead in most things, but he usually went further. So James bade farewell coolly enough to the Catholic church, but Stanislaus continued throughout his life to shake his fist at it. He became, even as a young man, so extreme in his apostasy that James, though seldom the peacemaker, suggested he moderate his revolt a little in the interest of family harmony.

Stanislaus recognized his indebtedness to James, but he also exhibited a sporadic independence of him that was by turns heroic and pathetic. In his diary for September 1903, when he was eighteen, he tried to analyse the problem:

My life has been modelled on Jim's example, yet when I am accused by my unprepossessing Uncle John or by Gogarty of imitating Jim, I can truthfully deny the charge. It was not mere aping as they imply; I trust I am too clever and my mind too old for that. It was more an appreciation in Jim of what I myself really admire and wish for most. But it is terrible to have a cleverer older brother. I get small credit for originality. I follow Jim in nearly all matters of opinion, but not all. Jim, I think, has even taken a few opinions from me. In some things, however, I have never followed him. In drinking, for instance, in whoring, in speaking broadly, in being frank without reserve with others, in attempting to write verse or prose or fiction, in manner, in ambition, and not always in friendships. I perceive that he regards me as quite commonplace and uninteresting—he makes no attempt at disguise—and though I follow him fully in this matter of opinion I cannot be expected to like it. It is a matter beyond the power of either of us to help.

This self-portrait is unduly harsh; a little later he notes that his brother has praised his criticism as brilliant, yet even praise fills him with doubt. The diary contains also a portrait of his brother, written at the same time, and while its tone is a little censorious, Stanislaus is obviously under James's spell:

Jim is a genius of character. When I say 'genius' I say just the least little bit in the world more than I believe; yet remembering his youth and that I sleep with him, I say it. Scientists have been called great scientists because they have measured the distances of the unseen stars and yet scientists who have watched the movements in matter scarcely perceptible to the mechanically aided senses have been esteemed as great, and Jim is, perhaps, a genius though his mind is minutely analytic. He has, above all, a proud wilful vicious selfishness out of which by times now he writes a poem or an epiphany, now commits the meanness of whim and appetite, which was at first protestant egoism, and had perhaps, some desperateness in it, but which is now well-rooted—or developed?—in his nature, a very Yggdrasil.

He has extraordinary moral courage—courage so great that I have hoped that he will one day become the Rousseau of Ireland. Rousseau, indeed, might be accused of cherishing the secret hope of turning away the anger of disapproving readers by confessing unto them, but Jim cannot be suspected of this. His great passion is a fierce scorn of what he calls the 'rabblement'—a tiger-like, insatiable hatred. He has a distinguished appearance and bearing and many graces: a musical singing and especially speaking voice (a tenor), a good undeveloped talent in music, and witty conversation. He has a distressing habit of saying quietly to those with whom he is familiar the most shocking things about himself and others, and, moreover, of selecting the most shocking times for saying them, not because they are shocking merely, but because they are true. They are such things that, even knowing him as well as I do, I do not believe it is beyond his power to shock me or Gogarty with all his obscene rhymes. His manner however is generally very engaging and courteous with strangers, but, though he dislikes greatly to be rude, I think there is little courtesy in his nature. As he sits on the hearth-rug, his arms embracing his knees, his head thrown a little back, his hair brushed up straight off his forehead, his long face red as an Indian's in the reflection of the fire, there is a look of cruelty in his face. Not that he is not gentle at times, for he can be kind and one is not surprised to find gentleness in him. (He is always simple and open with those that are so with him.) But few people will love him, I think, in spite of his graces and his genius and whosoever exchanges kindnesses with him is likely to get the worst of the bargain.

Characteristically Stanislaus began to doubt the artistic precision of the description he had just made; and after it he wrote in parenthesis in his clear, methodical hand, '(This is coloured too highly, like a penny cartoon.)'.

When a year later, in October 1904, James Joyce abruptly decided to leave Ireland with a young woman named Nora Barnacle, whom he declined to marry, many of his friends and relatives thought him as much a fool as a dastard. Stanislaus had his own misgivings, but he staunchly defended James and kept up an active correspondence with him. James took up residence first in Pola, at that time the principal naval port of the Austro-Hungarian empire, and then nearby in Trieste, where he taught at the Berlitz School. He depended upon Stanislaus for news and even to some extent for subjects. With the avidity of an Oscar Wilde, plotting his fictional character as one might a course, he demanded every scrap of information about the response of Dubliners he knew to his rather histrionic departure. He frequently borrowed initial hints for his stories from Stanislaus: for 'The Dead', Stanislaus's description of an Irish tenor's way of singing a sepulchral chorus in a song of Tom Moore; for 'A Painful Case', Stanislaus's account of a meeting with a married woman at a concert. Inspired cribbing was always part of James's talent; his gift was for transforming material, not for originating it, and Stanislaus was the first of a series of people on whom he leaned for ideas. As he remarked in later life to Frank Budgen, 'Have you ever noticed, when you get an idea, how much *I* can make of it?'

The brothers were not separated for long. After James's departure Stanislaus had some meager employment as a clerk, but wrote so bitterly of Ireland that James invited him to come to Trieste at least for a visit. The invitation, made more and more importunately over several months, seemed to Stanislaus even at that time to be in part a plea for support. He had never been away from home before, and Trieste, then in Austria, must have seemed to his twenty years the end of the earth. Like James, too, he was fonder of Dublin than his excoriations of the city indicated. But he obediently packed up and left for Trieste, arriving there in October 1905.

His early letters to his family show him extremely homesick. He was alarmed, too, to find his brother drinking heavily. He had known too much drunkenness in Ireland to tolerate it here. He asserted a moral authority over James, which he was able to enforce by stronger muscles, in dragging him away from bars. James left him in 1906 and went to live in Rome for six months; but, not liking that city, he returned to Trieste in 1907 to be dragged away from bars some more.

The brothers quarrelled frequently and were the more bound to each other. They taught for a time at the Berlitz School, then, finding they could do better with private lessons, left it. Their styles of teaching reiterated their differences. Stanislaus was punctual and conscientious in his duties. James invariably arrived for his lessons late, and after a brief drill began to converse about all manner of subjects; the lesson would end with teacher and pupil singing an Irish song together, after which James would slide down the banister and leave, also very late. James was extravagant in fancy and in finance, and the proceeds of Stanislaus's lessons often ended—after James, smiling and smoking a Virginia, had presented his latest need—in James's pocket. The seasonal problem—that their pupils left Trieste during the hot summer months—was too much for James, who could not put by for the summer, and depended on Stanislaus to stave off disaster. When he revamped in *Finnegans Wake* the fable of the dancing grasshopper and the saving ant, who had a seasonal problem too, he drew upon his experience with his brother by letting the improvident grasshopper carry the day.

Stanislaus kept his brother in humour as well as in funds. He encouraged him when publishers sent rejection slips, as they did almost steadily from 1905 until 1914. It was he also who put the poems of *Chamber Music* into a sequence and thought of that title for them. In 1907, just before they were to be published, James suddenly decided that their sentiment was false, and went to cable the publisher, Elkin Mathews, not to bring them out. Stanislaus walked up and down in front of the Trieste post office arguing with him; he finally persuaded James to allow the book to appear because it would help him publish other books. The contrast of opinion was typical: Stanislaus's judgment was sound in practical terms, but James was right in that *Chamber Music* looks pale beside his other works. It was Stanislaus also who suggested the title *Stephen Hero* for the early version of the *Portrait*; he based it on the ballad 'Turpin Hero' that his brother loved to sing. He also advised him, when he began to rewrite it, to turn the book into an Irish *Faust,* and this suggestion may account for some of the ruthlessness with which Joyce endows his hero in the later version.

Until the First World War Stanislaus continued to play Sancho Panza, as Italo Svevo and other Triestine friends inevitably remarked, to James's Don Quixote. But his pleasure in the part waned. His sense of an absurdity in his thraldom had grown, and in his disaffection he was accidentally helped by the war, which divided him from his brother. In Trieste the Austrian authorities did not trouble British subjects at first, and according to one story which James retailed, Stanislaus in his doctrinaire way trusted too much to their indifference. He drove around the city with an irredentist friend and was arrested and then interned in an Austrian castle. James, as usual, made out better; through the intervention of powerful friends he was allowed to depart with his family for Switzerland, and spent the war years in comparative comfort in Zurich. There he wrote the greater part of *Ulysses*. He also returned to drinking, but this did not have the disastrous consequences foretold by Stanislaus; underneath the excesses, James was able to maintain a secret discipline about his work.

Stanislaus's internment was not very rigorous, and as soon as war ended he returned to Trieste and resumed his teaching. It was like him to establish himself permanently in the city James first suggested to him, while James experimented with several others. By now Stanislaus had a group of friends who respected his obstinate, forthright personality, and liked his vigour of judgment and blunt humour. During his separation from James he had thought of not resuming the role of keeper, and James, for his part, had found other keepers whose discipline was less severe.

So when James arrived in Trieste late in 1919, their relations were altered. He had an income from a generous patron and was less dependent upon Stanislaus's aid; Stanislaus was understandably rather resentful of his brother's lack of gratitude. At one time James had talked of dedicating *Dubliners* to him, but when the book was published he had forgotten it. And in the transformation of *Stephen Hero* into *A Portrait of the Artist*, the main casualty, though for good artistic reasons, was Maurice, Stephen's brother. Stanislaus did not mention these or other grievances, but during the war he had written James that he hoped to take better care of himself after it. He received his brother rather coldly, listened to him less attentively, and allowed himself to be a little bored by the intricacies of the researches for *Ulysses*.

James spent nine months in Trieste, teaching at a commercial

school which had now become the Università di Trieste. The
city, so fallen from its former busy greatness as Austria's mer-
chant port, no longer pleased him. He quickly resolved to leave,
and was persuaded by Ezra Pound to go to Paris in June 1920,
so as to arrange more easily for the publication of *Ulysses*.

At first Stanislaus was passed over for his brother's position
at the university, but after a year it was given to him, and he
became a successful and popular professor. In 1927 he married
his student Nelly Lichtensteiger, an attractive young woman
from a comfortably situated Triestine family of Swiss descent.
The next year the two Joyce families met at Salzburg.

Professor Joyce's stubborn spirit never permitted him to
conceal his opposition to Mussolini's regime, and in 1936 he
was expelled from Italy. This punishment was later commuted
to dismissal from his professorship. James, who had been accustomed to receiving rather than doing favours for Stanislaus,
helped him on this occasion. He met him in Zurich and arranged for him to obtain a teaching post at a boys' school near
Zug; but Stanislaus decided that its rigid schedule was not for
him, and managed, through the intercession of a friend in Rome,
to be restored to his position in Trieste.

The brothers met only three times after 1920. These last
encounters were rather shocking to Stanislaus. When he began
to discuss fascism, his brother said impatiently, 'Don't talk to me
about politics. I'm only interested in style'. James, then working
on *Finnegans Wake*, seemed to Professor Joyce to be consciously *arrivé* and rather inaccessible, surrounded by admirers
and drinking more than ever. Stanislaus had not approved
wholeheartedly of either of the books his brother wrote away
from his side. *Ulysses* appeared to him at first to be wilfully
derogatory of human life, lacking in those moments of serenity

which he remembered as part of his life in Dublin. In after years, however, he saw more humanity in it than before, and gave most of it his praise. *Finnegans Wake*, however, struck him as the sorry effect of the adulation lavished on James in Paris; his brother seemed to him so sure of approval for whatever he did that he had lost interest in communication. He could hardly have sympathized, either, with the treatment of the theme of two brothers in that book. Shem, who resembles James, is a penman, while his brother Shaun, modelled to some extent upon Stanislaus (whose first name, which he never used, was John), is a postman; Shem is a madcap and Shaun a goodygoody boy; Shem is a profligate and Shaun a Tartuffe; Shem is a tree and Shaun a stone. Joyce of course had more in mind than his own fraternal relations, but these played their part too.

Back in Trieste, Stanislaus repeatedly wrote urging James to abandon *Finnegans Wake* and to write something of greater value. When the book was published in 1939, James offered Stanislaus a copy, but Stanislaus refused it, deliberately repudiating for the first time one of his brother's books. They continued to correspond, nevertheless, and it was fitting that James's last note to anyone, written five days before his death in Zurich in 1941, should have been to Stanislaus. It was a letter-card giving him the names of Italian and other friends who might be able to help him, for Professor Joyce had been put into semi-internment at Florence as an enemy alien. The subsequent news of his brother's death made Stanislaus physically ill; he regretted painfully not having accepted the last proffered gift.

Their estrangement was dissolved by James's death, and Professor Joyce made himself the keeper of his brother's reputation, repeatedly emerging from silence to denounce some distortion of his brother's youth by other writers of memoirs.

Stanislaus's only child, born two years after his brother's death, received his brother's name. During the war he became absorbed in setting down in a book his recollections of James. He conceived his brother's life in botanical terms as the story of a flower's burgeoning and then of its blasting—the blasting to occur after James's final departure from Trieste. He wrote on the basis of a good memory and of the diary which he kept faithfully throughout his life. The finished section, somewhat over half the book he intended to write, is remarkably frank and searching, but what gives his record its special force is that complex mixture of frustration, affection, resentment, and regret which Stanislaus had for the days when he was closest to his brother.

The exile of Stanislaus from Ireland was much stricter than James's. For forty-nine years he did not re-enter an English-speaking country, while his brother made a series of trips to Ireland and England. But during the summer of 1954, Professor Joyce decided to travel to England and perhaps even to Ireland. Not having money to waste, he arranged to go to London as guide for a group of Triestine students; they travelled as cheaply as possible and sat up on trains and boats for a day and a half. His health had seemed excellent but the strain affected his heart; yet he stubbornly rejected a diagnosis of heart trouble and shopped among doctors looking for one who agreed with him that the discomfort was of no consequence. Those who saw him then felt, nevertheless, the perplexity into which the sudden question had forced him.

Professor Joyce was invited to Dublin but decided not to go, feeling that if he went he would have to tell his fellow-countrymen that their only reason for respecting his brother now was his acclaim abroad, to which they could not entirely shut their ears. He returned to Trieste to find his health more seriously impaired than he had admitted. He tried various doctors and medicines, but complained that they made him feel worse, and in a characteristically broad gesture of renunciation dispensed with them. The day he died, June 16, 1955, was Bloomsday, the day his brother had made famous. Stanislaus himself was accustomed to celebrate the anniversary with a party. Coincidence helped to bind the brothers in death as they had been bound in life.

The book he left reveals his virtue. His Triestine friends thought of Professor Joyce as like Cato, and there is something of Cato's almost monumental integrity in his life. Incapable of anything less than honesty, he antagonized imperial and fascist authorities alike. In his liberal and anticlerical views, he was a democrat of the school of 1848. He struggled for a more personal freedom, too, attempting to find himself a character distinct from his brother's. In the end we may well feel that the most surprising aspect of this much humiliated spirit is his sturdy pride.

Stanislaus Joyce in Trieste about 1905

Stanislaus Joyce in 1955

MY BROTHER'S KEEPER

I · *The Soil*

MY RECOLLECTIONS OF MY
brother go back to such early years that I hardly dare say how
far back they go—at any rate to nursery days. I have a recollection, definite enough though vague in detail, of a dramatic
performance of the story of Adam and Eve, organized for the
benefit of his parents and nursemaid. I was Adam and a sister,
my elder by less than a year, was Eve. My brother was the
devil. What I remember indistinctly is my brother wriggling
across the floor with a long tail probably made of a rolled-up
sheet or towel. Of what he said I have, of course, no memory,
but it must have made the original myth seem funny, and, as
taking the gilt of myth off the gingerbread of reality was to
form so large a part of his work, may be worth recording.
There were other nursery theatricals that I remember more
distinctly, but they belong to a year or two later, and, though
one at least was comic in intention, were not so interesting as
the child's first attempt to visualize the sacred history stories
he had been told, and his instinctive realization of the fact that
the most important part dramatically, which he reserved for
himself, was that of the Tempter.

We lived at that time at Bray within a stone's throw of the
sea in the house on Martello Terrace next to the baths. The
"terrace" ran straight down to the water's edge, and in winter
the sea sometimes dashed over the sea-wall and flooded the

3

road in front of the house till it was awash with the door-step. From our windows we had a long view of the Esplanade, which stretched along the sea-front half the way to Bray Head, and behind it there was an equally long green enclosure with a band-stand, and—Dickensian touch!—rude donkey-boys. Behind Martello Terrace were lanes and fishermen's cottages and a long strand reaching to Killiney. About the earliest impression I can recall is that of standing ankle-deep in the thin flat ripples on that strand on an early summer morning while my father, swimming a long way out, was lost in the dazzling reflection of the sun on the level sea.

My brother's fear of dogs and preference for cats dates from the time when he was badly bitten by an excited Irish terrier, for which he and I were throwing stones into the sea on the beach near the sea-bathing establishment which is, or was, in the middle of the Esplanade. The wounds, 'which looked both sore and sad', were medicated by a Dr. (or Mr.) Vance, a friend of my father's, who had a chemist's shop somewhere on the sea-front. He was a cheerful, hard-working chemist, whose wife suffered from heart disease and spent the greater part of the day on a sofa reading novels. His devotion to her was often the subject of comment amongst his friends, most of whom habitually neglected their wives, but the comment was not altogether hostile because he was too clever and vivacious in company to incur contempt. In a jerky, humorous manner like that of the comic actor Edward Terry (Ellen Terry's brother), whom he somewhat resembled in appearance, too, he would tell stories of the disasters which he and a stupid servant, a female Handy Andy, caused in his house; as, for example (when he failed to turn up at a card party), that she had put so much pepper in an Irish stew that the whole family, including the servant, had been obliged to spend the rest of the evening sitting around the kitchen tap.

Vance's elder daughter, Eileen, who comes into the early part of *A Portrait of the Artist*, was a couple of years older than my brother—a pale, oval-faced girl with long dark hair, which she often wore in plaits over each shoulder in front, framing her face. She was already well aware of the effect. She seemed cold and distant, but she was not so by any means. When my brother was at Clongowes, she wrote him a letter, happily intercepted by my mother, which concluded with this verse showing the hand of her father:

> *Oh, Jimmy Joyce, you are my darlin',*
> *You are my looking-glass night and mornin'.*
> *I'd rather have you without a farthin'*
> *Than Johnny Jones, with his ass and garden.**

Though my brother has borrowed this verse and some uxorious traits for the making of Bloom, Vance did not otherwise resemble Leopold. He was spare and sprightly and always welcome because he was 'good company'. Moreover, his wife was really ill; she died young a few years later. That they were Protestants in no way interfered with the friendship between them and our family. My father and mother never gave the matter a thought, but there was one member of our household who seemed to think that she imperilled her precious soul by

---

* Vance adapted the lines from Samuel Lover's chapter, 'Ballads and Ballad Singers', in his *Legends and Stories of Ireland*, where they are given:

> *Oh Thady Brady you are my darlin,*
> *You are my looking-glass from night till morning*
> *I love you betther without one fardin*
> *Than Brian Gallagher wid house and garden.*

sitting down to play cards with the Vances, and who, whenever she could do so, made trouble. It was the woman who
appears in *A Portrait of the Artist* as Mrs. Riordan, and of
whom I shall speak presently.

Vance was one of a small group of friends who shared my
father's high hopes for his precocious youngster. After all they
were not so greatly mistaken. He died while my brother, as a
schoolboy in the upper classes, was still fulfilling those hopes.
My brother liked him, and introduces him by his right name
into *A Portrait of the Artist*. The mention bears witness here,
as elsewhere in *A Portrait* and *Ulysses*, to a grateful memory.

In the case of a writer whose early impressions were so vivid
and lasting, and who, moreover, deliberately chose the Dublin of his adolescent years as the main, if not the sole subject matter of his artistic production, it is not idle to ask how
these impressions became so firmly fixed in his mind. In this
regard, the ingenuous admiration of those simple-minded people, untinged with envy though some had children of their
own, is a factor not to be overlooked. He was not the first-born
—the first, a boy, died in infancy—but he was the eldest of the
family, handsome and clever. He amused friends of the family
in much the same way that Dickens is said to have done at
about the same age. His precocity and independence as a very
young child were remembered when he had passed out of the
University and was beginning to be known as a young man of
promise, or rather, to say it with *Dubliners*, as 'a young fellow
with a great future behind him'. Stories were told of how, when
not yet four years of age, he entertained relatives, who had
turned up unexpectedly in his parents' absence, by 'playing'
the piano for them and singing, or of his habit, at a still earlier
age, of coming at dessert time down the stairs from the nursery
one step at a time, with the nursemaid in attendance, and

calling out from the top of the house until he reached the dining-room door, 'Here's me! Here's me!' (It was an appropriate entrance for the author whose last creation was to be H. C. E.—Here Comes Everybody.) Or again, when he was seven, of his riding on his tricycle from the outskirts of Dublin to Bray to visit a nurse, while his sorrowing parents sought him among kinsfolk and acquaintance. The effect of such a heady diet of admiration in childhood might have been to make the boy a prig, but the natural attritions in a large family, soon to be in a state of gradual impoverishment, were unfavourable to the growth of such a characteristic. In the tense sensibility and raw realism of the parts of *A Portrait of an Artist* that deal with those years, there is no trace of priggishness.

His first educator was the woman who in *A Portrait of the Artist* is called Mrs. Riordan, and whom he, and the rest of us after him, called 'Dante'—probably a childish mispronunciation of Auntie. She had, in fact, in embryo, an influence not unlike that of her great namesake, for besides teaching my brother to read and to write, with some elementary arithmetic and geography, she inculcated a good deal of very bigoted Catholicism and bitterly anti-English patriotism, the memory of the Penal Laws being still a thorn in the flesh of Irish men and women when I was a boy. Her name was Mrs. Conway, and she seems to have been some distant relative of my father's. She lived with us for several years and it was owing to her preparation that my brother was accepted at Clongowes Wood College, the principal Jesuit College in Ireland, when he was little over six years of age.

Mrs. Conway was unlovely and very stout. She used to wear in the house one of those funny little caps which in photographs enhance the fading beauty of Queen Victoria. As I remember her, she seems always to have been sitting down somewhere imposingly, and she had a surliness of temper that in Ireland is associated, no doubt unjustly, with the Reformed Church of Christ. She may have suffered from sciatica, I fancy, because she always had great difficulty in sitting down and standing up, and performed both feats to the accompaniment of exclamations of pain—'Oh, my back, my back, my back!' *— which I used to imitate pretty accurately for the amusement of the nursery. She had her bursts of energy, however, for I remember the scandal, mentioned in *A Portrait of the Artist*, that she created one fine summer evening when a military band was concluding its programme of music on the band-stand behind the Esplanade. While the band was playing 'God Save the Queen', she interrupted the loyal rapture of an elderly gentleman who was standing up, hat in hand, listening to the anthem, by giving him a rap on the noddle with her parasol.

Many years before she had entered a convent with the intention of becoming a nun, but before she had taken her final vows a brother of hers died and bequeathed her a rather large sum of money. She left the convent and soon got married to a husband whom she must certainly have considered a judgment sent from heaven. I have heard him described as being tall, solemn, and bald-headed. He had a good position in the Bank of Ireland, where he used to keep a pair of trousers to wear in his office so that he could always appear in public with his best trousers elegantly creased. When the young couple were invited to dinner he would read a book before leaving home in order to have matter for conversation. Besides this, he had the commendable habit of getting up in the middle of the night to pray, and incidentally to suck raw eggs. After a couple

---

* 'O, my back, my back, my bach!' *Finnegans Wake* (London: Faber and Faber, 1939; New York: The Viking Press, 1939), p. 213.

of years of married life he decided that he could do better in South America. He certainly did. He left for Buenos Aires with the greater part of his wife's fortune, and she never saw him or it again. She was to have followed him, but his letters, always few and far between, became rarer and rarer. In an elephantine attempt to be playful, his wife wrote to him, quoting a popular song of the time:

> *Jumbo said to Alice:*
> *'I love you',*
> *Alice said to Jumbo:*
> *'I don't believe you do;*
> *For if you really loved me,*
> *As you say you do,*
> *You'd never go to Yankee Town*
> *And leave me in the zoo'.*

This pachydermatous frolicsomeness so outraged his sense of propriety that after a last indignant letter he never wrote to her again, and she lost all trace of him. It was an embittering experience and it befell an appropriate subject. Perhaps she felt that she had some leeway to make up with her conscience. Whatever the cause, she was the most bigoted person I ever had the misadventure to encounter.

She was thought to be a very clever and shrewd woman—in fact, she was by no means stupid—and was allowed to have more than her say in the conduct and education of the children. It was a generation of large families, but with scant understanding of children. Dante was only more definite and consequent than others in her belief that children come into the world trailing murky clouds of original sin. In her brighter moments, she used to take us during the Christmas holidays to see the crib at Inchicore,* with the wax figures of the Holy Family and Magi and the shepherds and horses and oxen, sheep, and camels stretching all round the hall in cheap and dusty grandeur. In a sterner mood, she brought us to see a picture entitled 'The Last Day', in the National Gallery. It represented a tremendous cataclysm, black thunder-clouds lowering, lurid lightning flashing, mountain-tops crashing down, and little naked figures of the wicked in all the contortions of despair—Oh, why did I do it!—imploring mercy, while huge rocks fell on them. In another corner of the picture, the blessed were being catapulted up to heaven with their arms crossed on their breasts. I don't remember whether God Almighty was in the picture or not, but in any case He was evidently having the time of His life—or perhaps I should say of His eternity—squelching sinners.

Another incident is impressed on my memory. One day I was out with the nursemaid, walking beside the pram in which there was I don't remember which younger brother or sister. We happened to pass through Little Bray when a funeral was starting from one of the two-storeyed houses there. Perhaps the nursemaid stopped to watch, but just at the moment when they were carrying out a diminutive coffin, a woman rushed screaming to an upper window and made as if to throw herself out, had not people within the room held her back. In the discussion of the incident which took place when we came home, someone, probably the nursemaid, said that the cause of the mother's despair was that the infant had not been baptized.

---

* '. . . drinking the champagne out of her slipper after the ball was over like the infant Jesus in the crib at Inchicore in the Blessed Virgins arms sure no woman could have a child that big taken out of her . . .' *Ulysses*, p. 711 (736-37). [In this and subsequent notes the page references are first to the standard English edition (London: John Lane, The Bodley Head, 1936), and then in parenthesis to the standard American edition (New York: Random House, 1934).]

Dante then explained to us that the child could never go to heaven. Her attitude was: 'So now you see what happens. The child can never go to heaven. Now you see what comes of not baptizing immediately'. We were all duly impressed, for it seemed the most natural thing in creation that God should be some kind of drunken ogre with less mercy even than the small mercy of men. But somewhere in my mind the incident seems to have been filed for reference. I remember one of our Jesuit teachers at Belvedere College stating impressively during religious instruction when discussing confession and the use of reason that it had been revealed to I don't recollect now which sainted ruffian, possibly St. Augustine, that there was a child of seven years of age in hell. My brother makes some of the Catholic university students in *A Portrait of the Artist* discuss the point and puts some of his anger into the mouth of 'Temple'. Jim used to say that the Church was cruel like all old whores. In the novel he modifies the phrase.

However, Dante was not altogether without tenderness, for she used to tell the children to bring her the tissue paper that came wrapped round parcels,* and when they presented her with some sheets of it before visitors, her economical soul would shake its fat all over with laughter when the visitors had gone. She died very fitly of fatty degeneration of the heart many years later, and no doubt, after a suitable quarantine in purgatory, will sail up to heaven on the Last Day in a glorified body (that needs no tissue paper) to join the chorus of angels in singing 'For He's a jolly gay Fellow' for evermore.

The sincerest of the little group of my brother's well-wishers

---

* 'Dante gave him a cachou every time he brought her a piece of tissue paper.' *A Portrait of the Artist as a Young Man*, p. 7 (2). [In this and subsequent notes the page references are first to the standard English edition (London: Jonathan Cape, 1924), and then in parenthesis to the standard American edition (New York: The Viking Press, 1916).]

was the man who appears in *A Portrait of the Artist* as 'Mr. Casey'—John Kelly of Tralee. He had been in and out of prison several times for making speeches in support of the Land League agitation. In fact it was in consequence of these terms of imprisonment that he fell into the decline from which he died some ten or eleven years later. After he had served a sentence, my father used to invite him to come down to Bray to recuperate at the seaside. I remember his coming to stay with us three or four times, and the hugger-mugger after his escape up to Dublin to avoid arrest, an escape at night that put an end to what must have been his last visit to Bray. The sergeant who came after dark to give warning that a warrant for Mr. Kelly's arrest had arrived and that he had delayed its execution until the following morning was a very tall, sinewy Connaught man who dwarfed my father and Mr. Kelly when they used to talk with him. He hailed from the Joyce country—his name was Joyce, of course—and he was clannishly devoted to my father. There is mention of the incident in *A Portrait of the Artist*.

I do not think that the family of—so far—six young children spoiled John Kelly's enjoyment of the rest and sea air at that pretty seaside resort. Seaside resort seems too big and too modern a name for Bray with its hundred or so modest summer visitors, though the Queen of Rumania, 'Carmen Sylva', did honour us with a visit one summer. Mr. Kelly used to take me out walking and give me donkey rides. My brother cannot have been at home or I should not have been preferred, so that I reckon it must have been after he had gone up to Clongowes for the first time. If so, I was not yet four at the time. I remember very well, however, that on one occasion the donkey ran away with me. When the donkey-boy had put me in the saddle and for a moment left his beast unattended, the donkey started off at a gallop with John Kelly and the donkey-boy in hot pursuit. It must have been a smart gallop, for they could not overtake the donkey. John Kelly, in any case, was not in training. The road wound up a slight incline at the top of which there was a level railway crossing. John Kelly, who often used to recall the incident, said that when he saw the red cap I was wearing disappear with its bobbing tassel round the turn of the road, he gave me up for lost. He feared the gates at the level crossing might be shut and that I should be pitched over them in front of a passing train. But the way was clear and the donkey continued his gallop. I stuck on and was delighted that at last the donkey had galloped, for I had never been able to cajole the lazy donkey-boy into doing more than a jog-trot of forty or fifty yards with his 'baste'. In retrospect, not so blurred even after more than sixty years, my Gilpin ride does not seem to have been so short. After the level crossing, it was past a park or large garden with high railings and then, I think, to the left up the Main Street of Bray to the fountain in front of the Town Hall. He was an Irish donkey and his outburst of energy was due to the fact that he wanted a drink.

John Kelly of Tralee must, I think, have been of peasant stock. He was pale and handsome, slow of speech and movement, with regular, clean-cut features and a mass of black hair. The fingers of his left hand were permanently cramped from making sacks and picking oakum in jail.* He had an old-fashioned courtesy, a peasant eloquence—in later years more than once in exercise on my brother's birthday—a natural gift of friendship, and a passionate loyalty to his country and his Chief, Parnell. His great expectations for my brother were hardly

---

* '. . . and Mr Casey had told him that he had got those three cramped fingers making a birthday present for Queen Victoria.' *A Portrait of the Artist*, p. 31 (27).

outdone even by my father. What he thought my brother might become I cannot guess. Something in political life? I hardly think so. At any rate he never tried to influence him as Dante did with her narrow, restless, partisan bigotry. If the boy liked to listen, let him listen. He did.

Whenever John Kelly came to stay with us, he fell easily into place. He was amused and could be amusing. In a family in which all the children had tunable voices, each one down to the youngest that could speak had his or her song, some of them comic songs which were considered stupid enough for children. Mine, by the way, at this time or a year or so later, was 'Finnegan's Wake'. Mr. Kelly, also, when pressed by my father to do so, would recite 'The Auld Plaid Shawl' or 'Shemus O'Brien' —and recite it so movingly that my father would get busy with the tumblers of punch to hide his emotion—or sing for the children his ballad 'The Goat':

> *'Oh Pat', says me mother.*
> *'What's that, ma'm', says I.*
> *'Take the goat to the market*
> *And sell her do try'.*
> *Sure, the words was scarce spoke*
> *When the goat gave a jump,*
> *And hit me poor mother*
> *A ter-r-rible thump.*
> *With a whack fol the lardle-lie, lardle-lie, lay,*
> *Whack fol the lardle-lie, lardle-lie, lay.*
> *Sure the words was scarce spoke*
> *When the goat gave a jump,*
> *And hit me poor mother*
> *A ter-r-rible thump.*

He had a pleasant mellow bass and sometimes could be induced to sing 'The Diver' or 'In Cellar Cool' to my mother's accompaniment. Once after they had been up to Dublin in a small party to hear some opera, John Kelly said to my father reflectively:

—Do you mind what I'm telling you, John. If you got three months in jail, you'd sing any of those fellows off the stage.

'Uncle Charles' was William O'Connell, a maternal uncle of my father's. He formed part of the household as early as I can remember and remained with us until we moved up to Dublin after my father had lost his position owing to the closing down of his offices. I have heard my mother say that in the case of his uncle my father returned good for evil; for when his father died, his uncle, William O'Connell, then a prosperous businessman in Cork and a bachelor, refused bluntly to take any interest in his orphaned nephew of seventeen. When I knew him he was a large, white-haired old man, imperturbable and quietly religious. He took a cold tub and went to Mass every morning, and made himself useful by doing my mother's shopping in the town of Bray, which was at some distance from where we lived. He took me with him on these excursions, but I went unwillingly because he had distressing habits. He would remain for what seemed to me an age, though it was perhaps only an hour, in talk with the proprietors of shops where he went to order things, while I wandered around the shop looking at labels and advertisements that I knew by heart; or he would take me with him into some chapel on the way home to say three 'Hail Mary's' for his 'intention'—whatever this might be was a mystery to be respected.

He used to sing, too, in an old man's voice but not unpleasantly, 'Oh! Twine me a bower all of woodbine and roses' or 'In happy moments day by day'. They all used to sing. The singing of sentimental ballads was a backwash of that ebbing wave of romanticism, in which poetry and all it is wont to express had degenerated, Tommy Moore assisting, to a drawing-room accomplishment. Whatever happened, nothing could ever upset him; he had his magic formula at all sticky points: 'All serene, ma'am, all serene'.* And his serenity was sometimes put to a rather severe test. During the first summer holidays when my brother had come home from Clongowes, we wanted to play football one afternoon with other young boys on the large green in front of the terrace, but we had no football. My brother had a wild idea—a very rare thing with him. He ran into our house, fetched Uncle William's tall hat from the hall-stand, and with that relic of old decency we played football. Then, adding insult to injury, we filled it with stones and hung it up on the hall-stand again. After a first brunt of the storm had passed, my mother and Uncle William, two instinctive peacemakers, were at their wits' ends to conceal the mishap to the tall hat from my father, for there was to be a picnic on Bray Head in a few days' time, and some relatives and friends had been invited. Fortunately, Uncle William knew a hatter in Bray who undertook to recondition the hat and restore it to its pristine beauty in time for the picnic. It arrived punctually looking as good as new, but on the day of the picnic towards the afternoon the flies discovered it and began to gather on it. Whatever stuff the hatter had put in it, it was just their tipple. When one fly had had enough, he flew away to bring the glad tidings of his find to his chums.

—My God, man, said my father, who was rather short-sighted, peering at the cluster of flies. What's the matter with your hat? All the flies on Bray Head are swarming over it.

—Musha, let them alone, John, said Uncle William. Sure, the craythurs are taking their tay.

---

* 'Very good, Simon. All serene, Simon. . . .' *A Portrait of the Artist*, p. 67 (65); and 'Where's punch? All serene.' *Ulysses*, p. 405 (417).

A few years later, but before we left Bray, we used to go with other warlike heroes of the same age to engage the enemy, urchins who lived in the lanes behind Martello Terrace. They were almost always bloodless clashes, of which there is a reminiscence in 'Araby', but they were sufficient at that age to give the thrill of adventure. These incidents, trivial as they are and such as might happen to any boy, suffice to show that my brother was not the weak, shrinking infant who figures in *A Portrait of the Artist*. He has drawn, it is true, very largely upon his own life and his own experience, and the vividness of his early impressions is due in great part, no doubt, to the fact that at college he suddenly found himself among boys bigger and older but less intelligent than himself. But *A Portrait of the Artist* is not an autobiography; it is an artistic creation. As I had something to say to its reshaping, I can affirm this without hesitation. In Dublin when he set to work on the first draft of the novel, the idea he had in mind was that a man's character, like his body, develops from an embryo with constant traits. The accentuation of those traits, their reactions to hereditary influences and environment, were the main psychological lines he intended to follow, and, in fact, the purpose of the novel as originally planned. As the other characters are often blends of real persons fused in the mould of the imagination, so for the character of Stephen in both drafts of the novel he has followed his own development closely, been his own model, and chosen to use many incidents from his own experience, but he has transformed and invented many others. The first chapters show a boy of subtle and penetrating sensibility, who from his earliest years seizes the images of things to ruminate on them and clarify them in his memory, and who finds, in his need to compose the life he knows in a pattern he can understand, a certain by-product of courage of a kind unknown to his hardier schoolmates. Though the treatment is objective, we are, as it were, from first to last in the centre of Stephen's brain. The picture is an interior. The purpose of these present reminiscences is to give a picture of the model from the outside, to be the other eye that adjusts focuses and rounds off contours.

The only real weakness my brother showed as a boy was a terror of thunderstorms—a terror excessive even for his years. It was not merely a boy's fear of thunder, it was the realization and terror of death, that dominant passion of the Middle Ages that makes *Everyman* such a poignant masterpiece and the retreat in *A Portrait of the Artist* hardly less poignant. Until he was twelve or thirteen, my brother was always beside himself with fear during thunderstorms. He would run upstairs to our room, while my mother tried to calm him. She would close the shutters hastily, pull down the blinds, and draw the curtains together. But even that was not enough. He would take refuge in the cupboard until the storm was over.

It was a direct result of the religion of terrorism that Dante had instilled into him. She used to teach us to cross ourselves at every flash of lightning and repeat the rigmarole, 'Jesus of Nazareth, King of the Jews, from a sudden and unprovided for death deliver us, O Lord', as if she were the canvasser for some kind of religious insurance company. Though almost three years younger than my brother, I was entirely unmoved by thunderstorms, and even his terror did not, as often happens with very young children, communicate itself to me. This was due, I think, not only to my being less apt to learn and less imaginative in realizing the significance of what was taught me, but also to the fact that, though I was Dante's godson, I disliked the chuffy, domineering woman, and was unconsciously resistant to her ideas, religious and patriotic. Briefly, as I had no love for her, I had no love for what she loved. But my brother assimilated her teaching readily and vivified it in his imagination. She had made much of him from infancy, and, no doubt, in return for her care, he gave her if not affection at least respect.

His fear of thunderstorms never quite abandoned him. If they were violent he became restless as cats do, and could not work. In an article on my brother in the *Nuova Antologia*, Alessandro Francini-Bruni, with whom we shared a flat in the early bohemian days in Trieste, writes, 'When a thunderstorm came on, he quite lost his self-control. He became irresponsible and gave way to acts of cowardice like a child or a silly woman. Panic-stricken, he would clap his hands to his ears, run to crouch in some cupboard, or cuddle up in bed in the dark in order not to see or hear'. This is sheer waste of material for a grand opera libretto, *La Forza del Rimorso*. Either Francini was unable to distinguish in his memory hearsay from actual incidents, or he wanted to work into his article for literary effect the anecdotes of my brother's childhood that he had heard at that time, chiefly from me in my broken Italian, during the prolonged (and happy) evening gossips of the two young families. In any case it never happened so. At most, if I were standing at the window looking at the storm, my brother would say to me, with glittering eye and exasperated politeness:

—Will you be kind enough to close that window, like a good bloody fool?

And then to Francini in Italian:

—You know, my brother thinks that a thunderbolt knocks at the door before coming in.

Though he was always uneasy during bad storms, it took a really startling flash to make him do something demonstrative. One day in midsummer we were overtaken by a thunderstorm at the corner of via Fabio Severo. The thick masses of cloud seemed to be resting on the house-tops, but it had not yet begun to rain heavily. Suddenly there was a crash of thunder and at the same time a blaze of lightning lit up the yellow façade of the old Austrian barracks. My brother clapped his hands together and with a cry skipped out into the roadway. A workman who was passing said, not unkindly:

—Corajo, giovinoto, corajo.

And I, to make a joke of it, said:

—Take it easy, man. You needn't dance a Highland fling about it.

We found shelter before the cloudburst came on. He seemed a little mortified. But the next morning he came into my room with the newspaper in his hand to show me that a tree in a garden above via Fabio Severo had been struck by lightning. He pointed out the paragraph angrily as if it had been my fault. That was the only time that I can remember when he gave any outward sign of his agitation, and there was at least some reason for it. Somewhere he calls God 'a noise in the street'. It is a reminiscence of these shocks. He means that the idea of God is something that startles you when you are hard at work, and makes you jump up and look out the window. This is certainly a more perturbed approach than the peaceable 'something not ourselves that—' I forget now what.

My brother's major work came at the close of an epoch of Irish, perhaps one may say, of European history, to give a comprehensive picture of it in the daily life of a large city. He always held that he was lucky to have been born in a city that is old and historic enough to be considered a representative European capital, and small enough to be viewed as a whole; and he believed that circumstances of birth, talent, and character had made him its interpreter. To that duty of interpretation he devoted himself with a singleness of purpose that made even the upheaval of world wars seem to him meaningless disturbances.

Nature, it has been said, makes no sudden starts; and in a special manner, as the Proverb of Hell affirms, to create the little flower of genius is the labour of ages. That little flower is, with startling frequency, a flower of evil, springing up amid decay, the vigorous offshoot of a withering stock. As no man acquires his talents or his character overnight, some account must needs be given in this book of the stock which produced the curious but hardy blossom which is the subject of this study.

Though for the second half of his long life my father belonged to the class of the deserving poor, that is to say, to the class of people who richly deserve to be poor, he was born into a middle-class family which, for Ireland, was fairly well-to-do. His father was able to live the life of a gentleman, and that, dictionaries tell us, means 'a man of respectable position who follows no occupation'. My grandfather's portraits and photographs show him to have been a handsome man—'the handsomest man in Cork', according to my father. He was the only child of an only child, as my father was. The source of my brother's peculiar form of self-exploitation for an artistic purpose, that sublimation of egoism, may well be here in these three generations of only sons. A brilliant young man of promise, my grandfather lived beyond his means. He was fond of hunting, and, at one period in his brief career, seems to have owned a race-horse; I fancy from certain vague hints of my father's that he must have been a gambler. One hint was that, marrying at the same time as a friend of his, they had a bet of ten guineas on which of the two would have a son first. My father won the bet for him, but shortly after birth lost this useful talent for making easy money. In his weepy moments, my father used to say that when my grandfather rode out to

hounds they would run to look after him. It is to be hoped that
the police always had the situation in hand, and that the
women didn't let the milk boil over. What is certain is that
'he went through the hoop' twice—a circus metaphor which in
careless Ireland means to go bankrupt. It would seem that on
the second occasion it was with his wife's property, for the
Married Woman's Property Act had not yet been passed. After
the second bankruptcy he lived with his wife and young son
at Sunday's Well, a fashionable suburb of Cork, on an al-
lowance from his father, a prosperous builder and contractor,
and perhaps on some desultory occupation. His wife had an
annuity settled on her by her father. My grandfather died
young, in his early forties, and his death seems to have been
sincerely mourned even by his wife.

He had married a woman of some means, an O'Connell, one
of a family of nineteen, the daughter of the proprietor of one of
the largest general stores in Cork. Some of the nineteen became
priests or nuns, and one—the Reverend Charles O'Connell—
(again I quote hearsay from my father) was Dean of St. Finbar's*
and had some reputation as a preacher. It was a marriage arranged
by priests to steady the young man, as one imagines. In Ireland
'priests' marriages' have a bad name, and my grandfather's
marriage proved worthy of that evil repute. As a result, though
fervently Catholic, he became very anticlerical. He handed on
his antipathy to priests as a precept to his son, and found him
apt.

His wife was many years older than he. Her portrait towards middle age is that of a stout woman with few pretensions
to beauty. She had been educated by the Ursuline nuns, and in
the attic of our Martello Terrace house there were a number

---

* Another of John Joyce's exaggerations; he was curate of Carrignavar, near
Cork City.

of leather-bound French prayer-books that she had kept from her convent days, the symbol of culture in Cork when she was a girl. By all accounts she had a sharp tongue, and may have had good reason to exercise it. She seems very soon to have been aware that her tenure of the spouse she had captured was not in fee simple. Once when they were newly married, it came on to rain heavily while they were taking a walk in the country around Cork City. They took refuge in a peasant's cottage, but as the weather showed no signs of clearing up, my grandfather went to the nearest village to get a car to take them home. The peasant woman, who was standing at the door of the cottage looking after him, said, perhaps not so innocently:

—Sure that's a fine young man, God bless him. I suppose now, ma'am, you're his mother.

—No, faith, said the newly married wife with bitter wit, I'm his grandmother.

In the little household that was soon formed his son was his fervent partisan, but even 'Uncle Charles', still in his old age impressed by the memory of his brilliant, spendthrift brother-in-law, spoke of him as a man of 'angelic temper'. The night he lay dying he tried to persuade his son to go and hear the aging Mario, who was singing in opera that night in Cork. The serenity of temper, skipping a generation as often happens, descended to his grandson, who was named after him and who in boyhood and youth was of such a cheerful and amiable disposition that in the family circle he was given the nickname (borrowed from an advertisement for some patent food) of 'Sunny Jim'.

My father as a boy seems to have had a good treble voice, for he sang in concerts at an early age. He was taught the piano and had a smattering of music. He was, however, a delicate boy, and to strengthen him my grandfather arranged with the Harbour Master of Cork to allow him to go out on the pilot boats that went to meet the transatlantic liners, for which in those days Queenstown was a port of call. As a result, no crossing of the Irish Sea, however rough, ever upset him. But besides the robust health which he acquired from the briny Atlantic breezes, he learned from the Queenstown pilots the varied and fluent vocabulary of abuse that in later years was the delight of his bar-room cronies. In the pages of *Ulysses* it has shocked most of the censors of polite literature in Europe and America.

After the death of his father, who died of typhoid while still in the prime of life, my father's relations with his mother became more and more Byronic. He was inscribed in the Queen's College, in the faculty of medicine, and studied for three years, taking a few exams. It was in sports and university theatricals that he shone as a student. He rowed in his college fours, was an indefatigable cross-country runner and a useful man at putting the shot in spite of his short stature, and always boasted that his record for the hop, step, and jump (eighteen feet in the first hop) stood for many years after he had left the University. But it was in university theatricals that he chiefly distinguished himself. I have seen a dozen or so cuttings from Cork daily papers containing flattering notices of Mr. Joyce's performances in various comic parts. Out of vanity he preserved them for years, and lived, like his son, on the memory of a youth of promise. The dearest of all things in Ireland is the memory of the past.

Some of the notices which Mr. David Marcus, the editor of a Cork review *Irish Writing*, kindly took the trouble to seek out for me at my request show my father to have been a student of no little self-assurance and dramatic ability. In March

1869 the re-establishment of the Queen's College Dramatic Society was announced in the Cork newspapers, but at the first performance in the Theatre Royal on March 11 there was a rowdy demonstration for political reasons against one of the actors. My father, who was nineteen at the time, seems to have restored good humour by singing comic songs. The *Cork Examiner* says he 'was exceedingly funny' and 'intensely popular'. A few weeks later, in May 1869, he had the principal part in 'The Irish Emigrant', a farce in one act. The critic of the *Southern Reporter* says, 'To Mr. Joyce's acting in the latter piece it affords us pleasure to be able to refer in terms of unqualified approbation. It was full of quiet humour, genuine and racy of the soil and admirably sustained. Mr. Joyce is a young gentleman of considerable dramatic talent and excellent promise'. A staider paper, the *Cork Examiner*, says, 'Mr. J. S. Joyce played the part of O'Bryan, the Irish Emigrant, in a fashion which, though tinctured with burlesque—a fault of the inexperienced—was far above the rendering of the ordinary amateur. Mr. Joyce's really admirable singing was also applauded as it merited'. My father became the mainstay for comic parts of the Queen's College Dramatic Society.

After an abortive attempt to volunteer with three college friends for the French Army in 1870 (he was twenty-one then), including a flight to London with his mother in stern chase and a crest-fallen return, he got mixed up with a Fenian group in Rebel Cork, so that his harassed mother decided to leave Cork for good. She was influenced in this decision by the fact that in view of the approaching O'Connell Centenary, her cousin, Peter Paul M'Swiney, a cousin of the Liberator's, had been elected Lord Mayor of Dublin.* She hoped the Lord Mayor would make her son his secretary.

---

* M'Swiney was Lord Mayor in 1875.

Before John Joyce started for Dublin a dinner was given in his honour; to it, since he had been known as a singer on the concert platform in Cork from early boyhood, some members of an English opera company then visiting Cork were invited. After the dinner there was an informal concert at which the company's leading tenor and my father also sang. When my father had sung some operatic air then in vogue, the English tenor, who seems to have been free from the usual professional jealousy, congratulated him warmly and said he would willingly have given two hundred pounds there and then to be able to sing that aria as my father had sung it. Later when he came up to Dublin, he had many other encouragements of the same kind from people whose opinions in such matters were valued. Full of good intentions on his arrival in the Irish capital, he went to an Italian lady teacher of singing to have his voice trained. She listened to him singing a few pieces and then went into the next room to call her grown-up son. 'Come and listen to this young man. I have found the successor of Campanini'. Italo Campanini was the tenor who was then the furore of Covent Garden and later, in 1883, took the part of Faust to inaugurate the Metropolitan Opera in New York. The compliments flattered my father's vanity, but neither aroused any ambition nor stimulated any purpose in him. After middle age they became part of his stock of consoling recollections, which, unlike his son's ruminations, had no trace of self-criticism, reflection, or regret. Is it because I have become hostile to my own people by being cut off from them for so long that I regard this childish, futile vanity as typically Irish? I find it in Yeats, Shaw, Wilde. In Swift, whose breeding at least was Irish, it was almost a criminal instinct when wounded. Only in 'magnanimous Goldsmith' was it an amusing foible. It makes the Irish lovers of singularity. My brother was not without it,

but in him vanity was stiffened with purpose, and in his struggle with publishers and critics, it became a sort of protective
armature against opprobrium and neglect.

My father did not become the Lord Mayor's secretary, but
he invested what remained of a thousand pounds, a coming-of-
age gift from his grandfather, in a distillery, the Dublin and
Chapelizod Distillery Company, of which he became the secretary. Some of the shareholders were English, but the founders
were Corkmen, like my father. The manager, whose name my
brother has borrowed for the manager in 'Counterparts', had
been a friend of my grandfather's in Cork. My father used to
describe him as a kind of duodecimo Lord Chesterfield, a figure
still remembered in Ireland. He drove out every morning to
Chapelizod, where the distillery was, in a dog-cart with a tiger
sitting behind him with folded arms. The workmen hated him,
and once tried to kill him by dropping a heavy beam of timber
on him from a gallery when he was going his rounds. My father
was quick enough to pull him under a shed an instant before
the beam crashed just where he had been standing. My father,
instead, was a favourite with the men, with whom he used to
play bowls. I do not know how long the secretaryship lasted,
about three or four years it seems, until my father discovered
that the manager was embezzling the money of the firm. After
a very heated discussion and a torrent of abuse from the manager, which came to an end only when the young secretary was
preparing to use violence, my father called a meeting of the
shareholders. The manager decamped, and the firm was wound
up. At the meeting the shareholders voted their thanks 'to the
young man who had saved them from greater loss' and appointed him trustee. Whatever money was realized from the
winding-up of the distillery was lodged in his name in the
Bank of Ireland, and must still be there, I presume, unless

the statute of limitations has provided for its disposal. The papers of the firm until at least ten years later were kept in a confused mass in a trunk in the attic. At the nadir of his fortunes, he used to wonder half-humorously whether he could get at that money, but a worldly-wise friend advised him to let a sleeping dog lie.*

A position was found for him as secretary of the National Liberal Club, and he seems to have fulfilled his duties efficiently. At any rate the National Liberal Club took to itself all the merit of the Nationalist victory at a subsequent election, in which one of the ousted Conservative members for Dublin was Sir Arthur Guinness, afterwards Lord Ardilaun; and it rewarded its secretary with a gift of one hundred guineas for each elected candidate—quite a nice little present for a good young man in Dublin seventy-odd years ago. There was even some talk of his standing for a constituency, for he had a glib tongue and had been among the first to greet the rising star of Parnell. It was a fanatical lifelong devotion which he handed on to his eldest son. As for his 'gift of the gab', excepting the literary allusion which Gabriel Conroy considers above the heads of his listeners, the speech in 'The Dead' is a fair sample, somewhat polished and emended, of his after-dinner oratory. Nothing came of the suggestion. Very probably he had neither the patience nor the docility that elder politicians expect to find in their juniors in the party.

Meanwhile there was no pressing need to work and he could enjoy life. His mother was independent, and he had a small but sufficient income from house property in Cork. They lived outside Dublin somewhere down along the bay towards Dalkey. He had a little sailing boat and a boy to look after it, and he

---

* The Bank of Ireland reports that it has no money in John Joyce's name.

sang occasionally at concerts. At these it might happen, if there
was a bar near the concert hall, that he would delight his
friends in the audience by singing the second verse of a song
before the first. Yet he had the proper temperament for a concert singer, and though he did not often sing in public, he knew
as well as any old hand how to make an audience friendly towards him in advance by being perfectly at his ease on the stage.
At one of the concerts in which he was the star singer, the
accompanist was a professor of the Dublin Conservatory of
Music. One of my father's songs had an introduction, nearly a
page long, which he liked, but the professor, instead of playing
it, strummed a few chords of his own and nodded to my father
to begin. But my father stood there looking at him. The professor strummed the chords again and again nodded to him to
begin. This time my father turned round familiarly to his accompanist and said in loud approval, 'Bravo! Well done! Good
man!' There was so much laughter that it was some time before
the professor could at last play the music that was before him
and my father got on with his song.

In fact he had a jolly time of it with his hard-drinking friends
of that hard-drinking generation. But however uncritical of
himself he may have been, he must have suffered in his self-
esteem. He had failed in all the careers that had seemed open
so promisingly before him—as a doctor, as an actor, as a singer,
as a commercial secretary, and lastly as a political secretary. He
belonged to that class of men regarding whom it is impossible
to postulate any social system of which they could be active
members. They are saboteurs of life though they have the name
of *viveurs*. He had natural advantages enough, including the
health of an ox, but no character to quicken them. And by
character I mean just belief in oneself. It is astonishing that .
father with so little character could beget a son with so much.

Being at a loose end, he fell in love again, this time with a Dublin girl. That at least was easy and pleasant. Perhaps, too, he had the illusion that he would enjoy family life, which as an only child he had never known. He always liked very young children, and even when he had had a dozen of his own, he would stop in the busy centre of the city, if he saw a small child toddling on independently in front of its parents, and, indifferent as ever to his surroundings, begin a conversation with it:

—Isn't that a great little girlie (or mannie) for you now? And where might you be going this fine day?

The child would stop and look up at him while the slightly embarrassed parents waited for him to have done with it and move on.

One of the customers of the distillery was a certain John Murray of Longford, an agent for wines and spirits. He had an only daughter, a pretty girl of nineteen who played the piano well and had a tuneful voice. My father became a visitor at his house, and in a short time he and the girl, Mary Jane, were secretly engaged. Some rumour of John Joyce's previous engagements or perhaps of his drinking bouts must have reached the father's ears, and though John Murray was by no means a teetotaller, he forbade the match. The couple had little difficulty in finding the means to write to each other and to meet. It was the one and only display of obstinacy in the unhappy life of May Murray. The jealousy of rivals found expression in a nickname for the pair, Beauty and the Beast, which was quite unfair.* My father was quite passably good-looking, a dashing and debonair young man. Once the father met them walking together in Grafton Street, a fashionable shopping quarter.

---

* 'When you made your present choice they said it was beauty and the beast. I can never forgive you for that.' *Ulysses*, p. 425 (438).

He made a scene and called a cab in order to take his daughter home. While they were waiting for the cab to come a little group of inquisitive people gathered round them. A man in the crowd asked my father what was the matter.

—Oh, nothing serious, was the glib reply. Just the usual story of the beautiful daughter and the irascible parent.

But urbanity, except in public, was far from being one of his characteristics. In the bosom of his family he showed quite another face. Until his prematurely aged wife died when only forty-four, the wound to his vanity rankled and he pursued her father (and when the old man died, his memory) as well as her family with an unrelenting hatred and unremitting virulent abuse that amounted to an obsession. His epithets ranged from the comic—'bottle-washer in a paper hat'—to the vitriolic—'old fornicator' (because the old man, after the death of his first wife, married again). The only member of her family who was saved from his scurrilous tongue was her mother, who had been favourable to the marriage. She had been one of a musical family, friends of Balfe; they are parodied somewhat in 'The Dead'. She had a trained voice, though she never sang in concerts, and seems to have liked her son-in-law. And that unaccountable man, who never could agree with mother, wife, or children, always treated the memory of his mother-in-law with respect. She owed her immunity, in part at any rate, to dying in the early years of his marriage.

They were married on May 5, 1880, when my mother was not yet twenty-one, and went on their honeymoon to London. Already on the wedding trip the husband began to swear at his too patient wife. While they were boating on the Thames at Windsor he noticed that a fellow with a girl in another boat was trying to pass him. During the impromptu race that ensued he cursed his girl bride fluently for not steering the boat straight, and when he had outdistanced his rival and could ease off, he made a joke of the violent language he had used in the heat of his excitement. In fact, one of his maxims was, 'Never apologize'.

Through influence a job was found for him in the Office of the Collector General of Rates and Taxes, in order that it might be fulfilled which was spoken of by the prophet, that he should be numbered with tax-collectors and sinners. His own mother had been opposed to the match—'They are troublesome people, John'—and when her son, her only child, married, she went back to Cork. He never saw her again. She died alone.

My brother has made use of this incident in *Exiles*, for no writer in English since Sterne has exploited the minute, un-promising material of his immediate experience so thoroughly as my brother did, using it in order to delineate character or complete his picture of an environment. Some critics have insisted on a resemblance between my brother and Sterne, basing their comparison on whimsicalities of style, originality in the construction of the novel, the patient accumulation of de-tail for a purpose that at first puzzles the reader, and still more intimately on the dominant motives in the hearts in both writers —the devotion to a father's memory, the hostility to a mother's wishes, the hateful call to active life in a form repugnant to all their souls longed for. There was undoubtedly a vague Ham-letic complex both in Sterne and in my brother, but although Sterne, in the loss of his father as the result of a silly duel, suffered in early youth a heavy blow to his deepest affection, and thus might have had reason to cultivate a tragic outlook on life, he refused to do so. He chose to be Yorick, because he did not wish to be Hamlet.

My brother was of a far more inflexible mettle. His attitude towards his mother never reached the point of contempt as

Sterne's did, nor was it ever personally hostile. He was at loggerheads with her because he would have no truck with the religion to which she owed fidelity. Moreover the vagaries of his style are purposeful. For him literature was not a comforting pastime that half lulls, half encumbers the conscience. It offered other satisfactions, grim realizations that dethrone tyrannical secrets in the heart and awaken in it a sense of liberation. And of sympathy, too. In the mirror of his art the ugliness of the Gorgon's head may be clearly reflected, but it is cleanly severed and does not turn the beholder's heart to stone.

He shared with Sterne, however, an innate scepticism in regard to the resplendent events and sumptuous personages that novelists deal in. I often ask myself how it is that such personages do not become prime ministers not only of England—that would be too little—but of Europe. No less a destiny seems fitting for such outsized men and women. I have known at least a few people who have reached the highest plane of celebrity, but they have succeeded by believing in one or two things wholeheartedly. Nor were their relations with other men and women like a page of Henry James's neat and orderly prose.

In early youth, my brother had been in love, like all romantic poets, with vast conceptions, and had believed in the supreme importance of the world of ideas. His gods were Blake and Dante. But then the minute life of earth claimed him, and he seems to regard as with a kind of compassion his youth deluded by ideals that exacted all his service, 'the big words that make us so unhappy', as he called them. Yet he had believed in them wholeheartedly—in God, in art, or rather in the duty (he would not have called it 'duty') imposed on him by the possession of talent.

The faculty of ardent belief in the absolute is like the poet's gift. It does not come by fasting or praying or consuming midnight oil, but it hallmarks the man who possesses it. It hallmarked my brother even when he deliberately chose for his subject the commonplace person and the everyday incident, the things that are despised. All his work is permeated by a kind of litotes which is the antithesis of romanticism, it might be considered the distinguishing characteristic of modern writing which signifies much more than it says. There are still, however, some writers of very great talent who ransack the whole world for their subjects and their settings, and are immensely popular. To me they seem to be a good deal lacking both in subtlety and sincerity. They have gained the whole world but lost their souls. Moreover, unlike his friend Svevo, who was disappointed at not being a popular success, my brother never cared a rap who read him. I think he wrote to make things clear to himself. 'Why publish, then?' it might be asked. Well, the expression of our ideas and impressions, even when intended for ourselves, becomes clearer when addressed to others; and it is also a way to assume responsibility for them.

My brother's choice of subjects flatters my vanity in a curious way. When we were both very young and my brother was still in the thraldom of the big words, I wrote in my diary in bungling schoolboy fashion that there are scientists whose work is concerned with infinite stellar spaces and who are hailed as great, and others deemed no less great whose work is at the end of a microscope. I opined that on a far smaller scale an analogous difference existed between writers, and that my brother would belong to the latter class. He used to read my diary without permission and be rather jocular about it, but he said, when he read this entry, he thought I might be right.

In the beginning of their married life my parents seem to have been what Divorce Court judges call 'reasonably happy'. The children began to arrive at almost regular intervals of a

year, the first in Dublin, among whom were my brother (the
second) and I (the fourth). Then John Joyce went to live at
Bray in the hope, as he used to explain politely and frequently,
that the train fare would keep his wife's family away. I have
no recollection of the earliest years in Dublin, but I have vivid
memories of Bray. The removal out of range of his wife's too
affectionate family, including three adoring aunts, does not
seem to have mended matters very much. He had not quite
relinquished his sporting life. He rowed stroke of a four-oared
boat at Bray regatta when he was forty and won (I don't remember the race but I remember seeing him training for it);
he used to go fishing for plaice and flounders and bathing from
the boat with the above-mentioned Vance and some fishermen
of Bray, as hairy-chested as himself and as fond of the contents
of the stone-jar in the stern-sheets of the boat where his bored
and silent second son used to sit. At that time his income was
sufficient, his work light, even too light, his children healthy and
one of them precociously clever, his wife, who shared his taste
for music and sang in the choir in Little Bray, patient in all
things, resourceful, and not at all deficient in a sense of humour.
I have a programme of a public concert given by the Bray Boat
Club in the Assembly Room of the town in 1888, at which
Mr. J. S. Joyce, Mrs. Joyce, and Master James Joyce (then six
years of age) all sang. Friends frequently came down from
Dublin to see him.

Yet at home he was a man of absolutely unreliable temper.
How often do I remember him sitting at table in the evening,
not exactly drunk—he carried his liquor too well then—but
sufficiently so to have no appetite and to be in vile humour. He
had a horrible habit when half seas over of grinding his strong
teeth with a noise that I used to think was caused by the creak-
ing of his stiff white collar. In later years my mother told me

that she was often terrified to be alone with him, though he was not normally a violent man. Fat Mrs. Conway always retired early to her room on an upper floor, and the nursery and the servants' room were at the top of the house. He would sit there grinding his teeth and looking at my mother and muttering phrases like 'Better finish it now'. At one time she thought of getting a separation from him, but her confessor was so furious when she suggested it that she never mentioned it again. The perverted morbid jack-in-the-box had bullied her out of seeking a separation which, probably, would not have been permanent and would undoubtedly have been good for both.

He had a nagging memory for petty offences to his pride that, with perverse constancy, kept his resentment green for years and years. When I was so young that this particular recollection is one of the vaguest and most remote that I have, we drove out with a few guests—amongst them my mother's stepmother, to whom all her family, except my mother herself, were hostile—to Powerscourt waterfall to picnic there. I remember the excursion very well. We were not alone; there were other groups. As I saw everything in inverse proportion to my height, my recollection is of a waterfall immensely high, and of a picnic on a greensward, immensely wide, stretching away somewhere below it to a row of stately trees. I have never been back to Powerscourt, nor have I any curiosity to know how it may be in reality. When the lunch-basket was opened, it was discovered that the tablecloth had been forgotten. The stepmother suggested as a joke that one of the ladies should sacrifice a petticoat. Voluminous white petticoats were worn in those days. My father appeared to take the joke gaily, but for some mysterious reason it rankled, and became another point in his perpetual indictment of his wife's family, even some twelve or fourteen years after the death of the offending party.

On another occasion he was crossing the Fifteen Acres, an open space in the Phoenix Park, with his brother-in-law, when a company of cavalry, at exercise in the morning, came galloping towards them at full tilt. The brother-in-law, my Uncle John Murray, started to run towards a clump of trees, but it was too far away and the cavalry was almost upon them. My father ran after him, seized him, and forced him to stand still. So it was easy for the company of cavalry to divide and leave the two men standing between the lines. My father used to boast that as they charged past the officer in command gave the order and the soldiers saluted him with their sabres. This happy combination of his brother-in-law's panic and his own presence of mind was far too favourable a trine to go unrecorded. It was recorded perennially.

But my mother was not of weak character, except in regard to her husband, and not without resource or energy in the government of her household when the occasion called for it. I have a clear recollection of her dealing capably with a dangerous fire in the nursery chimney. Telephones were a rarity in houses then and the fire brigade was not easy to call. I remember her sitting in the hearth, quickly but calmly ramming up the chimney brooms swathed in wet cloths, which the servants kept handing her from a tub of water on the floor beside her. I have better reason to remember another energetic intervention. One day in early summer—Jim was already at Clongowes—the whole nursery was out walking. The group consisted of four or five children, the nurse named Cranly, a young woman whose people were decent fisher folk from Bray, and a girl of fifteen or sixteen, a younger sister or cousin who came to help her. We caught the eye of a photographer on the Esplanade who asked to be allowed to take the group. The nurse girls were delighted—photographers were rare birds in those days—

and that evening they got permission to have the photograph taken. The following afternoon the girls put on their Sunday finery and we all went out to meet the photographer, who arranged us in an artistic group on the green behind the Esplanade. I, five or six at the time, was to sit on the grass in front with my legs crossed, but when the photographer said 'Now, don't stir', I began for devilment to turn my head jerkily from side to side, and neither the photographer's persuasions nor the nurse girls' entreaties could induce me to stop. The photographer had to give up the idea of taking the group, and we all went back home. The nurse girls were furious, and when they told how I had deliberately spoiled the opportunity, they were almost in tears. My mother listened to their report, and then promptly adjourned the session to the nursery, where I got a spanking, which must have been exemplary, seeing that I still remember it.

My father and mother had many friends in Bray and in town, and at about Christmas time and the New Year they often went up to dances in Dublin and stayed overnight at a hotel, as the Conroys do in 'The Dead'. My mother would give the servants many anxious recommendations about what they were to do during her brief absence, which seemed to me like a parting for ever. As long as she retained her good looks, he made trifles excuses for scenes of jealousy. One night at a dance one of the guests asked the hostess to introduce him to 'that pretty young lady'. 'By all means', said his hostess, 'but let me tell you that "that pretty young lady" is the mother of four children'. When the lady retailed the joke to them at the dance, my father laughed at it, but not when they were at home again, not for many months.

For his part he danced, and he was a good dancer, with all the best-looking girls in the room and took no notice of his wife.

My mother, instead, had not a particle of jealousy in her composition. The photographs of my father's former sweethearts still stood on the piano when I was a child. I remember the names of two of them: Hannah Sullivan, a dark energetic-looking girl, and Annie Lee, like the song. In each case he had broken off the match in a fit of jealousy—unreasonable jealousy, according to my mother. One day the photographs disappeared from the top of the piano. The next time my father had occasion to go into the drawing-room he at once noticed that they were missing.

—Where are the photographs? he asked.

—Burnt, was the answer.

—Who burnt them? he asked again.

—I did, said my mother defiantly.

My father put up the monocle he sported in those years and looked at her.

—No, you didn't, he said. It was that old bitch upstairs.

'That old bitch upstairs' was an elegant description of Mrs. Conway. He was right. Mrs. Conway had persuaded my mother that it was downright improper to keep the photographs in the drawing-room where the children, who were growing up and beginning to observe, could see them. Of course, my father knew very well what kind of submissive wife he had. His scenes of jealousy were just a form of satisfaction that his male truculence required. My mother was sorry afterwards that she had yielded to the insistence of the elder woman, 'Because', she said, 'they were all nice-looking girls'. And perhaps, too, it had given her a sense of triumph to adorn her wigwam with their scalps.

II · *The Bud*

MY BROTHER WENT UP TO CLON-
gowes Wood College when he was six and a half years of age,
and during his first year there was nicknamed 'Half Past Six'.
When my parents brought him up to Dublin to buy the list of
things the College required him to be provided with, and a
trunk inscribed with his initials J. A. J. to put them in, I, almost
three years his junior, was attached to the group two or three
times as a usual though unnecessary appendage. Going to college was a new experience for my brother, and though he must
have had some presentiments he welcomed new experiences
even at that age. There may have been some weakness at the
moment of saying good-bye in the hall of the college (I was
not there), but my recollection is that when my father decided
to send him to Clongowes, he was eager enough to go and enjoyed being the centre of such important preparations, including
visits to shops up in Dublin and lunch and tea in town. Unlike
me in this, too, he always liked new adventures, new scenes,
new people. The illusion of stability never seduced him.

I was taken down to Clane a few times on visiting day to see
him. Clane is a little town on his much-loved Liffey near
Clongowes, 'the meadow of the smith'. There was a drive of a
few miles by old-fashioned jaunting-cars to the college. Of
course he was happy to see us, but the impression that has
remained on my mind is not that of a boy who was lonely or
felt out of place. He seemed to be perfectly free of his sur-

roundings, a boy amongst boys. There was no reason why he
should not be so. He was always at the top of his class and always in good health. His letters home usually ran, 'Dear Mother,
I hope you are very well and Pappie also. Please send me . . .'
During his second or third year at the college he was chosen for
the honour of serving as an altar-boy at Mass. Even in sport he
distinguished himself. When after four years or so he left
Clongowes, we had at home a sideboard full of cups and a
'silver' (electro-plate) teapot and coffee pot that he had won
in the school hurdles and walking events. He disliked football
but liked cricket, and though too young to be even on the
junior eleven, he promised to be a useful bat. He still took an
interest in the game when he was at Belvedere, and eagerly
studied the feats of Ranji and Fry, Trumper and Spofforth. I
remember having to bowl for him for perhaps an hour at a time
in our back garden in Richmond Street. I did so out of pure
goodness of heart since, for my part, I loathed the silly, tedious,
inconclusive game, and would not walk across the road to see
a match.

In running he had a turn for both speed and endurance. Pat
Harding, a friend of my father's, who was Irish champion for
the 110-yard hurdles at the time when the American Kranzlein
was champion of the world, offered to train my brother for the
hurdles when he was in his last year at Belvedere, but my
brother already had other fish to fry. They remained friends,
and after my brother's elopement to Trieste my father wrote,
'In the whole city of Dublin you have only two friends, Pat
Harding and Tom Devin'. In the story 'Grace' Tom Devin appears as 'Mr. Power', but the down-at-heels trainer in *Stephen
Hero* is not Pat Harding, who was a lively young solicitor. As
for training, the most Pat Harding himself ever did was for a
week or two before a meeting. My brother was very fond of

swimming, too. He was a splashy swimmer but fast. Over a short distance he could beat his burly friend Gogarty, who was, of course, a far stronger swimmer. And he was an indefatigable walker. On one occasion he wished to go to Celbridge to interview an Irish American millionaire, who had bought an estate there and was reputed to have the intention of playing the part of Maecenas to young Irish geniuses. As my brother had not the train fare, he walked from our house in Cabra to Celbridge* to propose himself as a suitable subject, but was repulsed at the gates by the lodge-keeper, who was unsympathetic and slow of wit. My brother went to the post office and wrote a letter to the Irish American millionaire, whose name was Kelly, and then on the same day walked back to Dublin. I hope on the Day of Judgment to find out definitely whether it was stupendous cheek on the part of my brother or bad business on the part of the Irish American millionaire. At the time I took the former view, my brother the latter, but now I am inclined to think that my brother may have been right. At any rate the Irish American, who was not responsible for the repulse, wrote my brother an apologetic letter, and, getting no reply, wired to know whether his letter had been received. I have both the letter and the telegram.

My brother detested rugby, boxing, and wrestling, which he considered a training not in self-control, as the English pretend, but in violence and brutality. When most of the newspapers of America and England and even of Trieste carried five-column banner headlines on their front pages about Jeffreys, 'The White Hope' in that epoch-marking event, the Johnson-Jeffreys boxing match at Reno for the heavyweight crown, his ironical comments were a rough draft of the description of the

---

* A distance of about fourteen miles each way.

Myler Keogh-Bennett fight in the 'Cyclops' episode of *Ulysses*. There, however, it is used not to express personal bias but to associate violence and brutality with patriotism. Moreover, his first interest as a boy in the figure of Ulysses was aroused when his class was reading Lamb's *Adventures of Ulysses*. The boys were asked to say which of the heroes they admired most. My brother chose Ulysses in reaction against the general admiration for the heftier, muscle-bound dealers of Homeric blows.

My father had, no doubt, begun with the intention of giving his promising young son the best education the country had to offer a boy of his class and religion, but after a very few years that good intention, unfulfilled, formed just a minor item of the wreckage in the gradual ruin of his affairs. His office hours were short, from ten in the morning to half past three or four in the afternoon, and his work was light and easy, but such as it was he neglected it. To judge from his own reminiscences, he seems to have spent his time in the office drinking and telling 'good stories' with convivial companions of the same kidney whom he found there. They even played practical jokes on respectable old gentlemen who came to protest about their rates and taxes. If his work took him out of the office, the brief fiction of business soon ended in the bar of some hotel. Urgent work, such as the sending out of final notices to taxpayers, was neglected, and at the last moment he would have a couple of unemployed old clerks scribbling in his house from morning till midnight to help him to catch up on his arrears of work. When, finally, he succeeded in getting the notices out in time, he would lean back and take things easy again. Then, being an excellent mimic, he would tell his friends at home and in bars good stories about the poor devils he had got in to help him; about the boozy one, whose wife used to beat him, who turned up one morning with a black eye and a scratched face, and told a stale lie about colliding with the door of a cupboard in the dark (story in dialogue: sympathetic question and circumstantial answer with running commentary); or about the other, who, owing to the high cost of handkerchiefs, used to blow his nose in sheets of tissue paper.

I dare swear that government work could be done in that way only in Ireland, or perhaps somewhere in the Balkans, or in some place at the back of God-speed in Tsarist Russia before the Inspector General paid his surprise visit. Nor was the brown leather bag in which he carried the taxes he collected always inviolable, though he did defend it against two thieves who set upon him one night. He succeeded in beating them off with his blackthorn stick, and so had another story to tell over and over again in after years. His own borrowings from the bag, however, became more and more frequent and made it necessary for him to have recourse to money-lenders for fairly large sums at short notice. His property in Cork was gradually covered with mortgages, the interest on which ate up most of his rents. The end was already in sight when my brother was withdrawn from Clongowes and we moved up to Blackrock, a little nearer Dublin.

I liked the house in Blackrock—'Leoville' was its name because of a stone lion over the porch—better than the one in Bray. It stood in Carysfort Avenue next to the garden that surrounded the Protestant Church. I had been at an infants' school in Bray, and at Blackrock I was sent to a nuns' school, Sion Hill Convent, but so far as I can remember my brother was left to his own devices at home. Nobody in our house ever cared whether the children studied or not, though Dante and Uncle William were still with us. The latter, however, used to read us fairy stories, working his way steadily through Grimm and Andersen, and when the story was of the misadventures of some beautiful princess, he would interpolate pathetic asides, which escaped us, but were intended for my mother sewing in another part of the room.

My brother was not among his listeners. He had begun to read very much for himself, and was eager to study. He used to ask my mother to give him lessons to learn in the books which he had brought back with him from Clongowes and to examine him on them. My mother did so, giving him long lessons which she hoped would keep him busy for a couple of hours so she could get on with her housework. But in half the expected time my brother would come back to be examined and ask for more. The habit of examining him on his home-work at his own request continued until much later, when we were both at Belvedere and he was in the junior grade, so between thirteen and fourteen.

I believe his first essays to write were made here at Leoville, Blackrock. He began to write a novel in collaboration with a Protestant boy, Raynold, a year or two older than himself, who lived next door. I have no idea what strange adventures were to form the plot of the book, which was soon abandoned, but I remember the two boys discussing it and my brother writing in the afternoon till tea-time at the big leather-covered desk in the corner of the dining-room. He tried poetry, too, in the style of the drawing-room ballads to which he was accustomed ('My cot, alas!, the dear old shady home'), but the most successful was a piece on the death of Parnell, which I see mentioned, apparently with my brother's sanction, by the title of 'Et Tu, Healy', though I do not remember that it bore that title. It certainly was a diatribe against the supposed traitor, Tim Healy, who had ratted at the bidding of the Catholic bishops and become a virulent enemy of Parnell, and so the piece was an echo of those political rancours that formed the theme of my father's nightly half-drunken rantings to the accompaniment of vigorous table-thumping. I think it was in verse because of the rhythm of bits of it that I remember. One line is a pentameter. At the end of the piece the dead Chief is likened to an eagle, looking down on the grovelling mass of Irish politicians from

> *His quaint-perched aerie on the crags of Time*
> *Where the rude din of this . . . century*
> *Can trouble him no more.*

The production was much admired by my father and his circle of friends, whose judgment, in questions of literature at least, was as immature as the budding author's. My father had it printed, and distributed the broad sheets to admirers. I have a distinct recollection of my father's bringing home a roll of thirty or forty of them. Parnell, however, died when we were still at Bray, so the piece must have been written some months or a year after Parnell's death, because I am positive that the broadsheet was printed when we were living at Blackrock. My brother was, therefore, between nine and ten years of age when his ambition to be a writer bore its first timid blossoms. The lines I have quoted have stuck in my memory because 'the dear old shady home' and the blandly appropriated 'quaint-perched aerie' were standing jokes between us as late as when we were living at Trieste. Moreover, in the first draft of *A Portrait of the Artist*, now called *Stephen Hero*, the poem was assigned to the period I have indicated, and, further, describing a hasty packing up and departure from Blackrock, my brother referred to the remaining broadsheets, of which the young Stephen Dedalus had been so proud, lying on the floor torn and muddied by the boots of the furniture removers.

In Blackrock the disintegration of our family set in with

gathering rapidity. Dante left us and went to live with other
friends. In the few years that still remained to her before she
died, she changed frequently from one friend's or acquaintance's
house to another's, and I conclude that she could not find again
a family so tolerant of her dictatorship as we were. She had
adopted my elder sister, now a nun, then a little girl going on
for nine, as a kind of apprentice lady's maid, and succeeded, as
only thoroughly embittered religious people can, in making her
life a ceaseless round of tedious duties. While Dante remained
with us we still had the Rosary and the Litany of the Blessed
Virgin, at which she presided seated, every evening in the
conservatory at the back of the house. The least I can say is
that these two words rosary and litany do not mean for me
what they mean for sentimental Protestants who have sojourned
in Catholic countries. Yet when she had gone, perhaps in her
sour way she missed the children. Uncle William left us, too,
and went back to Cork.

I have a few scattered but significant memories of that brief
interlude between relative prosperity and real poverty. I remember, for instance, returning with my father to Blackrock
in the train from Dublin. In the third-class compartment the
only other passenger was a red-coated English soldier. My
father, being in the quarrelsome stage of drunkenness, began to
mutter quite audible curses at him. The soldier looked hard at
him and edged nearer to us. I was on tenterhooks between them,
fearing a row, and tried to distract my father's attention from
him by asking childish questions, but the soldier said:

—I see you don't remember me, Mr. Joyce.

My father, mollified, said, 'No, faith, I don't'. The soldier
then explained that he was the boy whom many years before
my father used to pay to look after his boat, and told a story
of the time when, during a storm in the bay, he had begun to

cry to be put ashore. My father had dropped him somewhere near Ringsend and sailed the boat back to Dalkey alone. My father, now very friendly, pretended not to remember, but when we got out at Blackrock, I was sent on home, and the rebel and the red-coat adjourned to a pub to talk about old times.

It was still less agreeable when, coming back in the evening from playing with other boys along the foreshore at Blackrock, I caught sight of my father, quite drunk but still elegant and with his eye-glass fixed, playing a piano-organ in the main street of the town and crooning 'The Boys of Wexford'. Meanwhile the Italian organ-grinder stood looking at him, with legs crossed and one hand resting on the organ, wondering at what he no doubt called mentally '*questi matti d' inglesi*'. We passed discreetly—the other boys as discreet as I—on the other side of the street, and I hurried on to bring the joyful tidings of his home-coming.

I wish I could see now, or could have seen then, the funny side of such happenings, as my brother did. And yet in *A Portrait of the Artist* he writes that 'any allusion to his father by a boy or a master put Stephen Dedalus's calm to rout and the smile waned on his face'. It did not seem so, but, of course, Stephen Dedalus is an imaginary, not a real, self-portrait and freely treated.

In the Jesuit schools he attended, the masters used to dwell rather heavily on the dangers of 'human respect', by which they meant doing something or leaving it undone against one's conscience for fear of what people might say or think of you. Their vague words were clearly understood. They desired to put their pupils on guard against a certain inferiority complex that might invade them when, in the little world of Dublin, they came in contact with a dominant Protestant class. In my

brother they found an apter pupil than they expected, or, indeed, wished for. It is no idle boast to say that at that time
there were very few youths, not only among the second-rate
middle class of Blackrock but in Europe, destined to go their
way so unperturbed as he, so callous against obloquy, or so determined to set completely at nought any praise or blame that
might come to them for the work they considered they had to
do.

I had neither such moral courage nor such love of my father.
On the contrary, my antipathy to him seemed to have been
born with me. There are some wise people who derive great
benefit to their health and peace of mind by sleeping with feet
and head in line with the earth's rotation. Conversely, I believe
most firmly that when the heart feeds on hatred and contempt,
the human being is facing the wrong way. But how is one to
blink facts and maintain one's honesty? When my brother read
Hardy's story, 'A Tragedy of Two Ambitions', which is about
a drunken millwright and his two serious, clerical sons, he
animadverted almost petulantly on Hardy's 'incredible wooden-
ness'. But I, having our own case in mind, attempted a generalization. I said that it was a proof of Saxon earnestness and Celtic
frivolity that a situation that suggested tragedy to an Englishman produced only low comedy in Ireland. My brother received the quip in silence, because he liked neither generalizations nor the implied reference. But he probably chewed upon
both.

It is not surprising that the usefulness of a public office served
by employees of the kind I have endeavoured to describe should
sooner or later be questioned by the higher authorities on whom
it depended. Furthermore, it was under hybrid control, partly
governmental, partly municipal, and hardly destined to a long
life. In 1891 or 1892 the office was abolished and the clerks

pensioned off. Because of his bad record, it was at first doubtful whether my father would be granted any pension, but on the personal intercession of my mother, the people at the top, whoever they were, assigned to him a pension equal to about one-third of his salary, and amounting to eleven pounds a month. At about the same time his house property in Cork, or what was left of it, was sold, apparently to make good defalcations, but it was so heavily mortgaged that little or nothing came to him from the sale. We left Blackrock abruptly and moved up to Dublin.

My father was still in his early forties, a man who had received a university education and had never known a day's illness. But though he had a large family of young children, he was quite unburdened by any sense of responsibility towards them. His pension, which could have taken in part the place of the property he had lost and been a substantial addition to an earned income, became his and our only means of subsistence.

The wish to shuffle off one's mortal load of responsibility is one among a number of common, human, quite unrealizable wishes. That, however, does not invalidate it as a literary theme. One of the world's masterpieces—*Faust*—is based on such a longing. In *Ulysses* Simon Dedalus, for whom my father served as model, is a battered wreck in whom even the wish to live carefree has become a vague memory, but if the facets of his character that are presented make the figure an effective and amusing literary creation, that is possible only because the tolerance of literature greatly exceeds that of actual life.

In Dublin the steps of our rapid downhill progress, amid the clamour of dunning creditors on the doorstep and threatening landlords, were marked by our numerous changes of address. I have before me a list of nine addresses in about eleven years, though I cannot be sure of the order. In the beginning two furniture vans and a float were required for the moving; in the end it was just a float. The *bourdon* of these recollections is my father's tipsy boasting:

—I'll show them a trick. Just you wait. I'm not dead yet. No, by God, not half dead. Who-op! What do *you* think?*

The weariness of it was partly relieved for his children by that unquestioning acceptance of all things which is the grace of childhood and by a capacity for simple happiness that could be satisfied even with fine weather, but under the strain his wife aged rapidly.

According to my reckoning we moved up to Dublin in 1893. For the first months of our stay in lodgings there was no question of our attending school. We had a long vacation which my brother enjoyed exploring Dublin, with me at his heels. Then my father took a large sombre old house in Fitzgibbon Street off Mountjoy Square, at that time quite a good residential quarter for well-to-do families. To judge by the size of the rooms, the house had seen better days. Our subsequent changes of address were due to my father's thoroughly Irish repugnance to paying any rent. I do not know what kind of landlord he himself had been in his time, except that during the Split, as it was called, when the overwhelming majority of the eighty-three Irish nationalist members, egged on by the clergy, turned against Parnell, and left him with only eight followers, my father quitted his office without leave during an election, and travelled down to Cork to persuade his tenants to vote for 'the Chief'. It was one of the things held against him when the office was closed down. The nine addresses which I recollect over a period of at most eleven years, besides representing a descending step on the ladder of our fortunes, are each

---

* '—I'm going to show you a little trick, Mr Dedalus said. I'll leave you all where Jesus left the Jews.' *Ulysses*, p. 225 (235).

of them associated in my memory with some particular phase of our gypsy-like family life. From Fitzgibbon Street, after a few months at a Christian Brothers school, we were sent free of fees at the invitation of the Jesuit Father Conmee to the Jesuit school, Belvedere College, in Denmark Street at the other side of Mountjoy Square.

My vague memory of the Christian Brothers school is that my class was so large that I felt lost in it, and sitting in a back bench I heard little and understood less. In any case it did not matter. At Belvedere the classes were much smaller and surveillance closer. Before I had been there long, I was startled and awestruck to see our Jesuit teacher turn a boy of about nine across his knees and whack him with a leather pandy-bat for writing the 'Our Father' at dictation in pencil instead of ink. But after all, priests have so few pastimes. He had other simple pleasures in which a sporting spirit was blended with his religious zeal. Then he would come up to a group of boys, rubbing his hands, and announce breezily:

—A great day for the Catholics! The ladies of the North Side beat the ladies of the South Side at hockey. A great day for the Catholics!

Otherwise he was mainly bored. One evening when I was taking a walk with some other boys towards the Phoenix Park, we met him returning from it. He stopped to talk to us about the lovely evening and our nice little walk, and then suddenly opened his mouth wide in a hearty yawn. Quite unperturbed, he bade us good evening with yawning tears glistening in his eyes, and strolled off. There was a humorous allusion to him in the first draft of *A Portrait of the Artist*. This was the same man who at my First Communion in their private chapel in Belvedere House began the Mass by blessing himself in English. I suppose God understood all the same, although, of course, as all Catholics know, Latin is the proper diplomatic language to use in conversations with God; or perhaps he got Adrian IV, that great friend to Ireland, to interpret for him. He corrected his mistake, and then got on with his day's work, but I wonder was anybody waiting outside for scatter-brained Father Farrelly after Mass with a pandy-bat.

Unfortunately there was a boy in my class who lived at Blackrock and came into school by train. He informed our classmates that my father had run away from Blackrock because he had gone bankrupt. I considered myself in duty bound to call him a liar (though I knew I was) and to challenge him to fight me after school. The venue given was a quiet spot behind St. George's Church, and we were beginning to have quite a set-to when a woman, shocked at such precocious barbarity, began to shout from a window overlooking that side of the square and to call to a man who was passing to stop us. We scattered; but after that encounter my adversary, whose name I don't even remember, kept to himself whatever other first-hand information he had about our family.

Our stay at the Fitzgibbon Street address must have been short, for we were already at our second address when my brother won his first exhibition in the Intermediate Examinations, a prize of twenty pounds in the Preparatory Grade. He was twelve at the time and I was nine and still young enough to wonder how on earth he could prefer to stay at home with a book on a fine afternoon in summer rather than come out to play. I have again a distinct recollection of his refusal, absolute trifles having an exasperating habit of sticking in the memory while important events escape it. Before we left Fitzgibbon Street, however, my mother had time to get scarlatina and the youngest brother, Georgie, to catch it from her. They were isolated after a fashion, in a large bedroom on the second floor, but the rest of the family, except two very young children, remained in the house. I do not remember that any special precautions were taken during the dangerous period of convalescence, the undeclared principle of large patriarchal families being that there shall be an ample margin to allow for losses while the tougher or the luckier ones survive.

Our new house was a small semi-detached villa at Drumcondra in the outskirts of Dublin. I liked it because it was almost in the country at the foot of a low hill, and just near it were fields with a weir into the Tolka and woods where my school-friends and I could trespass at pleasure. Our neighbours in Millbourne Lane, except in the other half of the villa, were farm-hands and navvies who lived in dilapidated cottages. Though there were certainly no signs of wealth about the children of our family, the infant proletarians from the cottages were unfriendly, and displayed their hostility by name-calling in chorus and stone-throwing. It was quite unprovoked, due solely to that innate animosity, observable everywhere in the lower classes, to anybody who is not yet quite so lousy as they are. Our house was well down the lane and we had to run the gauntlet of the unwashed every evening coming home from school. In the end I had a fight with one of the most active of the cat-callers, a little red-headed rough-neck, who rejoiced in the sobriquet of Pisser Duffy. It was late in the afternoon, and the loungers from the cottages, and even the women, stood around without interfering. In the imaginary portrait for which I served as model, 'A Painful Case', my brother has given me the name of Duffy.

After my modest skirmish with P. Duffy, I used to go about with a little group of boys from my class. One evening when we were about to engage an enemy group of street arabs, we saw the rector of our college, Father Henry, coming towards

us. At the sight of a priest the street arabs made off. We saluted
him and he returned our salute, looking at us keenly from under
his dark bushy eyebrows, but did not stop. I fully expected
trouble the following day. We had Father Henry for Latin and
Greek, and as soon as the lesson began he called out my name.
I stood up.

—What were you doing when I saw you last evening? he
asked.

I gave the usual stupid answer:

—Nothing, sir.

—Do you call it nothing to go fighting ragamuffins on the
canal bank?

—I wasn't fighting, sir.

In fact we had only got as far as the preliminary 'angry
parle'.

—Oh, said the rector, I suppose you don't call it fighting
unless you have a black eye or a bloody nose.

Then he trailed off into the usual warnings and threats, but
I could see that he was not altogether displeased. He was
literary-minded, and imagined me to be a typical schoolboy.
That was far from being my description. I was a scraggy, under-
fed boy with arms like the shins of thrushes, and too conscious
of my weakness to be quarrelsome, but there is hardly any way
out of it when you have been grazed by a stone.

Even my brother, in spite of his poise and unruffled temper
as a boy, could not escape the aggressive jealousy of his companions. The discussion about Byron and heresy and the tussle
with three of his classmates in *A Portrait of the Artist* is neither
invented nor exaggerated. He must have been thrown heavily
against barbed wire, for my mother had to mend the rips in his
clothes so that he could go to school the following morning.
It was one of the unpleasant memories of Millbourne Lane.

A boy was born there, who lived long enough to be christ-
ened Frederick and then, after a few weeks, died, leaving in me
at least a sense, though not yet the idea, of futility. The infant
had been in the care of a certain Dr. Tuohy, the father—so my
mother told me—of the artist Tuohy, who long afterwards
painted an excellent portrait of my father as an old man. It was
at Millbourne Lane, too, that my father made a vague attempt
to strangle my mother. In a drunken fit he ran at her and seized
her by the throat, roaring, 'Now, by God, is the time to finish
it'. The children who were in the room ran screaming in between them, but my brother, with more presence of mind,
sprang promptly on his back and overbalanced him so that they
tumbled on the floor. My mother snatched up the two youngest
children and escaped with my elder sister to our neighbour's
house. I remember that a police sergeant called a few days after
this pretty scene, and had a long talk in the parlour with my
father and mother. We were, at last, on the same level as the
navvies and farm-labourers around us. Nothing else came of it
except that there was no further actual violence, though we
lived amid continual threats of it.

My brother was less affected by these scenes than I was,
though they certainly influenced his attitude towards marriage
and family life. Half-hushed-up stories reached us of somewhat
similar happenings in the families of friends of ours, whose
material position, at least, was assured and normally comfortable;
poverty cannot, therefore, have been the root of the evil. The
main struggle of the various Mrs. This-bodies and Mrs. That-
bodies with whom we were acquainted was to conceal carefully
what went on at home, but not more than a couple of years
later it became my brother's set purpose to reveal it. The first
short stories he wrote at school—*Silhouettes*—were neither

adventurous nor romantic. They were already in the style of
Dubliners. But that attachment to his father, which was to be
one of the dominant motives in his character, remained un-
changed. When he went up to Clongowes, the home he left
was moderately prosperous and happy. He came back to it
when a holiday atmosphere prevailed at Christmas and, so well
as I remember, at Easter, and during the long summer vacation.
Summer is always a boon, and 'the wild freshness of morning'
clings about early memories. As he remained at college until
he was almost ten, he knew only the more gracious aspect of
our family life, the more amiable side of my father's character,
and the image of him formed in those years was never to be
effaced. Moreover he could escape from it all into the domain
of fiction. A little later he noted a memory of his reading of
novels by Erckmann-Chatrian—*L'Invasion* at school, *L'Ami
Fritz*, *Le Juif Polonais*, and others for himself—in which these
collaborators do not seem to have produced the effect they
desired.

No school to-morrow: it is Saturday night in winter: I sit by
the fire. Soon they will be returning with provisions, meat and
vegetables, tea and bread and butter, and white pudding that
makes a noise on the pan. . . . I sit reading a story of Alsace,
turning over the yellow pages, watching the men and women
in their strange dresses. It pleases me to read of their ways;
through them I seem to touch the life of a land beyond them,
to enter into communion with the German people. Dearest
illusion, friend of my youth! . . . In him I have imagined myself. Our lives are still sacred in their intimate sympathies. I
am with him at night when he reads the books of the philoso-
phers or some tale of ancient times. I am with him when he
wanders alone or with one whom he has never seen, that young

girl who puts around him arms that have no malice in them, offering her simple, abundant love, hearing and answering his soul he knows not how.

In those days my brother used to study so eagerly that, when we went picnicking to Howth or to the Bull, he would bring with him little note-books with summaries of history or literature or lists of French or Latin words so that my mother could examine him after lunch. It did not spoil the outing, though I sometimes protested. Before lunch we had a swim and in the afternoon a stroll round Howth Head or along the North Strand, and in the interval the examination occupied half an hour or so of a warm and lazy summer noon. The weekly English composition was his strong point. *A.M.D.G.—Ad majorem Dei gloriam—* was piously inscribed at the top of two leaves taken out of the centre of a copy-book, and then there followed four pages of bright ideas on such inspiring subjects as Love of Country, Independence, or Make Hay While the Sun Shines. He was never at a loss what to say, but wrote quickly without making a rough copy beforehand. Then came the conclusion—*L.D.S.*— not an anagram of L.s.d., but a Jesuit motto *Laus Deo Semper*, 'praise to God always'. His English teacher, George Dempsey, 'Mr. Tate' in *A Portrait of the Artist*, soon noticed his turn for composition. He pointed him out to the prefect of studies as a boy with 'a plethora of ideas in his head', and when my brother passed into the higher classes, Dempsey used to read his compositions to the class to serve as models. In the end he took it for granted that 'Gussie', as he jocularly called him from his second name Augustine, would be a writer. My brother seems not to have been unmindful of his encouragement, for I have heard that from Paris he remained in correspondence with the old man until his death. The rector showed less appreciation. What caught his attention was the signature at the end—*Jas. A. Joyce*, with a whirligig of a flourish underneath—on which he commented ironically. He would have appreciated modesty and submission. Well, he just didn't get them.

My brother was never subject to the moodiness or plain tantrums that so often impelled me to go up to my room when my father came home, followed by his sarcastic parting shot, 'What a loving son!' * Much more than his reputation for being clever, his good humour and gaiety made him a favourite with his many sisters and relatives. And neither brawling in the home, nor tireless political ranting to cronies, nor the near imbecility of tipsiness ever spoiled his accord with his father. The full twenty pounds that he won for his exhibition in the Preparatory Grade was handed over by his father to the young boy to do what he liked with it. My brother had no idea what to do with the money, for twenty pounds, in purchasing value equivalent to at least twice that sum today, was too much pocket money for any boy to handle. He bought presents for all of us, practical presents, a pair of boots for one, a dress for another, and there were frequent visits, in which I was occasionally included, to the cheaper parts of theatres, to see Edward Terry in his comedy parts, or Irving or Tree if tickets could be had, or the lesser lights, Edmund Tearle as Othello, or Olga Nethersole. Clever as he was, my brother was still little more than a child, and liked to play with the money. He opened a bank for the family in order to play at issuing receipts and making up accounts. I had unrequested loans of an odd sixpence or so pressed upon me, but his parents were the principal and most assiduous customers, and the money soon melted away in 'dribs

---

* 'By God, you're a loving pair of sons, you and your brother!' *Stephen Hero*, p. 207 (231). [Page references to *Stephen Hero* are first to the English edition (London: Jonathan Cape, 1944), and then in parenthesis to the American edition (New York: New Directions, 1944).]

and drabs'. Yet even so, at the beginning of those years of squalor, he could still be happy in the satisfaction of effort crowned with success.

My brother accompanied my father on a few rare trips out of Dublin, and seemed to enjoy travelling with him. At least he went willingly. When the property in Cork was sold, he had gone with my father on what I think was his last visit to his native town. In *A Portrait of the Artist*, the visit takes place later and awakens in Stephen a raw sense of unrest and spiritual discomfort, but my brother's letters home at the time were written in a tone of amusement even when he described going from one bar to another. While we were living in Millbourne Lane, there was a further visit of a few days in summer to Glasgow, at the invitation of the captain of one of the Duke liners, who was a friend of my father's. The great joke of the visit, which was spoiled by rain, was that my father, soused to the gills on the return trip, had a heated and noisy argument about politics with the captain, an anti-Parnellite. Fortunately the captain was a teetotaller on board though not one on shore.

—By God, man, my father would conclude in telling this wonderfully good story, if he had been drinking he would have thrown me overboard.

I can picture my brother as a handsome young boy, all eyes and nerves, traipsing about in the muggy drizzle of Glasgow after his tipsy father. In Dublin I have more than once seen children, younger than my brother was at that time, trying to lead a staggering mother home. Why, I wonder, seeing that people pretend to hold by the decalogue, has it never been thought fit to add a postil, enjoining some kind of consideration for children, to the fourth commandment? Can Moses have forgotten it in the hurry of jotting down more important matters such as the commandment not to covet one's neighbour's house, nor his wife, nor his man-servant, nor his maid-servant, nor his ox, nor his ass?

I do not know how long an indulgent landlord allowed us to occupy the house in Millbourne Lane, but it was long enough for me to find out for myself the fascination of books. It was there I first read a whole book alone, though it took me about six months to do so. The book was *David Copperfield*. Much of the novel was beyond my comprehension, but its sentimentality and oddity were within my reach. More than half of it was vivid; it awoke and satisfied some longing in my imagination. In the attempt to cast the parts among the people I knew, the one about which it seemed to me there could be no discussion was that of Steerforth for my brother. But my brother never cared for Dickens. Before we moved out, the big bony father of Master P. Duffy called to say good-bye. He was received in the dismantled parlour, and over a bottle of stout expressed his regret for past misunderstandings and offered the good wishes of the cottagers, so that we left in a halo of peace re-established.

I have a clearer recollection of our next house, as I was already about ten years of age when we moved into it. It was the house in North Richmond Street described in 'Araby'. It stood in a quiet neighbourhood, 'North Richmond Street being blind', and, as my brother says, 'an uninhabited house of two storeys [really of two storeys and a large basement storey] stood at the blind end, detached from its neighbours in a square ground'—a garden with apple-trees. The rest of the story of 'Araby' is purely imaginary. In the preface to the American edition of *Dubliners*,* Padraic Colum says that this story and 'The Sisters' are evidently recollections of childhood. This is

---

* New York: The Viking Press, 1925.

a mistake. In fact, only two of the stories—'An Encounter' and 'A Mother', describing a concert at which my brother sang with John McCormack—are based upon his actual personal experience. The remaining stories are either pure fiction or elaborated at second hand from the experience of others, mostly from mine, as I shall show later.

In 'An Encounter', my brother describes a day's miching which he and I planned and carried out while we were living in North Richmond Street, and our encounter with an elderly pederast. For us he was just a 'juggins'. Neither of us could have any notion at the time what kind of 'juggins' he was, but something funny in his speech and behaviour put us on our guard at once. We thought he might be an escaped madman. As he looked about fifty and had a military air, I nicknamed him 'the captain of fifty' from a phrase I had seen somewhere in a Biblical quotation. My brother did not write the story until after he had come to Trieste. I was still in Dublin, and when he sent me the manuscript, as he always used to do when he completed a story, I suggested my nickname for the fellow as the title for the story, but my brother preferred his own title for it.

It was one of the stories to which great exception was taken when in 1912 the tug-o'-war began with Roberts, the shifty manager of the Dublin publishing firm, Maunsel and Company. My brother's solicitor in Dublin, George Lidwell, pleading with him for a less rigid attitude in respect to changes in his work, said to him:

—You see now, your father, who has read that story and is a man with experience of life, has no idea what kind of individual you are writing about.

I was in Trieste then keeping the Triestine end up. I wrote back suggesting that my brother should have replied, 'Neither do I, but I have my suspicions, and I put them into the story'. Tom Kettle, a man whose opinion my brother valued because his Catholicism was an intellectual conviction, not just a phase of nationalism, also declared against the book. He kept saying:

—Oh, I'll slate that book when it comes out. I'll slate it!

That was a fair fight that my brother accepted, and that Kettle, by the by, would have lost had the First World War not claimed him as one of its wasted victims. My brother pointed out that it was an actual experience, but Kettle waved the reply aside.

—I know, he said. We have all met him.

I think it was Kettle's words that decided my brother to keep his own title for the story. He wrote to me that he would like to dedicate it to the author of 'The Voyage of the *Ophir*'.* But why pitch on poor George Meredith as a typical exponent of English educational methods and their suspected effects? Why not the author of *Ralph Roister Doister*?

My father now became or had already become an easy-going canvasser for commercial advertisements in the employment of the *Freeman's Journal*. (My brother has used this financial background for the makeup of Leopold Bloom.) He also did odd jobs in connection with the revision of voting lists, and got a few guineas now and then for acting as presiding officer at municipal elections. But these small additions to his pension made still smaller difference in satisfying the most urgent needs of his large family. My brother's prize money from the Intermediate Examinations, nominally left at his disposal, went in what it is far too dignified to call domestic expenses, and served only to confer on the household a month or so of effortless ease, in which my father bloomed again like a wilting flower in the rain.

* Meredith's poem written for the voyage around the empire taken in 1901 by the Prince and Princess of Wales.

He was always looking for a job, one suitable, of course, for a man who does not want to work, and now during spells of sobriety, for it must not be imagined that he was not occasionally sober, he would make optimistic calculations of how much he could earn 'between hopping and trotting'.

During these halcyon days when he was temporarily, though not bigotedly, 'on the water wagon', Sundays and holidays were spent, weather permitting, in taking long walks in the lovely surroundings of Dublin. My brother and I were always in the group, which usually included a friend or two of his, for whom he was better than a guide, though they were truer Dubliners than he was. We would stop to look in at the gates of a country house.

—A delightful spot, my father would say enthusiastically. I wouldn't mind ending my days there.

—Whom does it belong to, John, do you know?

—Well, it used to belong to old So-and-so.

—Is it the solicitor in Dame Street you mean?

—Yes, that's the man.

Then would follow the life, death, and miracles of old So-and-so or it might be scraps of information regarding more important people, the place where Addison used to walk, or Swift's supposed residence, or the house of the infamous 'Sham Squire', Francis Higgins, on Stephen's Green,* or Surgeon Wilde's house (Oscar was never mentioned) on Merrion Square. He had an inexhaustible fund of Dublin small talk, and

---

* Higgins (1746-1802), an attorney's clerk in Dublin, married a respectable young woman whom he led to believe he was a country gentleman. He was prosecuted and imprisoned, and afterwards owned gaming houses and got possession of the *Freeman's Journal*, in which he libelled Henry Grattan and other patriots. He received a thousand pounds for revealing the hiding place of Lord Edward Fitzgerald.

my brother shared with him this interest in Dublin lore, which distance and the lapse of time served only to increase.

When friends dropped in on Sundays or of an evening during the week, my father was unaffectedly delighted to see them and unwilling to let them go home even when the night had worn on—'Why, man, the night is young yet'. He was genial, amusing, hospitable. He had more talk, more stories, more reminiscences than the rest of the group, and they seemed to look up to him. Of course they asked him to sing. His voice was still good, mellow and rather dark in colour with resonant high tones. Many of the songs he sang were rubbish, such as that insufferable 'Yes, Let Me Like a Soldier Fall' (from which perhaps Verdi got the idea for '*Di quella pira*', though the Irish aria will not stand the comparison), sung, not quite seriously however, for the sake of the high C at the end. But ballads he sang well and many operatic airs in English but known by their Italian names—'*M'appari*' (very well), '*Ah si, ben mio*', '*Salve dimora*', '*A te, o cara*', which I liked best though he did not think much of it and rarely sang it. My brother, also, was beginning to have a voice, and singers of the past were often discussed, as in 'The Dead'. In the first years at Trieste, my brother found the same atmosphere in the Tuscan family with whom we lived. The wife of his friend Francini had been on the operatic stage before her marriage and had sung *Sonnambula* and other light soprano parts. She always urged my brother to have his voice trained as a sure solution of his difficulties. In the course of these evenings at home we became acquainted through my mother with a good deal of romantic piano music: Chopin, Mendelssohn, Liszt, Schumann, Schubert. The interest in these moody men, once the idols of the élite, was not so strange for our family as might at first appear. Indulgence in moodiness is one of the cheap luxuries of youth. I understood the spell of their melancholy perhaps better than I do in these crude days, and my brother was evidently not immune to the *maladie du siècle* either, for *Moods* was the title that he gave to the first volume of poems which he began to write about this time or a little later.

Towards the end of the summer holidays that were to furnish either the idea or the emotional environment for the few stories of childhood I have mentioned, two Dominican priests called to see my father. They were shown into the parlour, and when my father appeared they soon declared the purpose of this visit, couching it in a few words of flattery to his paternal vanity. The results of the Intermediate Examinations had just been published, and it appeared from them that my brother had again won an exhibition, this time in the Junior Grade. The two Dominicans had come to offer him free board and tuition in a college belonging to their order in the country. My father called my brother into the room, and, after explaining the proposal to him, told him that he was to decide for himself. My brother did so without hesitation. He rejected the offer.

—I began with the Jesuits, he said, and I want to end with them.

Whether the decision in itself was good or bad, my father did right, I think, to leave it to his son, for he believed such decisions tempered the will. My brother learned to come to a decision without regretting it. My father called it 'making a man of him'.

The Dominicans, for their part, were not above engaging in a little underhand, clerical competition with a rival order; and they were certainly very alert businessmen. The addresses of students were not given in the lists published by the Board of Education, only the name of the colleges they attended. To find us out so quickly, especially since my father's traces were not easy to follow, they must have had an informant in the offices of the Board, where names and addresses were registered when the trifling entrance fees for the examinations were paid.

A later rector of Belvedere College seized the opportunity afforded by an interview with Patricia Hutchins, the author of *James Joyce's Dublin*, to assert with some emphasis that my brother was given his breakfast at the college. Some other anonymous source adds also his dinner. But so far as I can recollect, in all the seven or eight years I remained at Belvedere College, breakfast was never served there for anyone.

'It was a mistake', said the same misinformed spokesman of his Order, 'although well meant by Father Henry at the time, to educate a boy here when his background was so much at variance with the standards of the school, cultural and religious'. (The suggestion was Father Conmee's, not Henry's; we were then at one of the Christian Brothers schools, and Father Henry didn't know us.) I remember my classmates. If by 'cultural background' he means independent, out-of-school interest in literature, music, painting, religion, history, or even politics, my 'cultural background'—not to speak of my brother's—was considerably higher than that of my classmates, and by a complexity of causes as much a result of our kind of family life as theirs was of their kind. In fact, this is a very cheap boast, for their cultural background hardly went beyond tennis and dinner-jackets. To me at least it seems that there is a reasonable suspicion that this is just the 'cultural background' that the rector of Belvedere College had in mind.

Clerical orders, the most unabashed beggars in the country, exposed a little later by Michael McCarthy in his *Priests and People in Ireland*, monopolize secondary education, thrive on it, and yet consider it a favour if they impart it. That, at least, is the attitude of the Jesuits of Belvedere College towards the most brilliant pupil their school has produced in over one hundred years. Even as a boy he won three exhibitions, and twice, in the Middle and Senior Grades, he won the prize for English composition. In any civilized country in Europe, the son of a large and impoverished family (we were ten at the time) is admitted free of school fees to the state schools as a right, not as a favour, and it is high time secondary education was in secular hands in Ireland, too.

About the time when we moved into the house in Richmond Street, and so when I was between nine and ten years of age, an incident took place which was typical of Jesuit educational methods and had considerable influence on my 'religious background'. One day the rector, Father Henry, sent for me without any reason that I have ever been able to imagine. He began by asking me questions about my work in class, which aroused some forebodings, but soon changed to more intimate questions. Though he was a priest and there seemed to me to be nothing unusual in the turn his questions had taken, I was a good deal bewildered. Then, changing again, he began to question me about my brother's morals; and such was (and is) the dominance of the priest in Irish life that it never entered my head that he had no right to do so. At any rate I could not answer because I did not know; and I said so. It was something new that I had not thought of. He seemed to suspect that I was evading his questions, for he warned that it was 'as in the confessional', and that the lips of a priest are sealed. He was a sallow-faced man with jet-black hair and a deep voice. It was rumoured amongst the boys that he suffered from heart disease, and might drop dead at any moment. Looking at me with the searching suspicious eyes of a fanatical convert from Protestantism, and laying his finger solemnly on his lips he promised that 'no word of what I might say should ever pass them'. He spoke earnestly—and he was reputed an eloquent preacher—of the most terrible of all sins, the sin of telling a lie to the Holy Ghost. I was impressed. I tried conscientiously to remember something in the Holy Ghost's line, but could think of nothing but some horseplay between my brother and a hoydenish young servant girl we had then, a kind of catch-as-catch-can-cum-spanking match. So I hawked that out for the Holy Ghost's benefit, hoping it would be enough on account. The rector evidently thought it was, for he dismissed me, and sent me back to my classroom. Another hour was already half over, but the teacher, a Jesuit of course, asked me no questions either about my long absence or about the lesson for the day. I sat there with my head in a maze, almost oblivious of the curious glances of my companions, and much more upset than I had been during the cross-examination.

The following day the rector sent for my mother, and, without alluding to any specific fact or mentioning me, gave her clearly to understand that she should watch her elder son who was inclined to evil ways. My mother was astonished and shocked, but at the same time incredulous. On her return from the college she said only that the rector had called her to speak to her about Jim. Floundering in doubt whether or not it was a sin to speak, I told her about the long interrogation of the day before, omitting nothing; but though in the course of my account I mentioned the pledge of secrecy 'as in the confessional', it was still only remotely and in the vague background of my mind that I felt, not so clearly as words express it, that I had been put upon, and that there had been some breach of faith. I was too young to appreciate the subtle but useful difference between 'in the confessional' and 'as in the confessional'; and in any case at that time there could be no shadow of a doubt in my mind that in such a matter a priest, especially the stern and devoutly pious rector of the college, could not be wrong. But my reactions lose nothing by being slow.

My mother was certainly not pleased with what she had heard, but in a way she was relieved, for from the rector's earnest admonitions she had been led to fear worse things. Of course, she blamed the servant, who was a girl of twenty-three or twenty-four, and so about ten years older than my brother. She had already left us, and we never had another. My mother had long before that time ceased to confide in my father about anything, but he observed that something was amiss, and inquired what all the hugger-mugger was about.

—I am under a cloud at school, said my brother.

—What about? asked my father.

—I don't know, said my brother. You had better ask the rector.

My father went to the college, but again the rector limited himself to solemn but vague warnings.

—That boy will give you trouble, the rector told him.

—No, he won't, said my father, because I won't let him.

Neither of them knew whom he had to deal with; but for years after, intermittently, until my brother left Dublin, my father would rehearse the story of the rector's thrust and his own clever parry. Nobody seemed to think that I had done anything at all open to criticism, but I was uneasy and brooded on the trouble in which, under duress, I had been an unwilling agent.

As for my brother, he just laughed at me and called me a fathead. His imperturbability, not only at home, but in various interviews with the rector, was far beyond his years, and deeply angered the rector, who considered it a mute challenge. It is true he had just won a second exhibition and was studying hard to win a third. My father, apparently guessing nothing in spite of his reputed shrewdness, cursed the rector's 'tawny soul'

roundly every night for 'putting the boy off his studies'. The
boy, however, was not put off his studies; he applied himself
to them quite regularly. My brother never undervalued himself. That is certain; but it is not a sufficient explanation of his
calm. To judge by his unaffected imperturbability, he might
have been assisting at a badly rehearsed comedy that did not
concern him. That 'cold lucid indifference', which, he says in
A Portrait of the Artist, reigned in the boy Stephen's soul after
his first sexual experiences, seemed never to forsake him. But
I fancy there was a further reason. I fancy he grasped at once
what I understood only long afterwards by brooding on it,
that the rector had gone parlously near a breach of the vowed
secrecy of the confessional, and that he had the rector in the
hollow of his hand. He knew he was the victim of a Jesuit
intrigue, and was coldly determined to out-Jesuit the Jesuit.
Even at that early age the rumpus could not throw him off
his balance. He gave proof even then of that wariness in fence
that later stood him in such good stead in his struggle with
hostile authorities in various lands and in times of upheaval.

The storm blew over as unexpectedly as it had sprung up
because, of the two people who had the matter in hand, one had
already said too much and the other kept her counsel. But it
was the beginning of an almost open hostility between the
rector, Father Henry, and my brother which lasted until my
brother left Belvedere. The hostility, however, was mainly
one-sided. I find no trace of it in the portraiture of the rector
in the Belvedere chapters of *A Portrait of the Artist*. My
brother considered him the victim of his own fanaticism; and in
any case justice towards the characters of his own creation,
or imaginative re-creation, became an artistic principle with
him. That year or the next, my brother won an exhibition in
the Middle Grade, as well as the coveted first prize for English

composition, but though the other teachers were smiling and congratulatory, the rector was silent. It is interesting to note that in the Middle Grade his marks in mathematics were high— he was placed about thirteenth in Ireland, so well as I remember. He detested mathematics; it was his weakest subject, but he tackled it resolutely because he wanted to win an exhibition, and he succeeded. He had, in fact, the kind of cleverness which is supposed to be distinctive of successful lawyers, that of acquiring at short notice, when necessary, a temporary mastery of some subject in which they have not a particle of personal interest.

Before we left North Richmond Street my brother and I were often invited to go on Sunday evenings to the house of school-fellows of ours, the Sheehys, who lived not far from us in Mountjoy Square, a locality which seems to have declined as a residential quarter. This friendly relationship lasted some years and was practically the only experience of what might be called social life that my brother had in Dublin. The father was a member of Parliament, and the family consisted of two clever brothers and four clever sisters, one of them a really handsome girl. David Sheehy, the father, was a vigorous-looking man, who lived to be about ninety. I liked him, but my brother thought him pompous and inclined to lay down the law. He preferred the mother.

I must still have been a young boy when we first went there, for I remember a girl student, a university friend of the eldest sister's, who took possession of me, and talked to me almost all the evening about gymnastics and sport. I was a minor member of the college team which had won the inter-school shield for gymnastics, and she, a pretty girl with a lithe figure, was keen on sport, too. To me she appeared to be a young woman, but I was captivated, and disappointed time after time not to meet her again. On another occasion, after I had been partnered with his youngest daughter in a dance by Mr. Sheehy, we both sat, when the dance was over, on separate arms of a large arm-chair, she looking west-south-west, and I looking east-south-east.

My brother, for his part, never lost his poise and, though generally rather distant in manner, he was treated with easy familiarity as between successful students by the Sheehys, brothers and sisters, all of whom were then or later university students. The eldest son was professor in the University of Galway when he died. My brother was not only the most brilliant pupil in the college, and, at that time at least, of ex-emplary diligence, but also an omnivorous reader in English and French. His heterogeneous and mostly unorthodox reading often surprised them and was the subject of good-natured rail-lery. To improve his French he corresponded with some stu-dent in Vire, Calvados, whose name he had got from one of the many societies for improving Anglo-French relations. As the second daughter, Margaret, was just then beginning to make a name as an actress in amateur theatricals, charades were fre-quently arranged. My brother, too, almost always took part in them and discovered a real talent for mere clowning, unsus-pected in so serious a youth. Besides which, his voice was al-ready developing, and though the Sheehys were not musical, he was often asked to sing.

Until his fourteenth or fifteenth year he studied regularly according to the school curriculum, and altogether was in danger of becoming the model of a serious schoolboy in the higher classes, were it not that the works he borrowed from the Capel Street Lending Library sometimes seemed to the librarian open to question for a boy of his age. One of the books against which Old Grogan, the librarian, solemnly warned my father was *Tess of the D'Urbervilles*. My father had no notion what kind of book it was, or who the author might be, his own taste in literature wavering among *Tom Burke of Ours, Frank Fair-leigh,* and for breath-taking interest, *The Moonstone.*

—What kind of book is this I hear you are reading? he asked my brother.

—I have read many. Which do you mean?

—Old Grogan was saying something about the last book you took out, said my father.

—What! *Tess of the D'Urbervilles.* It's by Thomas Hardy. So I have to ask Old Grogan what I am to read. The ignorant old clod-hopper! He'd be much more at home in his native bog than in a library. I've a good mind to write a letter to the Corporation about him.

—Well, if you say it's all right, said my father, easily convinced.

As my father had often made Old Grogan, who had just the cut of a hedge-schoolmaster, the butt of his mimicry, the librarian was sacrificed conversationally on the altar of freedom of thought. But I, too, very nearly became involved as another comic victim in this first brush with a censor. The Capel Street Public Lending Library was a mile or so from where we lived, and my brother, with the excuse that he could not spare time from his studies, used to send me to change books for him, giving me a list of other books in order of preference in case the one he wanted should be out. Second or third on the list he gave me after the librarian's ineffectual attempt to act as censor was the name of another of Hardy's works, *Jude the Obscure.* I did not know the book, and, when halfway to the library I glanced at the list, I could not read the name aright. In my brother's scribbled handwriting, it looked like *Jude the Obscene.* I puzzled over it, but there seemed to be no doubt about it. The more I looked, the surer I was that that word was 'obscene'. At first I thought that I would say the book was out, but even in my own eyes I did not wish to be found wanting

in the rebellion declared against the librarian. Fortunately the
first book on the list was in, for I had screwed my courage to
the sticking point and was quite determined to call for *Jude*
boldly by the title as I read it. When I came home and told my
brother about my dilemma, he shouted with laughter. He was
sorry, he said, that I did not have to ask for it. He wished he
could have been there to see Old Grogan's stupid face and my
stupid face when I asked for *Jude the Obscene*.

By this time we had already moved once more. The new
house was in Windsor Terrace, Fairview, near the road that
winds round the wide shallow mouth of the Liffey to Clontarf.
It was the second last house on the left at the top of parallel
rows of two-storeyed houses, bordering on the rather extensive
grounds of some invisible suburban villa, and belonged to a
young clergyman named Love, a long-suffering Christian, who,
it is to be hoped, had other sources of income. He makes a
brief appearance in *Ulysses*. We remained for some years near
the sea, our next two removals being in the immediate neighbourhood. Clontarf, the scene of one of the most famous battles
in Irish history, was within easy reach by tram. The name Clontarf means 'the meadow of the bull', and the Bull is the long sand-
bank, which at high tide is completely cut off from the coastal
road by a narrow channel of water. The uneven green turf of this
sandy islet, overgrown with bushes and bitter-tasting bent-
grasses, had attracted golfers, who built a little club house,
putting greens, and artificial bunkers on the Bull stretching out
for more than half its length. Seaward a breakwater, partly
submerged at high tide, ran far out to the river mouth. Here
as before we used to spend the long summer holidays, bathing
almost every day when the weather was fine and the tide
served, the whole family often picnicking at the end of the
Bull or on Howth Head, which we could reach on foot from

the tram terminus at Dollymount. Haunting memories of this
wild, little-frequented strand, with its tang of sunbaked sea-
weed and stinging sea-breezes, occur in various places in my
brother's work, but chiefly in *A Portrait of the Artist*, where it
is the scene of Stephen's sudden resolution to live his life as an
artist freely and boldly.

Until fourteen or fifteen years of age, as I have said, my
brother had been a docile and diligent pupil, but from this age
onwards his systematic studies, which had followed the pre-
scribed curriculum obediently, gradually gave way to a line of
reading, as my father generally preferred to call it, of his own
choice. The last examination for which he studied regularly
was the Middle Grade. He used to go up to our room a couple
of hours after our return from school at about three and remain
there until ten o'clock, when he would come down in high
good humour for some light supper before going to bed.*
Meanwhile, on four or five nights a week, I had the pleasure of
my father's drunken company in the kitchen or in the parlour.
I had succeeded somehow in winning a book prize in the Preparatory Grade (a small credit with a bookseller of which a
student could avail himself), but it was considered unworthy
of any mention at home. My own private impression at the
time was that the examiners had given me some other fellow's
marks by mistake. In spite of the book prize, I went through
that school year (and others) without some of the principal
text-books. I had a rather good memory and used to cram
during the brief intervals and even during the lessons, and
generally succeeded in getting the smattering that was sufficient
unto the day like the evil thereof. I had a special grudge against
a Greek grammar by a Jesuit, Father Brown. I remember, too,

---

* (His mother to Stephen:) 'Get Dilly to make you that boiled rice every
night after your brain work.' *Ulysses*, p. 548 (566).

that the rector, Father Henry, who was our teacher for Greek, altogether disregarded the accents. With my classmates I earned the reputation of being a 'hard case', an adept at cribbing exercises under the teacher's very nose, and unblinking under exasperated tirades and threats when I did not succeed in getting away with it. In the end I managed to scrape ingloriously through examinations.

The school hours were hours of high tension, and there was little relaxation at home. It does not facilitate a boy's study to have a drunken man at the other side of the table asking him:

—Are you going to win?

—Well, I'll try.

—That'll do. That's all I want. [Repeated about a dozen times.]

And then again *da capo:*

—Are you going to win?

—I'll try.*

How long the third-degree examination continued with the same question and answer, I do not remember, but certainly long enough to seem incredible to people who are not familiar with the imbecility of drunkenness, that malodorous mixture of partial paralysis and semi-insanity. In the end the 'Chinaman' and 'hard case' collapsed in tears. Afterwards my mother arranged that I was to study in the room I shared with my brother.

Another more boisterous interlude to homework comes back to my memory, the evening when my father and the skipper of a fishing smack, both very drunk, brought each other home. This sea-captain was reported to be the one who had taken James Stephens, the Fenian organizer, away to France in 1865 after his escape from Richmond Prison. The story was that he

---

* 'Ho, boy! Are you going to win? Hoop! Schatt! . . . Head up! Keep our flag flying!' *Ulysses,* p. 540 (557).

had brought James Stephens, dressed as a woman and disguised as his bride, aboard his fishing smack. The vessel was stopped and searched by an English cruiser in Dublin Bay shortly after setting sail. With presence of mind Stephens, apparently in great distress, clung to the captain, who appealed to the officer in charge of the search party not to frighten his newly married bride, and that gallant officer and gentleman apologized for the trouble he had given them and let the vessel proceed on her way. Unfortunately, my admiration went not to the quick-witted Irish skipper, but at least equally to the gallant English officer and gentleman.

At the time I speak of the captain was a stocky man with a pointed grey-white beard, who walked steadily even in his cups, but seemed to be invaded by a kind of *rigor vini* that made it necessary for him to move all of a piece when he turned this way or that. I have in my mind's eye the picture of him sitting stiffly on my father's knee, like a ventriloquist's stooge, while they crooned in unison, 'I dream of thee, sweet Mado-line'. Every now and then my father would interrupt the duet to pluck the captain's beard and shout, 'Who-op! You're the best bloody man that ever scuttled a ship', until the rickety chair gave way under the double weight and they fell sitting on the floor. After this abrupt end to the concert, the captain took his leave with dignity, without forgetting his umbrella, which he had stood in a corner of the room.

I observe that it is usual in the pseudo-scientific jargon of our days to classify such people as weaklings. But if the story about the captain was true—and it probably was true, though he himself always avoided speaking of it—he had risked a long term of imprisonment in a minority cause and shown presence of mind in the face of danger. My father, for his part, had been a more than average all-round sportsman, and an amateur actor and singer immune to stage-fright. He lived to be eighty-three and had more than a dozen children. If such people are weaklings, the word must have very elastic connotations.

In such circumstances I had little wish to study, and even my brother's inflexibility of purpose seemed to weaken. I used to read a good deal, for the most part plodding in my brother's tracks. He devoured books, while I was a slow reader. It sometimes surprised me, however, to find both that my brother remembered little or nothing of most of the books he read so voraciously and that at need he could make good use of the one or two things he did remember from his reading. He read quickly, and if the book or the author did not appeal to him he forgot them both. If a book did, on the contrary, make some impression on him, he tried to read as many by the same writer as he could lay his hands on. Whenever I struck out for myself, I always felt a little guilty, as if I were indulging an inferior taste. That questionable taste included Scott and Dickens, whom my brother could not stand. In fact, I read ten or twelve of the Waverley novels running and cried 'Hold, enough!' only when I reached *Count Robert of Paris*. This habit of reading in tandem continued when we were in Trieste; not, of course for all books (he read far too much for me), but for many, and even for some foreign authors. My reading, which had to serve instead of regular study, may have been useful to him as a kind of revision, for occasionally in our endless discussions I happened to point out things he had passed over and to re-arouse his interest. He said frankly that he used me as a butcher uses his steel.*

There is an example of this revision in *Ulysses*. Stephen Dedalus sends Malachi Mulligan a telegram which runs, 'The

---

* 'Where is your brother? Apothecaries' hall. My whetstone.' *Ulysses*, p. 199 (209).

sentimentalist is one who would enjoy without incurring the immense debtorship for a thing done'. My brother had paid no particular attention to the epigram when he was reading *The Ordeal of Richard Feverel*. To me, struggling to understand the sentimentalists by whom I was surrounded, one of whom wept when he sang 'The Bells of Shandon', it seemed far too superficial to dismiss their sentimentalism, in such bewildering contrast with their conduct, as mere silliness. Meredith's epigram was a sudden illumination, and I drew my brother's attention to it. At least I could think I now understood why I detested 'The Bells of Shandon', as well as those other old favourites, 'The Lost Chord' and 'Thou'rt Passing Hence, My Brother'.

I cannot, of course, remember the religious crisis which is the central theme of *A Portrait of the Artist*. The impression it leaves is that it was an actual experience, and I have a vivid memory of many outward signs that confirm this impression: the long talks at the college, not with the rector, but with the preacher of the Lenten sermon, Father Jeffcott, who had known my brother at Clongowes College, and with Father Conmee at Gardiner Street; a brief interview of friendly admonition with the Provincial; the early morning Mass which he attended with my mother after which he would stay on in the silent chapel, where Mass had come and gone so quietly, to say another prayer, while his mother whispered to him that breakfast was ready; as well as the self-imposed abstention from sweets, newspapers, and theatres during Lent.

I watched these mild austerities with surprise, but without admiration and without any inner urge to emulation. At that age (I was getting on for fourteen then) I still went to confession and Communion twice or three times a year at Easter, at Christmas, and perhaps once more at some other time, but always with distaste. I was always more upset by a blunder or

a gaffe than by sin. The offence to the Godhead never
troubled me, but faults in my relations with others did. When
at low Mass on Sunday, to which I always went because it is
shorter, the celebrant went into the pulpit to denounce the
perils of 'serious mortal sin', his words fell flat and echoless on
my ear. I felt that they really meant nothing to the preacher
either, that they were so much gospel gibberish, and that the
twenty minutes' sermon, which bored me into the fidgets, was for
him what the weekly English composition was for me, the squeez-
ing of a dry lemon. But I just thought to myself, 'Father Reynolds
is a bad preacher', and that for the moment was the end of it.

Neither had I ever been able to work myself up into anything like religious fervour in regard to Holy Communion. For
me the host was a thing like tissue-paper with a curiously taste-
less taste, that stuck to the palate and had to be dislodged carefully with the tongue. The prayer to be read after Communion,
which contained the quotation, 'Lord, I am not worthy that
thou shouldst enter under my roof', puzzled me like an ill-
timed pun. The roof of my mouth or the roof of somebody's
house? Some people are born hypocrites, and some have hypocrisy thrust upon them. The latter was my case then. Of course,
it was the body and blood of Jesus. Oh, of course! And then
the idea that it was an act of cannibalism came into my mind
to be bundled in horror out of the door and come back through
the window for an answer. It had always been dinned into my
ears that Jesus Christ was true God and true man, and that as
man he had a human body of flesh and blood. At Mass the host
was converted miraculously for the hundred-millionth time into
the flesh and blood of Jesus. Those were their words. When I,
together with other boys, was being prepared for my First
Communion they had taught us that the feast of Corpus Christi,
one of the greatest festivals of the Catholic Church, had been

instituted in the Middle Ages after a doubting priest had found blood dripping from the host over his hands and the altar linen. I could not get away from the conclusion that to deny in the teeth of such common doctrinal instruction that Communion was an act of cannibalism, at least in intention, at least in imagination, was downright lying. And there was always the danger of dying suddenly and going to hell if one did not believe, that permanent blackmail for vacillating believers. Of course, one was permitted to doubt, provided it was honest doubt and one had taken the utmost care to find out the truth of such a supremely important matter. So, I supposed, after a lifetime of study, at fifty or sixty, one might venture to harbour doubt about the Real Presence. Meanwhile, I was in a cleft stick, forced to tell myself lyingly that I believed what in my heart I disbelieved even with a certain disgust.

Although the Lenten sermons preached by Father Jeffcott stirred up no such brain-storm of terror and remorse in me as they did in my brother, I remember that retreat well. I listened to them with something akin to irritation as one does to a story which one feels to be an invention but which one cannot disprove. In order to illustrate God's horror of sin and how much it offended Him, Father Jeffcott told us that if all the natural catastrophes and all the wars and all the ills and evils of mankind could be avoided by deliberately committing one venial sin, it would be far, far better not to commit that sin. With a start of anger that deafened me for a while to the rest of his sermon, I thought 'A lie! A thumping falsehood!', and later, when my anger ebbed, 'Do the sufferings of men not matter?' When I began to listen to him again, what he said did not matter, for another thought amused me. Approximately it was this: if it is true that sin offends God so much, considering the amount of sin that is committed per minute per square mile, He must be in a constant state of divine apoplexy quite inconsistent with celestial bliss. My scepticism regarding the things revealed to 'one of our fathers' had one immediate effect; it startled out of his apathy our lay teacher, Dempsey ('Mr. Tate'). When we came up from the College Chapel, the boys were discussing the latest sermon. One of them told him that Father Jeffcott had said that it had been revealed to a Jesuit saint that the damned were pouring into hell like hailstones. Master and pupils were silent for a moment awestricken.

—Hailstones fall pretty quickly, said I. That must be about the rate at which people are dying all over the world.

—I suppose so, said Dempsey with the indifference of a man who does not realize what he is admitting.

—And that means, I concluded, that in the war between God and the Devil for man's soul, the Devil is winning all along the line.

Dempsey had been chewing his moustache and listening half-bemused to the talk about a religious question that he took for granted. Now he woke up. He was very angry to find that he had walked into a trap.

—I don't want to discuss religion with you. That's not my business, he said sharply. You should ask whoever teaches you Catholic doctrine.

But it was the rector that taught us Catholic doctrine and I had no intention of asking him anything. So I hedged.

—I don't believe, I said, that we are obliged to accept the visions of the saints as gospel truths.

It was not exactly hedging either, for at the time my groping doubts about Catholic doctrine hardly went beyond that point.

The reverent landlord of Windsor Terrace must have been as largely endowed with Christian charity as his name betokened, for our residence at that address appears to have been somewhat longer than elsewhere. I cannot be certain how long my brother's conversion lasted, rather more than a year I should say, for we were still at Windsor Terrace when the reaction set in and he came under what was to prove one of the dominant influences of his life, the influence of Henrik Ibsen. It seems to me little short of a miracle that anyone should have striven to cultivate poetry or cared to get in touch with the current of European thought while living in a household such as ours, typical as it was of the squalor of a drunken generation. Some inner purpose transfigured him.

One afternoon comes back to me distinctly, the afternoon when Ibsen's *Master Builder* arrived from Heinemann's in William Archer's translation with his excellent preface, a slim volume in yellow paper covers with a vignette of Hilde Wangel, Alpenstock in hand, on the outside. It was an event; and my brother stayed up that night to read the play. In the morning I must have been the first to come down for I found the large arm-chair pulled near to the extinguished hearth and the table to the arm-chair. The lamp had been pulled to the edge of the table so that the table-cover drooped on the floor. The whole room bore witness that he had read late into the night. My brother had been keeping vigil to hear the message from Norway of the younger generation that sooner or later comes knocking at the door.*

---

* Professor Joyce is echoing his brother's words at the end of 'The Day of the Rabblement': 'Elsewhere there are men who are worthy to carry on the tradition of the old master who is dying in Christiania. He has already found his successor in the writer of "Michael Kramer", and the third minister will not be wanting when his hour comes. Even now that hour may be standing by the door.'

III · *Raw Spring*

Some four years later Yeats wrote to my brother, in a letter dated December 18, 1902, 'Your technique in verse is very much better than the technique of any young Dublin man I have met during my time. It might have been the work of a young man who lived in an Oxford literary set.' * My brother was not the product of an Oxford literary set. His cultural background was of the kind I am endeavouring to describe in some detail. In spite of his seeming equanimity, he suffered from it more deeply than I did because of his attachment to his father and because his mind was haunted by clear visions of what life might be made to yield.

In his last years in Belvedere College he had begun to collect the poems I have already mentioned in a thick stiff-covered exercise-book, the fly-leaf of which bore the title *Moods*. It was evidence of the struggle to keep the spirit within him alive in the midst of all-pervading squalor and disintegration. The volume contained some fifty or sixty original lyric poems, a few of them rather long, and perhaps half a dozen translations from Latin and French. It was soon followed by another similar volume entitled *Shine and Dark*, a name borrowed from Whitman's line, 'Earth of shine and dark mottling the tide of the river'. Of these very early poems only five remain in a complete form, as far as I am aware: the poem he called 'The

---

* This letter is given in full on pp. 208-209.

Villanelle of the Temptress', postdated in *A Portrait of the Artist*, two translations quoted by Gorman in his life of my brother, a poem quoted in J. F. Byrne's *Silent Years*, and the second song in *Chamber Music*, originally entitled 'Commonplace'. I remember some longer and more ambitious efforts— one, for example, on the Valkyrie and another celebrating some joyous festival of youth:

> *And orient banners they outfling*
> *Before the ripple-bearded king.*

I objected to the image, because, as I said, it reminded me of a playing-card. My brother, a little put out, asked me ironically why I didn't write poetry myself, seeing that I evidently knew everything about everything. In fact I had made a few abortive attempts. It must have been during my brother's last year at Belvedere College, for in a junior grade we were reading Coppée's *Le Luthier de Crémone*, and I had secretly attempted to translate the first pages of it into verse, but contemplating the result and comparing it with my brother's verse I ruefully concluded that I was not a poet. But criticism is a free-for-all. Mine was usually unbounded admiration, but when it was not my brother either brushed it aside or took it in good part. He tried some half-humorous poems in dialect, too. The dialect consisted mainly in omitting the 'g' of the present participle.

> *Am I foolish to be hopin'*
> *That you left your window open*
> *To be listenin' to me mopin'*
> *Here and singin', lady mine?*

The name he had put on the serenade was 'Rebuking', and when he asked me what I thought of it, I told him in schoolboy fashion that I thought it was very nice but that he ought to change the 'b' of the title into 'p'. He laughed; but he wrote no more poems in the vernacular style except the one to the air of 'Molly Brannigan' addressed to Molly Bloom, which has a more genuine ring.*

It was in his last year at Belvedere College that he was seized with an overmastering admiration for Ibsen that was like a sudden wind in the sails of a becalmed yacht, like a rudder to a drifting bark. The other influences he had felt, though he had accepted them, had been imposed; this arose within him, keen and exultant, as if in answer to a call. When Mrs. Patrick Campbell produced *Magda* (Sudermann's *Heimat*), he went to see it with his parents, probably in a flush period after he had collected his last exhibition. Discussing the play with them the following day he announced:

—The subject of the play is genius breaking out in the home and against the home. You needn't have gone to see it. It's going to happen in your own house.

Mrs. Patrick Campbell had at least one listener for whom the play was not just an interesting postprandial pastime. For my brother the drama had become a thing of supreme importance, what the Mass had been. It would be wrong to dismiss this announcement of his as a mere piece of youthful arrogance. It was, at least, as much admiration of others as of himself. Ibsen's influence had determined in him a fierce contempt for the ignobility of falsity, and the cause of his inward exultation was not conceit, but his feeling that he belonged to the elect company of those who mould the conscience of their race.

At this time, too, his first ambition to be a dramatist began to take shape. He used to write critiques of every play he went

---

* This poem is given in Herbert Gorman, *James Joyce* (New York: Farrar and Rinehart, 1939; London: John Lane, The Bodley Head, 1941).

to see, and then compare them with the bored, platitudinous
notices of the performances in the newspapers. In his last year
he took part in the college theatricals, playing the part of the
headmaster in Anstey's farce *Vice Versa*. He was quite deliberate and self-possessed on the stage, showed a surprising talent
for acting, and added an unexpected interest to the part by
improvising, to the coach's horror, an excellent imitation of
the rector of the College, who was sitting in the front row of
the College theatre and seemed to enjoy it as much as his pupils
amongst the audience did.

Before he left Belvedere, however, there was a final clash
between Jim and the rector. The summer term at school had
come to an end, and the Intermediate Examinations were due to
begin in a day or two. My brother had been entered for the
Senior Grade Examinations, which corresponded to the final
school-leaving examinations in other countries, with the added
importance of being conducted directly by the Board of Education. The examinations being, of course, nondenominational,
the religious tests, if any, were set by the various colleges themselves. In that year the rector appointed the day before the
Intermediate Examinations for the school examination in Christian Doctrine. My brother did not present himself for it. He
said he had been studying all day, which, so far as it went, was
the truth. His desertion deeply angered the rector, as I think
it was intended to do—my brother had a long memory—
especially because my brother was the head boy of the school,
occupying a position equivalent to that of captain of an English school. There was little the rector could do about it except bluster, and that he did. He said that it was an act of
rebellion, and that he would not allow my brother to sit for
the Intermediate Examinations at Belvedere, and went off, leaving my brother standing in the quadrangle in outward appear-

ance unmoved. A young Jesuit, MacErlaine, the professor of
French and one of the most competent teachers in the school,
whose best pupil my brother was in those years, asked him to
wait and followed the rector to his study. Whatever arguments
he used, he prevailed on the rector to allow my brother to
sit for the examination, and after some discussion he was permitted to enter the examination hall late.

The incident, coming just at the beginning of his final examinations, together with the angry debate on the rights and
the wrongs of it at home, could not but upset my brother.
That year, though he again won the special prize for English
composition, he did not win an exhibition but only retained
the exhibition he had won in the Middle Grade. There can
have been but little sympathy between the young Jesuit, whose
good offices saved the situation, and my brother; for the Jesuit
was a thirteen-stone specimen of muscular Christianity, a first-
class gymnast and swimmer, and, moreover, an Irish-language
enthusiast. But he was a North of Ireland man, and these North-
erns, like the Scotch, respect brains wherever they find them.

My brother's two prizes for English composition were the
reward of a diligent study of style, which he began at school
and continued at the University. It consisted in writing essays
on subjects of his own choice, though occasionally he asked
me to make suggestions. Sometimes these essays were deliberate
imitations of Carlyle, Newman, Macaulay, De Quincey, and
others. He knew by heart long passages from the stylists he
most admired. When Ruskin died my brother's essay on him,
entitled 'A Crown of Wild Olive', was, as the title implies, a
studious imitation of the deceased author. As late as our meeting at Salzburg after the First World War,* he could tell me

---

* In 1928.

that the only thing that really interested him was style, and I regret to think that then it may have been true.

But more indicative of the trend of his thoughts were the sketches that he began to write while still at school and while we were still living at Windsor Terrace. He called them *Silhouettes* from the first sketch, and though I remember only two of them there may have been a few more. *Silhouettes*, like the first three stories of *Dubliners*, was written in the first person singular, and described a row of mean little houses along which the narrator passes after nightfall. His attention is attracted by two figures in violent agitation on a lowered window-blind illuminated from within, the burly figure of a man, staggering and threatening with upraised fist, and the smaller sharp-faced figure of a nagging woman. A blow is struck and the light goes out. The narrator waits to see if anything happens afterwards. Yes, the window-blind is illuminated again dimly, by a candle no doubt, and the woman's sharp profile appears accompanied by two small heads, just above the window-ledge, of children wakened by the noise. The woman's finger is pointed in warning. She is saying, 'Don't waken Pa'.

It was certainly not the kind of story that schoolboys who become writers produce in boyhood. The poetry of noble sentiments, the romantic music, and the dramatic passions, with a dominant love theme, which culture offered him as a truer poetic insight into the universal problems of human life, did not fit in with life as he knew it. That life was admittedly debased, but he suspected that a less debased life might have its secrets, too, and in any case the life he did not know did not interest him. He accepted the life he knew, as he accepted himself, as the rough-hewn matter for his sharp chisel and just as God had made them both (together with the Amazonian jungle and the foulness thereof) for His delight. He had no doubt that most artists, even the greatest, belied the life they knew, and offered the world a make-believe. Literature, he said, was a parody of life. He declared bitterly that he believed in only two things, a woman's love of her child and a man's love of lies—of lies of all possible kinds—and he was determined that his spiritual experience should not be a make-believe.

Nevertheless two of his schoolboy productions were what the editors of weekly periodicals call 'plotty'. In fact, one of them, suitably written down to the style of a weekly paper admired by Leopold Bloom, was to have been sent to *Titbits* as a joke and as an experiment in raising the wind. Not wanting to use his own name, he gave it to a young man of his acquaintance who rejoiced in the patronymic of MacGinty to send it in under that name. The last time I heard of the story, MacGinty was 'just going' to post it to *Titbits*. It takes so much out of one to put a manuscript in an addressed envelope with a brief covering letter!

The plot concerned a man who goes to a masked ball disguised as a prominent Russian diplomat, and, when returning home on foot, narrowly escapes assassination at the hands of a Nihilist outside the Russian Embassy. The would-be assassin is arrested, and the masquer, too, as a suspicious character, because in his confusion he forgets about his disguise. But he is rescued by 'the laughing witch who is soon to be his bride', who hearing of the attempt, at once guesses what has happened and hastens to the police station to identify him. He had been wakened from a reverie of the 'laughing witch' by the rude shock of the attempt, and the few sentences that described the reverie were not without grace. A similar magazine story of this kind is attributed in *Ulysses* to a Mr. Philip Beaufoy, of the Playgoers' Club, London, who, if I am not greatly mistaken was, and I hope is still, a real person who had various short stories accepted by *Titbits* in those years. 'That *Titbits* paper' was the only one my father used to read for general culture.

The first version of the story was written in imitation of the usual story with a plot when my brother was a schoolboy, the second faked version some three or four years later. But almost from the beginning my brother followed his natural bent, which was for the plotless sketch. He came to consider a well-ordered plot in a novel or story as a meretricious literary interest, like the story in a *tableau de genre*. 'Suppose' is a common word even in arid geometrical and mathematical problems; it seems to me that if an hypothesis is permissible in the exact sciences, an hypothesis, that is a story, is all the more permissible to an artist in order to help him to clarify the speculations on human life that are striving for expression in his brain. As, however, an hypothesis in logic may be almost purely speculative or have little connection with actual facts, so, too, a story may have little relation to the brute facts of life. There is no denying that in fiction even gross unreality is widely accepted.

More than he objected to the succession of thrilling incidents carefully worked out so as to keep the interest alive, my brother objected to the literary psychology which he found everywhere in fiction. He said that literature provided men and women with false consciences, literary consciences. *Silhouettes* was the first faint indication of that coming revolt of his against the hypocrisy of art. The life which he found in novels was not the life that passed before his steel-blue eyes and unblinking gaze at home and in the streets of Dublin, the emotions which he found in poetry were not those he found in his own heart, but sumptuous exaggerations to which the poets rose by dint of leading haughty and elaborate lives. These brief tentative sketches were the beginning of a revolt which was to be as much against literary as against religious ideals. His refusal to

compromise with the truth had begun. Some of the poorest na-
tions in the world—Armenia, Greece, Ireland—have given birth
to some of the world's richest men. The most secretive race in
Europe, the Irish, whose literature has never dared to express
any but academic ideas on anything, gave birth to one of the
most ruthless realists in literature. Idols, he was to write, 'silent,
stony sit in . . . our hearts: secrets weary of their tyranny:
tyrants willing to be dethroned'.*

By the time my brother was inscribed as a matriculation
student of the Royal University of Ireland, at University College, an affiliated Jesuit institution, we had moved again to a
house with many spacious rooms, gates, and a garden, or rather
a neglected field, large enough for me and my school-friends to
play football in, five or six to a side. It was a ramshackle build-
ing in bad repair, but I should have been glad if we could have
stayed there. My father entered as lodger, occupying about
half the house, while a big, lumbering Ulsterman occupied
the other half with his wife and child. The relaxing Dublin
climate must have sapped the native energy of this man from
Belfast, for he was as improvident as my father himself, so that
our residence together, though quite amicable, was brief; poverty
and a ruthless landlord put an abrupt end to this attempt at
house-sharing under a slightly faded orange and green flag.

We were living there when, in April 1900, my brother contributed his article on Ibsen to the *Fortnightly Review*, under
the title of 'Ibsen's New Drama'. He was at that time eighteen
years and two months old, and surely one of the youngest
contributors to what was then the most important literary review in England. The publication of the article by the *Fortnightly Review* in a way approved the discernment of the
Intermediate examiners who had twice conferred the prize for

* *Ulysses*, p. 26 (29).

English composition on my brother, and it attracted more attention to him at the University than his refusal about a year before to put his name to the protest against the production of *The Countess Cathleen*, when the budding mob-leaders amongst the students, egged on by a political intriguer, Father Finlay, S.J., were canvassing for signatures. This Jesuit is reported to have said that he was glad they protested for patriotic reasons since on theological grounds the question would have been highly controversial. My brother stood out against the protest alone. It was a mere skirmish, an easily repulsed attempt of the self-appointed leaders of massed intolerance to assert their influence, yet it showed that my brother was beginning to experience in his own person the truth that the hearty Dr. Stockmann had blurted out in *An Enemy of the People*: that the strongest man is he who stands most alone. Incidentally, the article on Ibsen encouraged certain undergraduates and at least one professor to try their luck with the big reviews, and the latter candidly confessed that he had his article sent back to him without comment.

My brother almost from the first spoke slightingly of the article, not from false modesty, to which he was not prone, but from a vigilant habit of self-criticism, to which he was strongly inclined. Ibsen wrote through his translator, William Archer, to thank my brother for the article:

2, Vernon Chambers,
Southampton Row, W.C.
23 April 1900

Dear Sir,

I think it will interest you to know that in a letter I had from Henrik Ibsen a day or two ago he says: 'I have read or rather spelt out, a review by Mr James Joyce in the *Fort-*

nightly Review which is very benevolent ("velvillig") and for which I should greatly like to thank the author if only I had sufficient knowledge of the language'.

Yours truly,
William Archer

Close on a year later in a long letter to Ibsen my brother spoke of his article as 'hasty' and 'immature', though guiltless of 'wilful stupidity'. That was his real opinion of it, often expressed to me, though naturally he was glad of his success. He had written the article rapidly after having read a French translation of *When We Dead Awaken*, the drama in question, and the proofs of the English translation, which had not yet appeared, were sent to him either by Archer or Heinemann, to serve him for the quotations in the article. As journalism, it was 'a very smart bit of business' for a youngster of eighteen who, by the by, was by no means lacking in business capacity. In spite of his admiration for Ibsen he was greatly amused by a parody of *When We Dead Awaken* that appeared in *Punch*. His admiration had no need to live a sheltered life.

What is still interesting to note in the article is that he admires in Ibsen just those qualities that he himself was to possess in such a high degree: the 'wonderful calm' that 'seldom condescended to join battle with his enemies', and never allowed 'conflicting voices to influence his work'. He commends Ibsen because he has dispossessed the 'legitimate hero' and 'chosen average lives in their uncompromising truth for the groundwork of his later plays'. He noted that the interest did not depend on 'action or incident but on some great ideal conflict of which we become aware as the play proceeds, and which rivets our attention'. In spite of Ibsen's sense of form and his realism, both rigid and inexorable, his young disciple found in him 'a fine pity for men' and a 'deep sympathy with the cross purposes and contradictions of life'.

The article came from the heart without much reflection. He himself was learning sympathy with the cross-purposes and contradictions of life in a hard school, and already knew the desolation of those ideal conflicts in which the sufferer is divided against himself, and which, as he said in his letter to Ibsen, 'must be fought out behind the forehead'. Bitter conflicts, which after his mother's death made his life an ordeal of the spirit.

So well as I can recollect, my brother was paid a guinea a page for the article, about twelve guineas (I have not the article before me), and went off to London with my father, who was always in high spirits at the prospect of amusing himself and squandering a little windfall. My brother liked to go on these trips with him; for my part I was glad that my father would be out of the house for almost a whole week. I forget what was the thin excuse for going to London, to present himself unnecessarily to the editor of the *Fortnightly Review*, Courtney, or to William Archer perhaps, but the main thing was that my brother saw London, which he probably wanted to see, though he did not say so, and that for a week or so they had a jolly good time. They stayed at a cheap boarding-house, whose one-eyed landlady my father called Cyclopia. They went to theatres and music halls, then in their heyday. My father came back with funny garbled versions of popular songs, and my brother declared that the music hall, not poetry, was a criticism of life. They were invited here and there by a cousin of my father's, named O'Connell, and some friends of his. My brother was a kind of five days' wonder. He was not lionized, but there seemed to be some idea that he might be a lion in his cubhood.

The Boer War was dragging its slow length out to a still

distant close, and my father, like all Irish Nationalists, was loquaciously pro-Boer. In the train from Holyhead to London, he had words regarding the war with another traveller, an English jingo, and only my brother's calm dialectic prevented their actually coming to blows. When they visited the Houses of Parliament and were looking at the statue of Cromwell, an elderly gentleman who was standing by thought it fitting to the occasion to hold forth on the greatness of Oliver, concluding with the words:

—There are no men like him today.

—I'm afraid not, said my father, except perhaps Paul Kruger. The Bible in one hand and the sword in the other, you know.

The Londoner glared at him and walked off, speechless with indignation. And yet my father was proud of his cousin's son, a young stockbroker's clerk, who was a lieutenant in the C.I.V., so much derided by the regular army. He was a tall and handsome young fellow, over six feet three in height, who had figured on the cover of one of the War Office propaganda publications of the time. My father brought it home to show it to his friends, with an inconsequence that must have added to the gaiety of the Recording Angel's office.

Another flitting deposited us at No. 8 Royal Terrace, still in the Fairview district. We always moved with great intentions, but each succeeding house had an emptier look. And yet some of the happiest recollections of those years are associated with that house, such as going for a swim with a younger brother Georgie in the very early morning in perfect weather. The sea, the summer haze, the silent radiance of the morning were an enchantment under which my memory still lies. Or trespassing in somebody's park, in which there was a little lake or large pond, that had at one end a high bank, as steep as a cliff and crowned with a spinney and tangled underwood. The place had fewer attractions for its owner than for me, apparently, for there was never anybody about and I could sit half hidden in the miniature wildwood for hours reading *Quo Vadis* and *The School for Scandal*. But generally I did not like reading in the open air.

In the midst of the sordidness of our family life, my brother endeavoured to seize such elusive eucharistic moments of life, more frequent and more vivid in his case, and express them in songs of his own relief and comfort. For the rest, he was reading eagerly, following some line of impelling interest, mainly at the National Library, every evening till it closed at ten o'clock. Sometimes when his admiration was aroused, he would send me there, too, to confirm his opinion of Tolstoy's short stories or Turgenev's novels or *A Sportsman's Notebook*. He just had to pass his admiration on to somebody. His bookshelves began to be peopled with cheap editions in foreign languages bought, I must suppose, with whatever was left of the fee he received from the *Fortnightly Review*: D'Annunzio's plays and poems in white paper covers with red lettering, and many other cheap editions of Italian and foreign dramatists; yellow-backed French editions of Verlaine and Maeterlinck, and translations from the German: Sudermann's *Frau Sorge* (*La Dame en Gris*), *Es War* (*L'Indestructible Passé*) and *Geschwister* (*Le Souhait*); and George Moore's novels from *Vain Fortune* to *Evelyn Innes*, that begins so well, and its just-published sequel *Sister Teresa*, including *Celibates*, a good part of which he translated into Italian when he was living at Trieste. He had read everything that Yeats had written in prose or verse, so far as it was procurable, and considered him, with Mangan, the only Irish poet worthy of that high title. I demurred to his

valuation of Mangan. I could hardly bring myself to finish
Mangan's humorous essays and poems, short as they are, and
rhymes such as 'Bosphorus' with the ugly phrase 'life has lost
its gloss for us' could only be excused, I said, on the plea of the
drunkenness of the author. But my brother insisted that at his
best Mangan was a true poet. Later on he set two or three of
Mangan's poems to pretty airs with appropriate lilts. As for
Yeats, though he thought very highly of him as a poet, he laid
the blame on Yeats's aestheticism for what he called 'the man's
floating will' and wavering, indeterminate personality.

Among the older poets he had progressed from his boyish
hero-worship of Byron through Shelley to Blake, where my
prejudice in favour of sanity prevented me from following him.
I could go as far as *Songs of Innocence* and *Songs of Experience*. Many of the proverbs, I was ready to admit, convince
by their condensed, incisive energy rather than by their real
wisdom, but in the mystical books I found nothing but sheer
raving, and any mention of Blake's name only elicited jibes from
me. It was Yeats's edition of Blake's poems that directed my
brother's attention to him. As my brother lectured on Blake at
Trieste, the interest he felt in him was clearly no passing enthusiasm. What spiritual affinity could there have been between
the uncompromising young realist and the lunatic poet 'of
imagination all compact'? Perhaps just that. The mystical Blake
was 'of imagination all compact', and at that time the imagination was fighting hard for its rights in my brother's soul. It
stirred him deeply that in an age of self-satisfied materialism,
Blake dared to assert the all-importance of the imagination and
to stake his long life on its affirmation.

His attitude towards Shakespeare was vitiated by his cult of
Ibsen and by his preference which, the more he read, grew all

the stronger, for the artistic tenets of classicism in the drama.
Yet he seemed to know by heart many passages and most of the
songs of Shakespeare's plays, and for some purpose he had
learned them or for some reason they had remained in his
memory. He had attacked *Macbeth* vigorously for its formal
deficiencies in an essay to which Thomas Arnold * had assigned
a high classification, but it was not the lack of form in Shakespeare's plays that he chiefly objected to. I should say that his
aversion sprang from something deeper than a sense of form,
and that he disliked in Shakespeare his total lack of faith or
its equivalent, a capacity for an all-or-nothing devotion to
something, regardless of whether it was conducive to his earthly
comfort or not. He considered Shakespeare a time-server, ever
ready to write what he hoped would please, but gifted with a
mastery of words that made him the mouthpiece of mankind.

When we moved into Royal Terrace, somebody found at the
end of the garden two books which the children nicknamed
'the ashpit books'. One was a song-book, the first pages of which
were missing. It contained a large and miscellaneous collection
of classical and traditional songs, popular ballads and many
so-called comic songs, the humour of which always remained
a vulgar mystery to me. The other was a closely and badly
printed collated edition of the four Gospels in a red cloth cover.
The former tenants of the house were Protestants, but evidently
their Protestantism was *animato ma non troppo*. As the little
volume was still quite presentable, though the cloth of one
cover was detached from the cardboard owing to exposure to
weather, I put it on the shelf and thought no more about it till
an incident at school drew my attention to it again. We were
reading Keats's 'Ode to a Nightingale', and at the lines

---

* Brother of Matthew Arnold and Professor of English at University College,
Dublin, from 1882 until his death in 1900.

Through the sad heart of Ruth, when, sick for home,
She stood in tears amid the alien corn

the teacher, Dempsey, asked the boy who was rehearsing them:

—Of course, you know the story of Ruth? You have read it in the Bible.

The boy nodded and said:

—Yes, sir.

But, of course, he did not know the story and had never seen a Bible at home. Dempsey, for his part, knew what everyone in Dublin and perhaps in Ireland knew then and knows now, that in Catholic homes and in Catholic schools the Bible is never read. In all the years from the time when I was at a nun's school at Blackrock to the time when I left Belvedere, never once was the English Bible, or Douay version, or Latin Vulgate opened or read or discussed in or out of class. The very brief and very inadequate excerpts in their prayer-books are all the vast majority of Irish Catholics ever know of that compendium of Jewish history and Hebrew literature, which they are supposed to consider of supreme importance. The Catholic Church has its own shrewd reasons for preferring to keep the Bible a sealed book in a dead language. Religions thrive on the ignorance of religion.

Dempsey's candid presumption of basic, all-round hypocrisy irritated me chiefly because, although the question was not addressed to me, I had let it pass. I afterwards wished I had said out bluntly that I had never opened a Bible, and that I had always been led to regard it as a Protestant book. On my way home most of these thoughts came pell-mell into my mind, and that evening I took up the 'ashpit book' with the four gospels, and began to read them in a desultory fashion at first (instead of studying) and some days later I read them right through. The immediate result was the uneasy prompting of doubt. I went to the library to read what the *Encyclopædia Britannica* had to say about the gospels. The contrasting opinions of presumably competent people regarding practically everything—authorship, date, place of origin, and even language of the primitive texts—produced eddies of confusion that settled down into one conviction: that no man in his right mind would buy a house with title-deeds like those relating to the edifice of the Church. Yet, while the gospels could hardly be considered at all as historical documents relating to events corroborated by contemporary evidence, the various Christian Churches had for centuries claimed for them what had never been claimed for authentic historical documents, that is, absolute 'gospel truth' in every detail.

In the course of a few months I lost my first keen interest because I realized that these questions were a matter for scholars, and not of general importance. In fact, that they were like the authorship of the *Iliad* or the *Odyssey*, a controversial subject of the kind that is a godsend to scholars and the source of their livelihood. I read Renan's *Vie de Jésus* in the cheap translation published by the Rationalist Press Association, and afterwards at Trieste, in French, without being moved either time to enthusiasm for his picnic Christianity or for the Gospel of St. Luke, 'the most beautiful book in the world'. In order to get an idea of the motives underlying the Reformation, I read Luther's conversations with Melanchthon, but Protestantism gained no proselyte in me. On the contrary, I thought I could discern in Luther fundamentally the mental attitude of some sturdy Irish parish priest, with the body of a Metropolitan policeman, a grey, unshaven chin, and no damned nonsense about him, the kind that would say, when speaking of women, 'Shure, marriage is a plaster for that sore', as Luther did. But at least, when I read Carlyle's essay on Luther, I was not reading about an unknown man, and when the rector, talking to the class about Protestantism, told us that it was only the shadow of a church, and that Luther left his monastery in order that he could marry a runaway nun, he had one listener who thought almost audibly to himself, 'I wonder whether the rest of your teaching is as reliable as those two statements'. A minor inconvenience of my dip into Protestantism was that one evening, when I was turning down by the canal at Charleville Mall on my way to the lending library that was now nearest to us, a small group of boys at the corner began to call after me, scanning the syllables, 'Mar-tin Luth-er, Mar-tin Luth-er'. Some junior assistant in the library had thought it his religious duty to inform his corner-boy friends, and perhaps others, of the kind of books I was reading.

My talks with my brother were so interminable that almost every other evening I used to accompany him across the city to the National Library, and then turn back home to begin my own homework. On one of these strolls I announced out of the blue that I would refuse to do my Easter duty. Jim made a half-hearted attempt to dissuade me from my purpose. He asked me:

—Why?

—Because I don't believe in it and I'm not going to pretend that I do, said I, excited in spite of myself.

—You mean that you don't believe in transubstantiation, said Jim with ironical emphasis on the polysyllable.

—Yes, said I, that's what I mean.

We walked on in silence for a while. Then my brother spoke in a different tone.

—Don't you think, said he reflectively, choosing his words without haste, there is a certain resemblance between the mystery of the Mass and what I am trying to do? I mean that I am trying in my poems to give people some kind of intellectual pleasure or spiritual enjoyment by converting the bread of everyday life into something that has a permanent artistic life of its own . . . for their mental, moral, and spiritual uplift, he concluded glibly.

—I don't know, I said, sticking to my idea and trying to collect the scattered thoughts of weeks, what symbolical significance the Mass may be made to bear. Your argument seems to me to side-track the real question. I know that the host is supposed to be the real body and blood of Christ, that people have been burnt for not believing that it is, and that wars have been fought mainly to suppress people who denied it. Well, I don't believe it. I think it is a literal interpretation of words that were intended figuratively, and in any case it is quite impossible now to sift the ounce of truth from the bushel of legend.

—What do you consider legendary?

—The virgin birth, for example. In Roman history, long before Christianity was heard of, the legend was told of the vestal virgin, Rhea Silvia, and the alleged father was a god.

—The Christian legend is more interesting, said Jim. The Mass on Good Friday seems to me a very great drama.

—Perhaps. I am not in a mood to appreciate it. At any rate, I don't feel in any way called upon to sift the legend, even if I were qualified to do so. And I don't feel in any way called upon to accept other people's findings regarding it. To make a long story short, I am not going to Communion any more because I don't believe that the host is the real body and blood of Christ. . . . And if it is, because I have no appetite, I added angrily.*

---

* 'Rum idea; eating bits of a corpse why the cannibals cotton to it.' *Ulysses*, p. 73 (79).

Jim stood stock-still in Ballybough Road, raised his chin in the air like a dog about to bay, and gave one of his loud shouts of laughter, and then, as we walked on, said, still smiling:

—Well, do as you please. I certainly don't want to influence you.

I added more calmly that I was satisfied in my mind that Communion was a ritual survival of cannibalism.

The mention of the Mass of the Presanctified was not made with the intention of diverting the discussion. I think this is the correct name for this particular mass, but I have been for so long out of touch with Catholic liturgy that I cannot be sure, and I am too uninterested to ascertain. It is celebrated on Holy Thursday or Good Friday morning, and was introduced, I believe, in the fifth or sixth century, no doubt to supplant the dramatic interest of the pagan mysteries, which the people still missed. It was as a primitive religious drama that my brother valued it so highly. He understood it as the drama of a man who has a perilous mission to fulfil, which he must fulfil even though he knows beforehand that those nearest to his heart will betray him. The chant and words of Judas or Peter on Palm Sunday, 'Etsi omnes scandalizati fuerint in te, ego numquam scandalizabor', moved him profoundly. He was habitually a very late riser, but wherever he was, alone in Paris or married in Trieste, he never failed to get up at about five in all weathers to go to the early morning Mass on Holy Thursday and Good Friday. Resenting my sarcasms at Trieste, he asked me:

—You think I'm too orthodox, do you?

—No, but I think you've seen the performance before.

—So you have seen Norma before [one of my favourite operas]. As for orthodoxy, I wonder which of us two is more orthodox in his way of living.

My mother blamed Jim for my blunt refusal to go to confession or Communion, but she was wrong, for in point of time, at least, I refused first. The painful conflict between my mother and my brother originated from my refusal. The tone of the conversation is more faithfully reproduced in *Stephen Hero*, though he told me of a talk he had with 'Cranly', which was much vaguer and briefer than the one in *A Portrait of the Artist*. My father, as usual, behaved like a fool. He declared he was going to write to the College in order to make a public example of me. I looked at him with a concentrated contempt that revives now when I call it to mind, and said, 'Oh, don't take it so much to heart'. He did not write to the College, either because my mother dissuaded him, or, which is much more likely, because his hand was too jiggy from drink. I did not care in any case. I remember that shortly afterwards I put into an essay some of the cruder sceptical ideas that I habitually confided to my diary. Jim read the essay, as he always did, and tore it up without compliments.

He used to read my diary too, without asking 'May I?' or even saying 'By your leave' and in the twenty-first chapter of *Stephen Hero* in the conversation with Cranly already cited, there are two borrowings from it. There is reference to the idea of 'an ugly, misshapen Jesus'. I had heard in many a Christmas sermon that Christ, who could have elected to be born the son of a king, chose rather to be the son of a poor carpenter in order to share the sufferings and hardships of the wretched. My idea was that if he had wanted to go the whole hog, he should have chosen to be born an ugly, misshapen little Jew instead of the perfect ideal of manly beauty that Italian painters have given us—a thoroughly reliable source! Health and beauty are more precious gifts than noble birth, and ugliness and deformity the cruellest and most irremediable of misfortunes. Perhaps he was ugly. A very unprepossessing appearance and the temporary nature of some of his faith cures might partly explain the sudden change of popular feeling between Palm Sunday and Good Friday. The beautiful Jesus of the Catholic Church was evidently invented in order to oust Apollo. That in any case was the idea to which a passing allusion is made in *Stephen Hero*. Moreover, his familiarity with Mary Magdalene and Joanna and the unchaste Susanna* and many others suggested to me the reflection that Christ was no eunuch priest, an idea of which my brother made somewhat larger use in the first draft, and eliminated afterwards.

In the essay on *Twelfth Night* that Jim tore up, I had maintained, speaking of Sir Toby Belch, and in double detestation of drunkenness and religion, that jolly drunkenness had the highest possible sanction, because at the marriage feast at Cana, when the guests had drunk well and finished all the wine provided for the occasion, so that there could be no doubt that some of them were drunk, Jesus, at his mother's request, but rather unwillingly, stood them another one. It was just as well Jim tore the essay up. I had no time to write another. When the teacher, Dempsey, collected the essays on Monday morning, I told him that I had none because my brother had torn it up, and such was Jim's prestige in the college he had left that Dempsey asked no further questions.

My brother's breakaway from Catholicism was due to other motives. He felt it was imperative that he should save his real spiritual life from being overlaid and crushed by a false one that he had outgrown. He believed that poets in the measure of their gifts and personality were the repositories of the genuine spiritual life of their race, and that priests were usurpers. He detested falsity and believed in individual freedom

* See Luke 8:3.

more thoroughly than any man I have ever known. There are people—and they are the majority who outvote us—whose aim in life is to attain stability and security by travelling along the tramlines of reason and experience to the terminus where they have to get off. The more intellectual ones among them endeavour, Procrustes-like, to make life fit a reasoned plan of their own, and willingly sacrifice freedom on the altar of the trinity of order, certainty, and security. They desire an order and stability that life only very rarely yields even to them, and that in any case preclude vast experiences without which life is all the poorer. The interest that my brother always retained in the philosophy of the Catholic Church sprang from the fact that he considered Catholic philosophy to be the most coherent attempt to establish such an intellectual and material stability. In his own case, however, freedom was a necessity: it was the guiding theme of his life. He accepted its gifts and its perils as he accepted his own personality, as he accepted the life that had produced him. His revolt was a defence of that personality against a system whose encroachments on the plea of obedience ended, like modern totalitarian systems which have copied it, only with the complete cancellation of character. By reaction, his personality was challenging, a rally-point for some, a comprehensible cause of jealousy in others.

While still a freshman at University College, he declared his intention of making his allotted span an experiment in living. He was determined to be the same in act as he was in his fixed desire; and, though he progressed from merciless dogmatism to merciful scepticism, he was temperamentally capable of absolute devotion to a mission to which he felt called by the accident of having been born with talent, even if, as he foresaw from the beginning, that mission should make him an outcast. He understood better than those who were wont to quote the text how inexorably an inner necessity can turn son against father and against mother, too; and yet it was inspiring to live with one so young and purposeful. His faith in life sustained him with the joyous certainty that in spite of the squalor that surrounded him, life had some not ignoble meaning.

In our world today, serious literature has taken the place of religion. People with liberty of choice go, not to the Sunday sermon, but to literature for enlightened understanding of their emotional and intellectual problems. And it answers in parables. My brother held that those parables for the most part falsified men, women, and issues—all life, in fact, as it is lived every day or as it is lived in the imagination, and that at best it was a literature of entertainment, the province of men of letters. Yeats's, Russell's, and the envious 'Eglinton's' * insistence on his arrogance is in great part a mistaken judgment. Nor can the mistake have been altogether in good faith, for my brother was outspoken in his lack of esteem for men of letters, who toyed with literature. He was far too self-analytical not to be fully aware of his limitations. He considered that he was more gifted than his coevals, but he recognized that Yeats had more poetical talent, and to me he said so repeatedly. What he condemned was their vacillating, compromising attitude towards literature and the host of issues it raised, their willingness to come to terms with the rabblement for the sake of a little peace and success, their literary simony. Falsity of purpose was the literary sin against the Holy Ghost, and he was vigilant to detect it. In his fashion not unlike Carlyle's ideal of the poet as priest, he watched, though he did not pray.

We continued to be fairly regular guests at the Sheehys', and there Jim met Francis Skeffington, who served him as a

---

* John Eglinton was the *nom de plume* of W. K. Magee, the essayist and editor.

model for 'MacCann'. The name, chosen for its corresponding suggestion of the North of Ireland, occurs twice in our family, once as that of a paternal grandmother and once as that of my brother's godfather. At the beginning of the First World War, Skeffington was arrested as he was going home one evening and shot without trial the following morning at dawn, though innocent of rebellion or any conspiracy to rebel. The English captain who murdered him was conveniently found to have been insane when he committed the act. At the time I speak of, Skeffington was engaged to the eldest daughter, whom he afterwards married, adding her name to his own, Francis Sheehy-Skeffington. He was considered one of the brilliant students of University College and something of a character, because he was a teetotaller, mainly a vegetarian, a feminist, and a pacifist. He was short and stocky, had an untrimmed, reddish-blond beard, and on all occasions wore a kind of shooting costume, for which reason his fellow-students, with flagging wit, called him 'Knickerbockers'. Jim and he sometimes acted in charades together for, barring surnames, Skeffington had some sense of humour, and Jim, as I have said, could keep people in fits of laughter with his dumbshow. In one charade that I remember, while Margaret Sheehy was reciting, he was sitting on the floor, half reclining, half resting on one hand, looking up at her with an expression of blank imbecility on his face. Then, following the recitation, his face showed indignation, or astonishment or happiness, always at an imbecile level. At any point of irony he would go into a kink of silly giggles, the perfect reproduction of the laugh of a girl friend of ours, and recovering himself to find that the point of irony was long past and that the tone was now pathetic, fall to weeping and blowing his nose loudly. I have seen performances far less funny than this impromptu dumbshow applauded on the stage, but except during these lighthearted evenings at the Sheehys', he did not indulge this vein. I find traces of it, however, in certain passages in *Ulysses*. I have mentioned Jim's good looks, but he was immune from personal vanity. He was by no means *soigné*. His thick hair was usually in disorder, and his clothes often looked as if he had slept in them. During a parlour game called 'Confession', when asked what was his pet aversion, he answered promptly 'Soap and water', and I believe it was the truth. In this, too, we were different, for I have been a devotee of the cold bath all my life.

One Christmas Margaret Sheehy produced *Caste*.* An upper room, with the folding doors removed, was the stage, while a large adjoining room served as auditorium for the many guests. Margaret Sheehy played Polly with native vivacity, and Jim played Captain Hawtree without making the part a caricature of military stiffness. The facile audience were generous with applause, for the great advantage of amateur theatricals is that it is not considered proper to criticize until you go home.

Most of us spend our middle age readjusting the values misplaced in youth, for one of the minor mysteries of life is that one never knows at the beginning who or what is going to be important. But I always believed in my brother, not as a younger brother who looks up to an elder one—I was far more inclined to be morose than admiring—but because I thought I recognized in him a different type of mind from that of any of the men or adolescents with whom he came in touch —something direct, keen, unyielding, indifferent to his career. About that time, I began keeping a diary, which was a record more of his doings and comings and goings than of my own. It is true that we were almost always together, for everywhere

---

* By Thomas William Robertson.

my brother went I was sure to go like a not too amiable little lamb. At the Sheehys' I did not shine. I was sometimes asked to sing, for I had some voice, too, but that was all. Sometimes, however, little accidents are revelatory. One of those parlour games that they liked so much and played so often in that family was 'The School for Scandal'. One of the company goes out of the room and the others say spicy things about him. When he is re-admitted he has to guess the author of the 'scandal'. It was Dick Sheehy's turn to go out; he was a big, stalwart, good-natured fellow whose jokes were sometimes on the heavy side. Maggie Sheehy was collecting the sayings, and when she came to me I registered that Dick was 'elephantine in wit and in person'. Maggie Sheehy looked at me, surprised out of her usual politeness, and said frankly:

—He'll *never* think you said that.

—Well, I replied apologetically, isn't that the point of the game?

I always accompanied Jim to the Saturday evening meetings of the University Literary and Historical Society, where the timid or patriotic debates were almost uniformly depressing to hear, for example, an unblushing time-server such as Hugh Boyle Kennedy, afterwards Chief Justice of the Irish Free State, read a paper on 'The War Machine, a State Necessity'.* A more unwarlike figure than the future Chief Justice it would have been difficult to find in that college. The Father Finlay I have mentioned, forgetful for the nonce of the Spanish officer who was the founder and of the military organization of his order, is said to have suggested that a more appropriate subject for him would have been 'The Sewing-Machine, a Home Necessity'.

---

* This paper was read on February 11, 1899.

My brother's contribution to the debate that followed the reading of the paper was an ironical modification of the eight beatitudes to suit the exigencies of the War Machine.* He spoke with calm vigour like a man who speaks from the heart. To his last days, when he was fleeing before the invading hordes in France, he regarded the European upheaval as one might observe a blizzard or a tornado, and only wondered whether it was still possible to get a book he needed from Paris, and then, too, as a young student, listening to patriotic blatancy, he loathed war. It was evident, moreover, that certain anti-militaristic aspects of the Christian legend still fascinated him. At another debate Arthur Chanel Clery, one of those creatures whom the Jesuits use with ill-concealed disfavour, blandly told his audience that 'though we [the Irish] may sometimes, occasionally, overstep the mark in convivial drinking [humorous coughing and laughter], we are totally free from a more desolating vice [a moment of silent self-approval and then applause]'.

There was at least one young Irishman who was an exception to that consoling generalization, and did not care who knew it. At that time Jim used to frequent music halls and musical comedies which had names like *The Gaiety Girl, The Circus Girl, The Singhalee,* and, having a quick ear, he would strum out their catchy airs on the piano. Among the music-hall stars, he showed a preference for damsels of a rather full habit of body, and confessed meekly that 'he liked them sizable'.† These lighter forms of theatrical performance exercised only a passing attraction on him for a year or two, perhaps because a little of

* 'British Beatitudes! . . . Beer, beef, business, bibles, bulldogs, battleships, buggery and bishops.' *Ulysses*, p. 406 (417).
† 'They like them sizable. Prime sausage.' *Ulysses*, p. 52 (59).

them goes a long way, though after his death I saw mention in some paper of his admiration for a Parisian star who was, however, also a prima donna with a fine voice. In fine, he found the frank vulgarity of the music hall less offensive than the falsity of most of the legitimate drama of his day: Jones, Pinero, Sutro, Phillips (verse was always a mitigating circumstance), and, most of all, Shaw.

While for school I studied only the indispensable minimum, I read my brother's English and French books. Maeterlinck was easy, even his so-called philosophical works, Verlaine not too difficult, but when Jim's correspondent at Vire sent him *Cyrano de Bergerac*, in its glossy green paper cover, it was heavy going to get through it. I had the satisfaction of finding, however, when Coquelin came to Dublin, that I was able to follow him with little difficulty. I remember quite clearly the vigour with which, squat back to the audience, he hurled defiance at the besiegers of Arras. I remember his clever brother who played the part of the poetical pastry-cook, and I remember Roxane, but I cannot recollect the actress's name, which is regrettable for I was half in love with her for long afterwards. Viewed across the gulf that separates the top gallery from the footlights, she was romantic, intelligent, beautiful, but for me the greater part of her fascination consisted in her not being Irish.

My brother's university career was undistinguished as regards his studies. He passed his honours examinations regularly without winning any scholarships, but was always in doubt, then and later, as to whether university studies were, after all, worth the trouble. No professor on the teaching staff enjoyed a reputation for anything more than average competence, and the sole preoccupation of the incumbents of the various chairs was to prepare students for the examinations in their subjects.

Anything beyond that was considered supererogatory and even a waste of the students' time.

It was while we were living at Royal Terrace, and during a brief holiday at Mullingar, where my father had found temporary work revising voting lists, that Jim wrote his first play, a realistic drama, in four acts, if I am not mistaken, which he called *A Brilliant Career*. He finished it towards the end of summer before returning from Mullingar. There was a reference to his work on it in an 'epiphany' and in *Stephen Hero*. I have little recollection of the plot, but as much as I recall of it was a rehash of ingredients borrowed, unconsciously I am sure, from *When We Dead Awaken*, *A Doll's House*, and *The League of Youth*.

A young doctor, Paul, for the sake of his career, throws over a girl, Angela, with whom he is in love, and marries someone else. He renounces the valiant purposes of his youth, and becomes a time-server. His career is a great success, and, still young, he has been elected mayor of the town, unnamed, in which the scene is laid. There is a serious outbreak of plague in the port (there were some sporadic cases of bubonic plague in Glasgow that year) and the town is thrown into a state of panic. The doctor-mayor copes with the situation energetically, and in a short time the threat of an epidemic is eliminated. From the outbreak of the plague till the end a woman has been organizing assistance for those stricken with plague, and after a public manifestation of gratitude to the mayor, the woman comes to see him. She is Angela, the girl the doctor had jilted. She, too, is unhappily married to a jealous husband. The doctor realizes that his brilliant career is dust and ashes. My recollection of the play, especially of the end of it, is vague. It ended in psychological disaster, though not in tragedy. After

While Jim was writing the play I had formed high hopes for it. He did not give it to me to read until he had finished it, though I had seen the manuscript on the desk in his neat, firm handwriting with the stage directions in violet ink and—symptomatic of his power of concentration—hardly a correction in the whole manuscript. When I read it first I admired it unquestioningly, but then I found in my admiration a vague sense of disappointment which I attributed to the resemblances to Ibsen which I fancied I had noted. When Jim asked me what I thought of the play, I said that my impression was that it would be powerful on the stage (that, in fact, was my first impression), and I made a joke about his beginning his dramatic career from the A.B.C.* I objected, however, to the dedication to 'his own soul' as being too flamboyant; I understood, of course, that he meant that in his own case he did not intend to let the care of a brilliant career interfere with his intellectual or emotional life. In one way or another he had often said so, but I did not like to see it proclaimed on the front page. And yet I admired his determination, while firmly believing that the spiritual, intellectual, and emotional life of the vast majority of people is so unimportant that they would be foolish to make any sacrifice to it.

William Archer's letter encouraged my doubts. Yet I did not find the characters too little individualized and the canvas too large. I, at any rate, recognized them at once because Jim had sketched them into the picture using, successfully it seemed to me, friends of our acquaintance and university students as his models. What I found less convincing was the strong scene between Paul and Angela. I was interested to see the effect it

* *A Brilliant Career.*

had made on Archer. The characters sketched from the life he considered insufficiently individualized, the purely imaginary characters, instead, impressed him. I knew there was no woman in my brother's life at that time. There were many unindividualized women, but no woman; and this point had already arisen between us; he used to call his poems 'love poems'; I retorted that, seeing the source of inspiration, it should rather be called prostitute poetry. Jim was unabashed.

—Well, why not? said he. Doesn't a great part of all lyrical poetry correspond to that description? You're a tiresome moralist.

—Very far from it, said I, but it is all to the good to give things their right names. And that's the right name for it.

—It is and it isn't, said Jim decisively to close the conversation.

Now returning to discuss the play and Archer's letter for maybe the twentieth time, I said that I thought that the weakness of the play was principally that the crisis was a plastic creation of the imagination with no basis in actual experience.

—Do you mean the plague scene? Jim asked.

—No, I said. That's not important psychologically. I was thinking really of the big scene between Paul and Angela.

—That Archer found strong and telling, added Jim.

—Of course, he must know what would be effective on the stage, I admitted, but I don't find it convincing, perhaps because I know you too well. Where did you get that scene?

—Here, said Jim, smiling and touching his forehead, all here.

—I think, said I, the scene would be more telling for me if I knew it had some basis in reality.

—How can you know, Jim objected, whether Ibsen's scenes have any basis in actual experience or not?

—I don't know, I admitted again, but I have that illusion. I fancy the reality of experience has a way of making itself felt.

—There are realities of the imagination, too, said Jim.

—Why, then, I retorted, do you pour such ridicule on the dreamy dreamers with manuscripts hidden away in their desks?

—Yerrah, what reality of experience do you think I could have in this city? said Jim, leaving my question unanswered. Is it with So-and-so and So-and-so (and he reeled off the names of girls he knew)? No, thank you. I leave flirting to clerks.

—I didn't mean flirting.

—Well, if you mean anything else, you are talking like an idiot, said Jim.

—You never know, said I hopefully.

Then, singling out the least appropriate girl amongst those he had mentioned, Jim began to describe in minute detail all the preparations, physical, spiritual, and financial that would be necessary before beginning to lay siege to her virtue. It was in his comic, Rabelaisian vein, like Leopold Bloom's antemeridian manoeuvres. The dénouement, the comments of all the members of both families, including the cooks, was very funny. Jim never seemed to be observant, but when he was in this mood one saw that he had missed very little. He used to say that he didn't see things, that he absorbed them. At any rate, his comic interlude put an end to the discussion.

I gave more weight, and perhaps so did Jim without saying so, to the phrase in Archer's letter in which he said that my brother seemed to him, possibly, to have 'more than talent'. He lent words to my conjecture and vicarious ambition. As for Jim, he did not believe in genius. He said it was a fake of vanity. He believed in talent, work, and what he called 'throwing himself into what he tried to do'. He quoted apropos something Catulle Mendès had written to the effect that among the French decadent poets there was no lack of talent, but that they were too indolent or disorderly to work. But I believed in genius, and even then knew that if he had only talent, he would follow the beaten track, but that if he had 'more than talent' he could be expected to be unpredictable and to blaze a trail of his own. And yet my influence, sometimes amounting to pressure, in all our many years together, was always deliberately towards the beaten track, because I felt that he ought not to leave it too easily.

My brother replied with some delay to Archer's letter, thanking him, of course, for his friendly criticism, but telling him at the same time that he himself thought less of *A Brilliant Career* than Archer did, but for a different reason. Jim did not specify the reason. I protested. I said that William Archer would ask himself, 'Why the devil has he put me to the trouble of reading it, then?' and be offended. But Jim paid no attention to my objection, and sent the letter off. He was right. Archer was not offended; he must have realized that the author was a boy of nineteen. His correspondence continued to be helpful and friendly. He took offence only after the publication of *Ulysses*, forgetting that men of 'more than talent' go their own way. But his criticism evidently made my brother aware of many deficiencies, for he thought seriously of abandoning his university studies and going on the stage in order to gain a practical knowledge of the production of dramatic works. Beginning with the easiest part of the project, he sometimes took a theatrical paper called, I think, *The Stage* and chose his stage name, Gordon Brown, a choice which bore witness to his admiration for Giordano Bruno, whose philosophical essays he was reading at that time.

During this time, we had moved once more. My father's

method, whenever a landlord could not put up with him any longer and wanted to get rid of him, was to go to the landlord and say that it would be impossible for him with his rent in arrears to find a new house, and that it was indispensable that he should be able to show the receipts for the last few months' rent of the house he was living in. Then the landlord, to get a bad tenant off his hands, would give him receipts for the unpaid rent of a few months, and with these my father would be able to inveigle some other landlord into letting him a house. In these auspicious circumstances we moved into a smaller house in a poorer neighbourhood. Between one moving and another so much furniture had been sold off that we were now reduced, as I have said, to a well-laden float. Some of the family had gone on ahead to the new house at 32 Glengariff Parade, and as the last of us to leave Royal Terrace towards evening walked slowly after the float, with the dray-horse straining under the weight, my father kept lilting to himself one of his songs:

> *Shall carry my heart to thee,*
> *Shall carry my heart to thee,*
> *And the breath of the balmy night*
> *Shall carry my heart to thee.*

The third 'heart' was, of course, a corona on a high note. The evening was balmy, and my father was pleased with himself at having pulled off his little trick again. In all these movings he used to make a great to do about the family pictures: his father (two pictures, young and middle-aged), his mother, grandfather, and grandmother. They were his credentials. Later at Trieste and in Paris my brother, too, following him in this, set great store upon them. In my opinion they were furniture-pictures, glazed and wooden portraits that looked as if the sitters had been seized with a catalepsy of respectability while being portrayed.

Glengariff Parade was in a depressing neighbourhood. One end of it led out on to a main road and we were near the corner. I don't think that I was ever curious enough to explore where the other end of it led to. It was during our short residence there that Jim composed his songs, consisting of at least half a dozen settings for his own poems and for some of Mangan's and Yeats's. Some of them were real songs in form, others were more like haunting liturgical chants, but all caught the spirit of the words they accompanied. One morning shortly after we had moved into Glengariff Parade, I was standing at the open and still uncurtained window of the only front room watching the butcher's boy walking in the middle of the road with his head in his empty basket; he was raising the dust with his feet, and intoning loudly:

> *Walkin' along the road*
> *Kickin' up all the dust*
> *And there's ne'er a wan in Glengariff Parade,*
> *Dar give him a lick in the pus.*

'A rival poet', I said unsmiling to Jim, who had come to the window. But Jim was amused. He called him 'the poet of the rugged glen', which he said was the meaning of the name Glengariff. (He had been studying Irish for a year or so.) Jim was not limitary in his sympathies as I was; they extended in Ireland from Mangan and Yeats to the unlettered poets of the rugged glens, where a few years later Synge was to stake out his claim. If he sometimes seemed to be limitary in his sympathies it was because he had no doubt as to their order of importance.

My brother did not go on the stage except as an amateur actor in a one-act comedy by Maggie Sheehy, in which he played the leading male part. The title of the comedy was *Cupid's Confidant*. Geoffrey Fortescue, a rake and adventurer, is paying his addresses to a wealthy girl, but just when he seems to be in the straight and winning comfortably, because Sweet Innocence has quarrelled with her True Lover, he is jockeyed out of position by the girl friend of Sweet Innocence, 'Cupid's Confidant' (played by the authoress). She beguiles the rake into making love to her and unmasks his villainy. The True Lover is recalled from an imminent voyage to the antipodes, and all ends well.

Jim, who often found relief for his feelings in stark English, said that even the virgin cheeks of his arse blushed for his part in it. It certainly did not seem so. He appeared to be quite unconcerned as if he were acting in a more elaborate kind of charade. It offered him the least possible opportunity for emerging, and yet in spite of the inexperience of life which I am labouring to describe, he acted exceedingly well the part of a handsome, polished, adroit, irresistible man of the world. The principal Dublin dramatic critic—not a young man—praised his performance highly, and compared my brother for poise and finish to Charles Wyndham!

Another experimental form which his literary urge took while we were living at this address consisted in the noting of what he called 'epiphanies'—manifestations or revelations. Jim always had a contempt for secrecy, and these notes were in the beginning ironical observations of slips, and little errors and gestures—mere straws in the wind—by which people betrayed the very things they were most careful to conceal. Epiphanies were always brief sketches, hardly ever more than some dozen lines in length, but always very accurately observed and noted, the matter being so slight. This collection served him as a sketch-book serves an artist, or as Stevenson's note-book served him in the formation of his style. But it was in no sense a diary. John Eglinton, in his short memoir of my brother in *Irish Literary Portraits*, mentions my brother's diary as if it were something the existence of which was known like that of *Dubliners* or *Ulysses*, and even describes him as cultivating the acquaintance of men of letters in order to gather diligent notes about them for his diary. The story is an impudent invention. Except in the case of one epiphany which regarded Skeffington, the subjects of the sketches were never people of any importance, and none of those men whom he met later were mentioned in the collection. Moreover Jim never kept a diary at any time in his life. That dreary habit was mine, and I have kept it up because I began it, as other people do cigarette smoking. (I consider my mania less harmful.) Nor was there reason to quote Burns:

> If there's a hole in a' your coats,
> I rede ye tent it;
> A chiel's amang ye takin' notes,
> An' faith he'll prent it.

My brother's purpose was different and his angle of vision new. The revelation and importance of the subconscious had caught his interest. The epiphanies became more frequently subjective and included dreams which he considered in some way revelatory.

Some of these epiphanies he introduced here and there into *A Portrait of the Artist* where the occasion offered and some into the imaginary diary at the end. The others he considered not to be of sufficient interest to be retained; but I did not share his opinion, and have kept several of them. As for his dreams, he was at no pains at first to interpret them subtly. The following note regarding a dream was one of the first of the collection, perhaps made before we left Royal Terrace.

A white mist is falling in slow flakes. The path leads me down to an obscure pool. Something is moving in the pool; it is an arctic beast with a rough yellow coat. I thrust in my stick and as he rises out of the water, I see that his back slopes towards the croup and that he is very sluggish. I am not afraid but thrusting at him drive him before me. He moves his paws heavily and mutters words of some language which I do not understand.

Which interpreted signified that I was the sluggish 'arctic beast'. In another of his dreams, haply by metempsychosis, I inhabited the body of a dog.

Dull clouds have covered the sky. Where three roads meet and before a swampy beach a big dog is recumbent. From time to time he lifts his muzzle in the air and utters a prolonged sorrowful howl. People stop to look at him and pass on; some remain, arrested, it may be, by that lamentation in which they seem to hear the utterance of their own sorrow that had once its voice but is now voiceless, a servant of laborious days. Rain begins to fall.

When the true inwardness of the dream was explained to me, I did not object to it very much, because I like dogs anyhow, but I suggested that the lugubrious howl might have perhaps come from some secret part of his own soul. Another note of a dream, in which Ibsen figured and Norway is confused with Denmark in a way Norwegians do not appreciate, was more amusing.

Yes—they are the two sisters. She who is churning with stout arms (their butter is famous) looks dark and unhappy; the other is happy because she has had her way. Her name is R. . . . Rina. I know the verb "to be" in their language.

—Are you Rina?

I knew she was.

But here he is himself in a coat with tails and an old-fashioned high hat. He ignores them: he walks along with tiny steps, jutting out the tails of his coat. . . . My goodness! how small he is! He must be very old and vain—maybe he isn't what I . . . It's funny that two big women fell out over this little man . . . But then he's the greatest man on earth.

The dreams are genuine, but they have undergone literary treatment, for otherwise why should he have written them? The literary treatment here consists in an attempt to reproduce dream impressions, as, for example, when a name is conveyed to us in a dream; there is no hint, however, that he considered dreams anything but an uncontrolled rehash of our waking thoughts, though he may have hoped they would reveal things our controlled thoughts unconsciously conceal. I preserved them because I suspected they might be his good-bye to poetry, an indication that prose was taking the upper hand. And I could see what he was driving at: the significance of unreflecting admissions and unregarded trifles, delicately weighed, in assaying states of mind for what is basic in them. The noise and pomp of big events and our own imagination are so apt to mislead us.

A further and stronger indication of the trend of his mind from the things that 'the piping poets solemnize' was the paper he read to the College Literary and Historical Society. Before reading it, however, he had spoken of Ibsen at length and with enthusiasm in a debate following some other student's paper, but as it was one of the very few such occasions when I was not with my brother, I do not remember what was the subject of the paper he spoke to on that night. Amongst the group of students whose interest he was beginning to arouse—within their college, too, students are always eager to back winners—the night was called his 'Ibsen Night'. Ibsen was so little known then in Dublin's minor centre of culture that when my brother, on being asked whom he would like to have preside at the reading of his paper, said in jest 'Henrik Ibsen', the secretary (W. P. Coyne) politely asked for his address. He had scribbled on his writing-pad the name 'Henry Gibson'.

The title of the paper was 'The Drama and Life', and my brother bestowed on it the same care that he bestowed later on 'The Day of the Rabblement' and on the essay on Mangan. His reason for doing so was also the same. In it he was defining his position to himself and against others—*contra Gentiles*. It differed from the other papers read before that debating society because it was not written in order to emerge from the ruck of students, but because he was fully conscious of having something to say that would clarify his claims as an artist. For these reasons the paper created an impression. He read it without emphasis in spite of its ornate style.

In his paper he repudiated the idea that art should have a moral purpose or a national purpose, as well as the vague theories of art for art's sake of the aesthetic school. He maintained that art had no purpose; that all fixed purposes falsify it, but that it had a cause, namely, necessity, the imperative inward necessity for the imagination to re-create from life its own ordered synthesis. He spoke of the importance of the artist in the community, and insisted on his right to develop his personality freely in accordance with his own artistic conscience, and without being drawn into movements or making himself

the mouthpiece of others. The artist inherits difficulties enough
to struggle with in his own soul.

Turning to the drama, he asserted that it was the highest
form of art because it was not static but presented life in action,
and further because of the discipline it imposed on the artist,
who must remain behind the scenes and allow his creatures to
live out their lives' crises on the stage. He derided the super-
human proportions of the heroes of romantic drama and the
clamorous and violent deeds of which they are the centre, all
'sound and fury, signifying nothing', and declared that more
intense drama of wider human significance could be enacted in
the anteroom of a Norwegian villa. Finally he defended the
realism of modern drama, but looked forward in the close to
a realism that should comprise the penetrating illumination of
the imagination, and be like the tree Yggdrasil, 'whose roots
are deep in earth but in whose upper branches the stars of
heaven are glowing and astir'.

IV · *Ripening*

It has become a fashion with some of my brother's critics (among them his friend Italo Svevo) to represent him as a man pining for the ancient Church he had abandoned, and at a loss for moral support without the religion in which he was bred. Nothing could be farther from the truth. I am convinced that there was never any crisis of belief. The vigour of life within him drove him out of the Church, that vigour of life that is packed into the seven-hundred-odd quarto pages of *Ulysses*. As a young man he was rather like Loevberg in Ibsen's *Hedda Gabler*, but with a steely firmness of will that Loevberg lacks. My brother was undoubtedly interested more in the Catholic Church than in any other organized system in Europe. He found its theologians ruthlessly logical, granting their premises, and suggestive of thought even when he did not agree with them, and something of the pomp and ceremony with which the legend of Jesus is told impressed him profoundly; but on almost all points of first importance, his attitude towards Catholicism was more like that of the gargoyles outside the Church than of the saints within it.

A Jesuit review published in Dublin wrote that his intellect was 'a great Jesuit-trained intellect that had gone over to the powers of Satan'; in other words, the Jesuits laid a kind of claim to him. The purpose of Jesuit training is to instil the belief that all our time and the use of our gifts belong to God, and further so to develop the conscience as to make cowards of us all. Their aim is to enslave the mind completely, and make it work for their ends. In my brother's case they failed signally. In all respects in which his personality was outstanding he made himself. Certainly his conscience was abnormally developed, but not in the way they desired. If it urged him to hold his gifts in unflinching fealty to something beyond his ambition for himself, it was in fealty to the truth of life as he saw it and understood it, and to the sincerity of his art in re-creating it.

He did, indeed, toy with theosophy as a kind of interim religion. His interest in it had been aroused by reading Yeats and Russell, and though he never belonged either to the Hermetic Society or to the Theosophical Society that existed in Dublin then and, for all I know, perhaps still exists, he read with serious intent expository works on theosophy by Madame Blavatsky, Colonel Olcott, Annie Besant, and Leadbeater, and I ploughed through them after him gathering scorn. I have a faint recollection of a poem called 'Nirvana', which described a state not of bliss but rather of what mystical writers call vastation of spirit. On the whole, however, I think his serious interest in theosophy lapsed very quickly, and that he was amused by my disrespectful transformation of the names of the most illustrious theosophists—Colonel Old Cod, Madame Bluefatsky (a name that suited her flabby, puckered face and puckered eyes that seemed to be peering through cigarette smoke), Any Bee's Aunt, and Mr. Wifebeaten. Theosophy may have been the only intellectual adventure of his nonage that he regarded as pure waste of energy. Nevertheless it brought him in contact with certain mystical writers whose personalities were less questionable—the anti-Jesuit Miguel de Molinos, St. John of the Cross, St. Teresa, St. Catherine of Siena, Thomas à Kempis. A cursory dip into these writers was enough to convince me that I could not work up any interest in them. I skimmed through the books, pausing to read here and there when I found an oasis.

—Why are you pottering about with the misty mystics? I asked him.

—They interest me, he replied. In my opinion, they are writing about a very real spiritual experience you can't appreciate.

—There you are right, anyhow.

—And they write about it, he continued, with a subtlety that I don't find in many so-called psychological novels.

It is clear, however, that at this time he felt very forcibly both the attraction of mysticism and the call of reality, and for a while he was interested in the figure of Paracelsus, scientist and mystic, who had laboured somewhat too boldly in both spheres. But the wilful thinking of the expositors of theosophy, a suspicion of deliberate self-deception in them, alienated his sympathies. The world they introduced him to was arid. Not only did the self-surrender and asceticism of mysticism, a bodily instead of an intellectual discipline, run contrary to his nature, but mysticism disappointed him also because it had allured him with the promise of intuitions of a reality beyond reality. In such a reality he could have believed. 'Life itself is a symbol', he said, quoting a reply of Ibsen's to one of his critics who had objected to the symbolism in his dramas. But mysticism, instead of enhancing the significance of life, required from the adept a total renunciation of it: instead of imaginative intuitions mysticism offered unsatisfying figments of the fancy. He knew at length that this path would lead him to no goal that he wished to attain, but how long he dallied with it I cannot say. Temperamentally he was not the kind of man to find his heart's ease amid a murmuration of mystics. At Trieste, however, he

lectured on two writers, a mystic and a realist, Blake and De-
foe.

Brief as our residence at each of our numerous addresses was,
it was still long enough in most cases to be marked by a death
in our family. At Millbourne Lane the boy Frederick died in
the first weeks of his infancy. At Windsor Avenue another male
infant came stillborn into the world, and while downstairs my
father was, as usual, assuring the sober friend who had brought
him home for the occasion, 'By God, he's not dead yet', upstairs
his last-born child was dead already. But at least these infants
may be supposed not to have suffered. At Glengariff Parade,
the youngest surviving son, Georgie, so named because he was
born on the fourth of July, died of peritonitis following typhoid
fever, in his fourteenth year, at the age when life, whatever it
may be, is sweet to all.

After Jim he was the most promising member of the family,
a handsome boy who had outgrown his strength a little, but
otherwise was not weak. He had always attracted attention, as
a child of two or three by his good looks and golden ringlets,
though his hair was darker when he died, as a boy by his in-
fectious laugh, almost too adult for his years with a spice of
malice in it. At school he did very well, skipping a class in the
year he went to Belvedere, and at the same time beginning
Latin without any apparent effort in a house where study was
rendered as difficult as possible. His memory was as good as
Jim's; his power of concentration was not yet developed, but
at draughts, at any rate, he could generally get the better of
me, if draughts is any test. He had little voice, but had, instead,
a fine ear for music, and was already beginning to strum on the
piano. He accepted as unquestioningly as I did the idea that
some day Jim would make his name as a writer, and whenever

he was present at our discussions, he would hang on their borders, like a skipping wicket. Though still a boy, he was one of those people whose presence banishes boredom.

When he fell ill, my mother was undecided whether to send him to the Mater Misericordiae Hospital, which was quite near, or to nurse him at home. He was her youngest, and, after her estrangement from Jim, her favourite son, and she resolved to keep him at home. He was a patient who never complained, but when during the crisis the pains became acute, he would put his arms around his mother's neck and remain so until they abated. She nursed him through the long weeks of typhoid fever until the doctor announced that all danger was over. My mother asked what diet she was to give the boy. 'Soup, meat, anything you like', he answered carelessly. Against her own judgment, she gave him some soup and a morsel of meat, but it was enough to prove fatal. After taking food for the first time for many weeks, he felt better. In his emaciated face his dark blue eyes looked larger than ever, but there was no wariness in their glance. They were alive to all that was passing. I had been reading 'The Bottle Imp', to him afternoons when I came home from school, but now he asked Jim to sing for him the setting he had composed for Yeats's poem:

> *Who will go drive with Fergus now,*
> *And pierce the deep wood's woven shade?*

Jim went downstairs to the parlour, and, leaving the doors open, sat down at the piano and sang the melancholy chant to which he had set the verses. Very shortly afterwards the symptoms of perforation of the intestines appeared. I was sent running for the doctor and someone else for a priest. Georgie was still quite conscious and calm, only saying to his terrified mother:

—I am very young to die.

He died that evening. In the first outburst of grief, when my mother saw that he was dead in her arms, her thoughts raced back to the time when he was an infant.

—When I took him out for a walk on the esplanade at Bray, she said sobbing brokenly, everybody used to turn and look after him.

Why an operation was not attempted at the last moment, I cannot understand. The then rector of the College, Father Tomkin, wished him to have a public funeral from the College chapel, and two of his Jesuit teachers were sent to offer condolence on behalf of the rector and to make the proposal. At the sight of the dead boy, one of them could not control his tears. No doubt it is contrary to Jesuit discipline, but I record it gratefully and in his honour: the Jesuit wept.

My father had kept fairly sober during his son's long illness, sometimes even reading to him in the evenings. He was a good reader, especially of humorous stories such as 'Mickey Free's Father and the Ghost'. But he did not feel his son's death very deeply. My mother never recovered from it. She could not forgive herself for having obeyed the doctor's instructions, especially since it had seemed to her sometimes that the big countrified blockhead had been drinking.

When I went back to school after the funeral, I felt raw and restless. For a couple of years before he died, Georgie, two and a half years my junior, had been a companion for me in ways that did not interest Jim. Long-armed and long-legged, he was a good swimmer, and we used to keep count of our bathes to see which of us would make the higher score by the end of summer. To hit some imagined staidness in my character, he nicknamed me Brother John.

Mother was certainly wrong in thinking Jim callous. He did not display his feelings as the others did, but he felt Georgie's death no less. When he thought everybody was asleep, he went softly upstairs to see 'the poor little fellow' where he lay alone with the blue of his eyes still visible under the lids that had been closed too late. And not long afterwards, at a mention of Irish rebellion, he exclaimed bitterly:

—Ireland is an old sow that devours her farrow.

It was a reflection on Irish history, but I saw in the expression his smouldering anger at Georgie's untimely death, and thought to myself, There goes what I was trying to say.

He thought that by the boy in the following dream-epiphany Georgie was intended.

> That is no dancing. Go down before the people, young boy, and dance for them. . . . He runs out darkly-clad, lithe and serious to dance before the multitude. There is no music for him. He begins to dance far below in the amphitheatre with a slow and supple movement of the limbs, passing from move-ment to movement in all the grace of youth and distance, until he seems to be a whirling body, a spider wheeling amid space, a star. I desire to shout to him words of praise, to shout arrogantly over the heads of the multitude 'See! See!' . . . His dancing is not the dancing of harlots, the dance of the daughter of Herodias. It goes up from the midst of the people, sudden and young and male, and falls again to earth in trem-ulous sobbing to die upon its triumph.

He called his son, born at Trieste, Giorgio.

In a letter of condolence to me, one of the Jesuits had asked me 'how my thoughts were running'. Since the funeral the course of my thoughts had been setting more favourably than usual towards them, but the letter was a sudden check. It an-gered me because I saw in it a pouncing readiness to take advantage of youth and grief and an open wound. I did not answer the letter. What could I have told him! The truth, and leave the college? A lie, or a conventional white lie, and feel a coward? I should have answered the letter without answering the question, but I was not sufficiently diplomatic to think of that.

Another younger brother, Charlie, little more than a year older than the boy that died, thought he had a vocation for the priesthood and entered a seminary. He had paired off with Georgie as children do in large families, and, being the less intelligent, had imitated him and followed him around. In his dumb sorrow and loneliness, the idea of being a priest comforted him, besides appealing strongly to his vanity. When I told the English teacher, Dempsey, why Charlie was leaving the school, he laughed.

—So, he said, he is provided for in this world and the next.

And I wondered how much anti-clerical animus might be lurking under the all-pervading sycophancy towards priests in Ireland.

I was no longer greatly disturbed by religious doubts. My position seemed to me clear enough. The Jesuits, like all priests, dealt largely in infinitudes, and the words 'infinite' and 'eternal' came easily to their lips. For my part, when I tried to imagine an infinite universe without boundaries anywhere, topless, bottomless, uncentred, my thoughts returned to earth baffled and bewildered by the vain quest for something which was 'beyond the reaches of the soul'. But it was also incredible that the universe somewhere should end, for where it ended something else must, I reasoned, begin. Time with a beginning and time without a beginning were equally beyond the range of my imagination. To speak of infinite space or infinite time, or of their opposites, finite space and finite time, seemed to me to be a mystification, a making play with syllables void of meaning, mere counters that did not correspond to any comprehensible ideas, words that were the disingenuous 'Hic sunt leones' of dim, unchartable regions of thought. The effort to imagine the infinitely little, too, arrested the heart like a hand of ice. And yet was it believable that the universe was finite at the small end and infinite at the big end?

Into this category of essentially incomprehensible ideas I put the idea of God. The Jesuits used this word glibly, too, and knew all the predicables relating to it. For me it was a mystery beyond the range of thought, co-equal with the universe. I needed no convincing that I was able to Think, if only the rudimentary thoughts that then occupied me, and that I had purposes, if only the purpose to try my ideas out on Jim. If thought and purpose existed in me, or broadly speaking in mankind, they existed in the universe in which I existed. I was driven to the dilemma of asserting either that thought and purpose existed only in me or also outside me. Less than a microbe in a planetary system, itself less than a microbe in the universe, I felt the absurdity of affirming that I, or man, was the only thinking and purposing being in it. Beyond that tentative 'Cogito, ergo Deus est', I could not see, but so far the argument was stringent enough for me. The rest was too vast for anything but cold speculation. I was altogether ignorant of philosophical systems at the time, but nothing that I have since read or heard ever changed that early attitude of benevolent agnosticism.

Jim listened patiently enough to my exposition of these ideas, but when I had finished he said in broad vernacular:

—Is that the kind of thoughts you do be thinking when you're goin' the road around Dublin's fair city?

—What's funny about my ideas?

—I didn't say they were funny, he answered more seriously, but you have a curious way of considering the whole question as if you didn't care a rap one way or another.

He missed the sense of supreme responsibility which is the sense of sin. I had never been God-intoxicated.

—As a matter of fact I don't care very much.

—Hasn't it occurred to you that you are not properly equipped for such a discussion?

—Strange to say, it has. But it has also occurred to me that if this discussion is only for properly equipped people, it cannot concern me. At the same time, I don't feel in any way bound to accept the learned opinions of such people.

—However you accept the opinions of popular astronomers.

—Oh, in a very different spirit. Or rather, in a very indifferent spirit. God interests me only a little more than astronomy. I'm a Home Ruler in the Universe, too.

Jim looked at me askance, and said comically:

—There's a queer, grim, Dutch touch about your phiz. I pity the poor woman who wakes up to find it on the pillow beside her.

Jim was arguing against himself. His own attitude was more or less the same, I am convinced, but my exposition of it had made it seem flat and distasteful to him. Moreover, he had little interest in the scientific or pseudo-scientific aspects of rebellion. He flouted the idea that science could supersede philosophy and considered science to be rather another kind of false religion, more inhuman and barren than the one he had left. And God had been once a living reality for him.

I was not grim, however, I was happier than I had ever been as an observant Catholic with doubts for ever popping up in my mind, and at school now I felt detached and untroubled. One of our teachers, perhaps noticing some change in me, told us in an impromptu homily, unconnected with our work in class, that when we went out into the world we should meet people who would be only too willing to undermine our faith. We were always to bear in mind, he said, that if a man is ill, he goes to a doctor, who has studied medicine; if he has a case at law, he goes to a lawyer, who has studied law; if a man has religious doubts, he should go to a priest of his Church, who has studied theology. I had ceased to be disputatious or eager to rebut the arguments of a preacher, but just for that reason perhaps, the obvious objections occurred to me spontaneously before he had ceased speaking: that we go to what doctor or lawyer we choose, and for advice and not for orders.

Still another flitting, not the last, but the last that Jim took part in, deposited us at 7 St. Peter's Terrace, Cabra—which in Irish means something like barren or blighted land. Today it is a good, middle-class residential quarter. My father, moved perhaps after Georgie's death by some transient twinges of conscience, commuted part of his small pension and bought the little two-storeyed house in Cabra and some indispensable furniture at auctions. We were now reduced in numbers, for Charlie, as I have said, had entered a seminary, and on Sundays his admiring sisters had the pleasure of seeing him, complete with soutane, biretta, and prayer-book, filing down from Clonliffe College with the other clerical students to high Mass at the Pro-Cathedral in Marlborough Street. My father moved into the new house with the usual programme of good intentions, but if he himself had any illusion that they would last beyond a fortnight, he was the only member of the family that had.

Jim's 'Ibsen Night' and paper on 'The Drama and Life' caused some stir also in the upper spheres of the University, for his English professor, Father Darlington, of whom there is a not unsympathetic thumbnail sketch as dean of studies in *A Portrait of the Artist*, thought fit to lecture on Sophocles, Shakespeare, and Ibsen, borrowing the books for his study of the third person of the trinity from my brother. I was present at the lecture, but remember only that his criticism of Ibsen was not hostile.

When we were coming out of the hall, one of a group of Irish-language enthusiasts, seeing me standing near him, said loudly in harsh Northern accent that suited his whey complexion and blunt features so well:

—I don't see how any man could know more about Ibsen than Father Darlington does.

When I told Jim, he laughed.

—Poor fellow, he said. Evidently he has had to swallow something that doesn't agree with him.

—That Magherafelt boor, said I angrily, is consumed with envy of you.

—It looks like it, said Jim carelessly, but I am sorry for him if he can't think of any better way to vent his spleen. Any girl of fifteen or sixteen could have told him how to do it sweetly.

In conversation with Jim, Father Darlington (another English convert) had said that he thought *A Doll's House* an excellent argument against mixed marriages. Jim wondered how he had worked that out.

Having seen in some review an announcement that William Archer was preparing a book on the poets of the younger generation Jim had written to him before we left Glengariff Parade to propose certain young Irish poets whose work he liked. If my memory does not betray me, he also sent him a thin green volume of verses by an Irish poet, Paul Gregan, who was personally unknown to my brother. So far as I know, Jim never met him. At the same time, my brother sent Archer his own unpublished poems and received in answer a painstaking criticism, which was not without some retarded effect.

Note new address: 71 Alleyn Park,
West Dulwich S.E.
[No date]

Dear Mr. Joyce,

I confess myself a good deal puzzled what to say about your
verses, and it is that uncertainty which has kept me silent so
long. I think, if you will forgive my saying so, that there is
as yet more temperament than anything else in your work—
you feel and you imagine poetically, but I do not find that
as yet you have very much to say. Perhaps this is a mere nar-
rowness of taste on my part; but I confess to a preference for
poetry embodying a definite thought, or a distinct picture,
rather than poetry which suggests only a mood. You will say
that this criticism would equally apply to most of Verlaine and
a good deal of Shelley. Well, perhaps it would; but you have
got to write as exquisitely as they before you can validly plead
their precedent.

The pieces I like best are *Wanhope, The Final Place, Commonplace, The Passionate Poet* and *Tenebrae.* In all these I
see very real promise. But do pray let me beg you not to
cultivate metrical eccentricities such as abound especially in
the opening poems of the collection. In the first place, for instance, I have marked four lines that seem to me mere stum-
bling-blocks and rocks of offence. I have also marked a line in
Tenebrae which I almost think you must have miscopied—
didn't you mean to write 'unto our call'? Also such rhymes as
'clothes' and 'those' will scarcely pass muster in serious verse—
and to my thinking you are much too fond of identical rhymes
—I mean ending two lines with absolutely the same word—a
trick to be very sparingly employed in English verse. But
enough of these pedantries.

My book of Poets, as you will see from the enclosed announcement, is long ago finished and will be out very soon. I
had heard of Mr. Gregan's work; but indeed my list of poets

was completed and the book to all intents and purposes finished two years ago.

Yours very truly,
William Archer

The tone of the letter is friendly and serious. The writer is
evidently trying to give the young poet the best advice he can
and the benefit of his large experience, but he did not consider
that at seventeen or eighteen neither Shelley nor Verlaine had
written exquisitely. A poem of Shelley's, written apparently
when he was twenty, 'On Robert Emmet's Grave', would deserve to pass unnoticed in an Irish country paper. What was
true, and what I was beginning to notice, was that not all Jim's
personality or even the most distinctive part of it found expression in verse, but only the emotive side, which in one respect
was fictitious. It is not so with true poets.

Jim wrote back defending some of his metrical devices, and
Archer replied, still patient and controversial. He advised my
brother against trying to have his poems published, as some day
he might regret it, if his talent developed freely and normally.
But, he added with Scotch balance, 'It is not always wise to
refrain from action in the present because we think we may
regret it in the future'.

The collection of poems which Jim had sent Archer was not,
of course, *Chamber Music* but either *Moods* or *Shine and Dark*,
juvenile poems of which, among those mentioned by Archer,
only 'Commonplace', the second poem in *Chamber Music*,
survives.

We had already moved into the new house, when my brother
wrote 'The Day of the Rabblement'. This short article, written
rapidly in one morning, accused the Irish Literary Theatre,
which had declared war on the commercialism of the English

stage, of prostituting the highest form of art (the drama) to the rabblement of the most belated race in Europe, which he called after Giordano Bruno '*la Bestia Trionfante*'. He insisted that as Ireland had no dramatic tradition of its own, Irish dramatists should look abroad for their models, and pointed out that eight years before Shaw took advantage of the fact that the English censorship was powerless in Ireland.

My contribution to the article, which he read to me in the afternoon of the Sunday on which he wrote it, consisted of two phrases, 'titter coyly' instead of 'smile archly' because, I objected, in a darkened theatre you cannot see how people smile, and 'Moore is drawing on his literary account'. The article was written for *St. Stephen's* magazine and rejected by a member of the staff, Arthur Chanel Clery, who alleged unalterable censorship. Without wasting time on Clery, my brother went hot-foot to the fountainhead, the rector of the University. He was chasing a shadow. The rector, nominally responsible, was amicable, but seemed to know little about the matter. He had not read the article. The incident was true in miniature to the pattern of clerical control everywhere. The nominal head is bland and sympathetic while his subordinates have a free hand for their silent work of suppression.

Whoever was the censor—Clery speaks vaguely of a Father Browne (still another converted Protestant, rumoured to have a wife and daughter somewhere in England) 'who had no little say in the conduct of the magazine'—whoever it was, he mistook his man and missed his mark badly. At my brother's suggestion, Skeffington, who had had an article of his on 'A Forgotten Aspect of the University Question' rejected by the same censor, joined him in publishing both articles together at their own expense in the form of a pink-covered brochure of a few pages. Skeffington was then registrar of the College, a position which he subsequently resigned because of the rejection of his article advocating the admission of women to all faculties of the University. He had been educated by his father on some system—so, at least, Jim told me—and was endowed with an enthusiasm that responded mechanically to all the more obvious appeals to justice, reason, and humanity. He had not yet considered the religious question, but he intended to devote a year to its consideration, he said, as soon as his work and studies left him time to do so. He was very methodical. Jim commented ironically that Skeffington was going to give his serious consideration to the problem whether laymen were permitted to think. Yet to me Jim spoke of him as 'the most intelligent man in St. Stephen's College after myself'.

In the end Jim's article, which begins with a challenging quotation from Giordano Bruno, 'No man, said the Nolan, can be a lover of the true or the good unless he abhors the multitude', got more publicity than if it had not been censored, more than the longer and better article on Mangan, for he and I distributed it to the newspapers and people in Dublin whom my brother wished to see it. A mention of it appeared in the *United Irishman*, and I remember handing it in at Ely Place to George Moore's pretty servant. My brother's strictures on the cultured and uncultured rabblement and on the Irish artists who, he maintained, had surrendered to the basest influences in national life—'your popular devil'—provoked in the following number of *St. Stephen's* magazine a comment apparently addressed to the students of the College but fitter for the urchins of a National School. It declared that 'the Irish rabblement' was willing in the interest of the traditional morality of the Catholic Church—outraged by *The Countess Cathleen*—to forego all that art might add to the surroundings of life.

Not long after the publication of the brochure, Father Dinneen, the professor of Irish and author of an Irish-English dictionary, went on an excursion with a group of students in the hills around Dublin. He was a little man with a pale, prematurely old face, like a pathetic leprechaun, but on this occasion, to show the lightness and innocence of his heart, he kept jumping up on the low stone walls along the way and off again, and every time he landed on the grassy border, he exclaimed amid the merriment of the students, 'Said the Nolan!'

Jim had kept the reference to 'the Nolan' advisedly, over-riding objections from me, his doubting Thomas. He intended that the readers of his article should have at first a false impression that he was quoting some little-known Irish writer—the definite article before some old family names being a courtesy title in Ireland—so that when they discovered their error, the name of Giordano Bruno might perhaps awaken some interest in his life and work. Laymen, he repeated, should be encouraged to think. As far as arousing curiosity goes, he gauged his effect accurately enough, but the rest is a matter of surmise. They certainly failed to notice that in the last sentence he proclaimed himself the successor of Ibsen. It was a proud boast for a youth of nineteen, but not an empty one, though not literally maintained.

Who the Nolan was may have been revealed by my brother's Italian professor, Ghezzi, with whom, after the publication of the brochure, Jim had discussed Bruno's philosophy. Ghezzi, thinking perhaps that the discussion had been too objective, said:

—But you must not forget that he was a terrible heretic.

—Yes, said Jim, I'll remember, and also that he was terribly burnt.

Jim was in spite of that on good terms with this young Italian Jesuit who, coming from a Kultur-Stadt in the producer country of Catholicism, was not in full sympathy with the ignorant obedience mixed with Puritanism, which is the Irish blend. They had read and criticized in lively disputes D'Annunzio's *Il Fuoco,* which my brother considered the highest achievement of the novel to date.

The distinctive features of the new-born conscience, which was already urging my brother's adventurous prow into troubled waters, were his inflexible sincerity as an artist and his firm belief that artists are the true spiritual shepherds of the flock. Yet, though he seemed weird to classmates who reacted only to herd instincts, as a university student he remained lively and by no means disinclined to gaiety. His abhorrence of the multitude was not uncompromising at all points. It did not, for example, prevent him from taking a rather prominent part in some ragging at the conferring of degrees. His loud laugh was characteristic and occasionally disconcerting, it appears, for once when he was laughing loudly in a group of students outside the gate of the National Library, a waspish old lady, who had just emerged from the office of some Bible Society or other in the same street, came over to the group and asked angrily:

—What is the matter with the young man? Why is he laughing in such a way? He must be ill. You should take care of him and take him home.

She confirmed, probably without knowing it, Leopardi's observation regarding the apprehension which the laughter of others can arouse in us. But the old dame knew her Bible, in which the only laugh that resounds is sardonic. My brother's laugh was not sardonic then. It was frank hilarity that gave no wry twist to the lips.

A striving after elegance of phrase sometimes gives sententious airs to the essays of his student days, but it does not impugn the sincerity of his indignation that the cultured rabblement should prefer 'a lying clamour' * (chiefly, patriotic art) to 'the splendour of truth' † (e.g., Ibsen's dramas). One consequence of his scorn of falsity and secrecy, collective and individual, written or acted, was his determination to maintain the closest relation between his life and his work, while yet remaining free to create artistically, unhampered by the shackles of autobiography.

A brief passage with Skeffington threw a curious side-light on his changing attitude towards lyric poetry. At about the time of the publication of 'The Day of the Rabblement', Jim and I were crossing Stephen's Green with Skeffington one afternoon, discussing a day's excursion to the Three Rock Mountains which Skeffington was planning to make with the Sheehys and some other students. Jim was invited to join them. Apropos of nothing, Skeffington, who liked to pose abruptly what he considered rock-bottom questions, asked him:

—Have you ever been in love?

Habitually when Jim was talking in earnest, he spoke slowly, not hesitatingly, but choosing his words with care, unless it was a matter he had thought out beforehand, in which case he spoke almost as he wrote. Now he rattled off an answer rapidly.

—How would I write the most perfect love songs of our time if I were in love? he asked. A poet must always write about a past or a future emotion, never about a present one. If it is a regular, right-down, honest-to-God, 'till-death-us-two-part' affair, it will get out of hand and spoil his verse. Poetry

---

* 'Be not sad because all men
    Prefer a lying clamour before you . . .'
        Chamber Music XIX.
† A phrase from Plato, quoted by Joyce in 'The Day of the Rabblement' and elsewhere. Joyce came upon it in a letter of Flaubert to Mlle. Leroyer de Chantepie, March 18, 1857.

must have a safety valve properly adjusted. A poet's job is to write tragedies, not to be an actor in one.

He spoke volubly, and what he said, though unoriginal, was not altogether nonsensical, but the tirade was quite evidently a turn put on for Skeffington's benefit. When there was a pause, I interposed acidly:

—In any case, if you fail as a poet, you can go on the stage as a patter comedian.

Skeffington laughed, but Jim unabashed went on in the same vein. When we parted from Skeffington at the door of the University, I asked Jim:

—Do you really think your poems are so perfect?

—Evidently I think highly of them; otherwise I shouldn't be trying to find a publisher for them.

—I think that nature abhors perfection, and that most readers agree with her.

—Is that a quotation from that brilliant diary of yours?

—No, but it will be.

—A coruscation?

He used to say that I reminded him of a sluggish saurian, whose scaly hide occasionally reflected glints of light.

—It occurred to me when I was reading Pope's *Essay on Man*.

—Pope's what? Why on earth are you reading that?

—Culture, said I briefly and grimly.

—You take my mistakes hostage, said Jim, dismissing the point that did not interest him and reverting to the one that did. Do you expect me to return an intelligent answer when Skeffington asks a damn silly question?

—Well, I suppose not, I agreed.

They made the excursion to the Dublin hills; and one of the results for my brother was the suggestion for two of the

songs afterwards included in *Chamber Music*: 'What counsel
has the hooded moon' and 'Lightly come and lightly go'. The
prettiest of the Sheehy girls furnished the inspiration for both.
Not that Jim was ever in love with her, though in *A Portrait
of the Artist* Lynch calls her 'your beloved'. They never met,
so far as I ever knew, except at the Sunday evening parties in
her father's house or on some very rare occasions such as this
excursion, and their relations were, on one side at least, always
rather diffident and conventional. This daughter rarely took
part in the charades they played so often, preferring to be an
onlooker. But the weather and the mood of the little group
conspired to make the excursion entirely successful, and the
girl was young, happy, and very handsome.

When they were returning late in the evening, all a little
tired, there was some talk about a pale rose-coloured moon
that had risen with a halo—a sign that rain was near, some
weather prophet predicted. The pretty Sheehy girl, who was
walking with my brother, thought it looked tearful.

—It looks to me like the chubby hooded face of some jolly
fat Capuchin, said Jim.

The girl, in too happy a mood to be shocked, gave him a
sidelong glance out of her large, dark eyes and said, basing
her conclusion, one may suppose, not exclusively on that observation of his:

—I think you are very wicked.

—Not very, said Jim, but I do my best.

After they had separated and she had gone off home, with
a brother and sister who had also been of the party, Jim strolled
on, in no hurry, because he had the idea for a song in his head.
Having no other writing materials, he tore open a cigarette-
box and standing under a street lamp wrote the two verses of
the song on the inside of the box in his firm, neat handwriting.

What counsel has the hooded moon
  Put in thy heart, my shyly sweet,
Of Love in ancient plenilune,
  Glory and stars beneath his feet—
A sage that is but kith and kin
With the comedian Capuchin?

Believe me rather that am wise
  In disregard of the divine,
A glory kindles in those eyes,
  Trembles to starlight. Mine, O Mine!
No more be tears in moon or mist
For thee, sweet sentimentalist.

In the fifth and last chapter of *A Portrait of the Artist* in which my brother shows the artist (the young poet) in the throes of creation, he uses the cigarette-box incident for the 'Villanelle of the Temptress', which was written a few years before the supposed date of the chapter, his first departure from Dublin, and belonged to one or other of the earlier collections. He also blends the figure of Mary Sheehy in the novel with an imaginary girl-child for whom Dedalus is supposed to have had a fleeting affection as a boy. I tell the incident faithfully as Jim told it to me. The song written on the inside of a cigarette-box was 'What counsel has the hooded moon', and I kept that curious manuscript for years, but when I came back to Trieste after the First World War, I could not find it again.

The key-word in the song is 'sentimentalist'. My brother was beginning to realize that he was not made of the proper stuff to be a lover, because he was not a sentimentalist. Mary Sheehy was the only girl who had ever aroused any emotional interest in him, but compared with the 'wild, radiant', enduring passion, of which he soon after showed himself to be capable, it could

not be called love. As for his love poems, the fact is that when
he did fall in love, he stopped writing them. His bosom friends
at that time predicted that he would pass unscathed from one
love affair to another, and they rather envied him his gifts for
winning women: good looks, a good voice, a good figure, and
the future they foresaw for him. In fact, some opinion of that
kind may have prompted Skeffington's question. I knew they
were wrong. Part, at least, of the attraction Ibsen's dramas had
for him may be traced to the secondary role that 'the love that
piping poets solemnize' plays in them. In love, my brother was
a realist, and even then in outlook 'a married man'; women
did not constitute his chief interest in life, nor did he expect
to be the main purpose of any woman's life. He knew that
sooner or later children would take his place. What makes 'The
Dead' such a fine story is the contrast between the lover and
the married man, presented not as the eternal triangle, but
compassionately—they have both loved the woman sincerely—
as the polar attitudes of the male towards women. He knew as
clearly as any rising barrister or doctor, divine or politician,
that he must first settle his marriage problem and then get on
with the work which he felt himself called upon to do. In
spirit he was still romantic enough or free enough, which may
be the same thing, to wish his marriage to be an adventure and
a challenge; but when he did settle the question in his fashion,
he became a family man. In spite of his struggle with poverty,
he believed in fatherhood and considered it a form of cowardice,
'too great a fear of fate', not to have children.

Meanwhile he was a bachelor undergraduate who loved
women and song—but wine not yet. With women his contacts
remained on a disappointingly low level, and he was already
growing tired of what he called after Swedenborg 'scortatory
love'. He concealed his disappointment by saying, in the semi-

scientific jargon he sometimes affected, that whores were bad
conductors of emotion, and moreover that he longed to copulate
with a soul. If such was his longing, he should have taken
proper precautions to be born in some other country. His life
showed that he was capable of loving one woman, and as long
as I knew him he took no kind of real interest, least of all
emotional or intellectual interest, in any other; but whether
because of his precocious sexual experience or other reasons,
he was temperamentally incapable of placing Woman on a
romantic pedestal to be, even symbolically, the object of his
service. He liked Yeats's poem 'The Cloths of Heaven', and
had set it to music, but for himself he would allow no woman
to tread, be it ever so lightly, on his dreams.

The truth seems to be that he who has loved God in youth
can never love anything that is less than divine. The definition
may change, but the sense of service due to something outside
himself *sub specie aeternitatis* abides. In boyhood my brother
had felt God to be a living presence, devotion to which had
given him a serenity that proved illusory. When belief in the
Trinity went the way of all dogmatic beliefs, the capacity for
devotion did not go with it. Not only was he still capable of
setting an ideal aim above his happiness and his career; such
an unquestioning sacrifice was even essential to his character.

His promiscuous sexual life was open and deliberate, for he
despised furtiveness in any form. He considered sexual contact
a necessary physical fulfilment and made no apologies for it.
He recognized that nature does not allow adolescent or adult
males to be continent, that in a less unpleasant way chastity is
as much against nature as homosexuality, and that, in fine, sexual
morality must adapt itself to the normal urges of nature, and
not the contrary. Nevertheless there can be little doubt that
his contempt for sentimentality was in great part instinctive

aversion to what he regarded as a clownish idealization of lust—
a remnant, this, of earlier piety. There were still other remnants
of earlier ideas: that the soul is awakened to spiritual life by
sinning—his interpretation of the Fall, and one of the main
themes of *A Portrait of the Artist*—and a lingering belief in
the innocence of girlhood, 'a simple rosary of hours'. He seems
to have compassionated young girls for the brutal incidence of
sex upon their virginal innocence. Even amid his drabbing, he
himself retained virginal airs, which were partly just the absence
of furtiveness. He was young even for his years. Despite the
squalor and unhappiness of his home and the torment of mental
strife within him, a certain air almost of youthful gaiety
hovered about his tall, slender figure. But besides vitality there
was a certain steely hardness in the short-sighted glance of
his perceptive eyes that forewarned all half-and-halfers. Among
the various nicknames that Gogarty's ingenuity found for him
there was also 'the virginal kip-ranger', further confirmed in a
limerick on him, by the same author, which ran:

> *There is a young fellow named Joyce,*
> *Who possesses a sweet tenor voice.*
> *He goes down to the kips*
> *With a psalm on his lips,*
> *And biddeth the harlots rejoice.*

Yet Jim, quoting prophetic couplets of Blake's, which declare
that

> *The harvest shall flourish in wintry weather*
> *When two virginities meet together.*
> *The King & the Priest must be tied in a tether*
> *Before two virgins can meet together,*

used to say that the only two virginities that he could imagine were the Holy Ghost and the Virgin Mary. It is a notable difference between him and the 'mummers', as he called his contemporaries, that he did not quote these lines because the rhymes chink, or because they sounded impressive in a discussion, but because he meant them. The priest and the king were both absent from his marriage.

In a world after his heart's desire men and women would satisfy their sexual instincts when they felt the urge, and marry when they chose to form a more enduring partnership—moral principles more in contrast, on the male side, with the morality that is preached than with the morality that is practised. He rarely mentioned or discussed marriage, but when he did, it was to pour cold scorn on the sexual morality which that confederacy of morbid bachelors, the Catholic hierarchy, has striven rather unsuccessfully for ages to impose on reluctant males. To make the heavy burden of marriage the exorbitant price of coition was, in his view, to sow the seeds of discord, while at the same time it debased what might be a franker and freer relationship between men and women. Especially repugnant to him was the vulgar sentimentality that plays the go-between in this bad bargain for the male. Commenting on the atrocious superstition that intercourse with a virgin will cure a man of a venereal disease, a superstition by no means extinct among the more ignorant masses, Jim pointed out that the same superstition lurks behind a great mass of literature. He cited as an instance the type of story, of which *Pamela* is the classic example, in which a rake is reformed by marriage with a virtuous maiden.

St. Augustine speaks of the cauldrons of lawless loves that seethed round him in Carthage. Talk, always slavering obscen-

ity about sordid adventures, which Irish humour made as unap-
petizing as possible, frothed around me in the company of Jim's
medical-student friends, and would have forced me to brood on
the sexual problem, if adolescence and their gibes had not been
enough. When I refused to accompany them to night-town,
where they were going to have their sottish fling—they generally preferred to range in groups and drink—one or the other
would say pointedly:

—Women are a great invention because they save a lot of
manual labour.

The suspicion was legitimate, but it was no longer true. I
warded off the attack by striking back.

—You exaggerate, Elwood. How often do you go down to
the kips, after all? I don't think women save you such an awful
lot of manual labour in the intervals.

It was another point on which my brother and I parted
company. He proclaimed his doings with Latin frankness, while
I determined to give continence a fair trial, and persisted till I
was twenty-four or twenty-five. I had no religious scruples;
I felt chiefly disgust for besotted satisfaction increased by certain social qualms regarding the white slave traffic. When I did
decide to change my practice, I had no sense of sin and no
respect for continence, which had come to seem to me the
straight path to abnormality. That presumably reasonable men
should think that in taking a vow against women they are doing
something pleasing to the Creator, who created women, and
continues to create them in greater number than males, seemed
to me an absurd and intolerable attitude far worse than class
hatred. It is the ostracism of a whole sex. In fact, this ridiculous
attitude has been the mainstay of low comedy for many centuries, so that obviously I am not the only one that has felt
that a renunciation of woman is the first step towards homosexu-

ality. Certainly the horror of women, which found expression in so many monkish diatribes, and which, though less vocal now, still exists today, would find a chorus of approval in all the sodomites that have ever lived.

Men invent their own tragedies. They invent a sadistic God with a sin-hunting mania, who, when

> *The pretty countryfolks do lie*
> *Between the acres of the rye,*

reacts to the scene like Betsy Trotwood to donkey-boys. What the pretty countryfolks do was His invention. It would be comedy instead of tragedy, if religious teachers did not queer the pitch by instilling their obsessions into children. Unromantic by nature, I now believe in frankness with women and soap and water, without making a fetish of either.

In her book *Poets and Dreamers*, Lady Gregory wrote that Irish peasants prefer any kind of song to a love song and quoted a Scotch-Gaelic saying, 'as loveless as an Irishman'. In fact, my brother may have been typical of his race in his attitude towards women and exceptional only in his recognition of it and in the logic of his conduct. When he did fall in love it was all in all, but that was not typically Irish. It was typical of any poet anywhere, and it did spoil his verse-making, as he had told Skeffington.

Irishmen are less prone to passion than given to gallantry. Dramas of passion are rare and find little sympathy among them. Their sudden revulsion of feeling and malignant outcry against their former idol, Parnell, when he became the protagonist of as genuine a love drama as modern history affords, could hardly have happened in any other country in Europe. Bigotry alone is not a sufficient explanation. Love gets a cold

welcome in Ireland unless it is obedient to priestly control
before marriage, and, through the confessional, after marriage
too. Unmarried mothers had better be dead than alive in the
greenest of isles. If it is known that there has been intercourse
between the couple before marriage it is remembered against
them as long as they live. Irishmen seem to marry for prosaic
reasons or to get it over, and are faithful rather than devoted
husbands. In Ireland more than elsewhere the hen-pecked husband is a rarity and a laughing-stock. For the most part, women
do not interest Irishmen except as streetwalkers or housekeepers.

It is in Anglo-Irish poets that this emotional deficiency is
most manifest. I do not know the poets in the Irish tongue
except in Douglas Hyde's translation from which it would not
be fair to judge them; but I fancy that the Irish word for
'love', pronounced 'graw' (to rhyme with 'gnaw') must always
have been a handicap. Scotland, too, has its Gaelic poets; but
it has a host of poets even before Burns, in comparison with
whose songs Anglo-Irish love poetry until Yeats is a very thin
vintage.

My brother has used the phrase, 'the asexual intellect of the
Irish'. He did not mean that Irishmen are less virile than others
(families are rather larger in Ireland than elsewhere), but that
sexual motives have little influence on their lives. Sexuality is in
their lives a thing apart which rarely 'gets entangled with reality'. This indifference or concealed hostility of Irishmen to
women is reflected in the character of their women. It would
be interesting to determine whether the coldness, bigotry, and
absolute lack of romanticism of Irish women are innate or unconsciously desired by the males of the race; for, in the last
analysis, women are always blamed by men for being just what
men themselves have made them.

About this time (1901) I went alone to a concert in the Rotunda given by Clara Butt and her husband, Kennerley Rumford, with an excellent supporting cast. It is difficult after such a lapse of time to remember the programme, but I am almost sure it included '*Mon coeur s'ouvre à ta voix*' and '*Che farò senza Euridice*'. She sang many songs, for she was called back again and again. After the concert when I came away, the music I had just heard went coursing through my veins; it seemed to me that the voice of a contralto was the only one worth listening to.

The concert-hall was crowded and among the audience I was one of the most enthusiastic. After a while I became aware that a lady who was sitting beside me looked at me several times. She was a handsome, dark-haired woman, between thirty and forty years old. I noticed her fair skin and the large pupils and very pure whites of her brown eyes. In one of the pauses she spoke to me, and we continued to chat in the brief pauses and the interval about the concert and about music, in which she seemed to be competent. At the end she shook hands with me, smiling placidly.

Afterwards I met her by chance at least once that I remember. She stopped me in the street; I was not yet eighteen and should not have had the audacity to accost her. She asked me some conventional questions about my studies, and her manner was pleasant and friendly, but I never met her again.

Out of this unpromising material, which he found in my diary, my brother made the story of 'A Painful Case', which he wrote much later in Trieste when the turbid life of Dublin was beginning to settle and clarify in his mind. He gave the woman in it, Emily Sinico, a Triestine name. Giuseppe Sinico was the composer of the 'Inno di San Giusto', the patron saint of Trieste. Mr. Duffy is the type of the male celibate, as Maria in 'Clay' is of the female celibate, but he is also intended to be a portrait of what my brother imagined I should become in middle age. The portraiture has 'the grim Dutch touch' he spoke of. He has used many characteristics of mine in composing Mr. Duffy, such as intolerance of drunkenness, hostility to socialism, and the habit of noting short sentences on a sheaf of loose pages pinned together. The title Jim suggested for this distillation of tabloid wisdom was *Bile Beaŋs*. Two of them are included in the story: 'Every bond is a bond to sorrow', and 'Love between man and man is impossible because there must not be sexual intercourse, and friendship between a man and a woman is impossible because there must be sexual intercourse', both of which, for some vague reason, were added after the chance encounter at the concert. Jim had also lent Mr. Duffy some traits of his own, the interest in Nietzsche and the translation of *Michael Kramer*, in order to raise his intellectual standard.

As my brother had burnt his play, the two collections of poems were now, with the exception of the article on Ibsen's play and 'The Day of the Rabblement' and a half-dozen epiphanies of a few lines each, all the literary work he had to show. He grew, however, more and more dissatisfied with the poems, and in the end burnt all but one or two of the earlier ones and a few recent ones which he had not yet included in either collection. I pleaded in vain for the lives of others, especially of those which Archer had singled out for approval. Beyond announcing his intention to burn them, he gave no reasons. He just read them over again critically and then tore them up one by one and burnt them without comment. As he had always animadverted on that class of poets for whom only what is imaginary possesses poetic value, it may be that in accordance with his new trend his principle was to reject such poems as seemed to him false emotionally and fit only to be chaplets for a 'piping poet's' brow.

Others, no doubt, were rejected for technical reasons. His personal preference was for poems the interest of which did not depend on the expression of some poetical thought, but on the indefinable suggestion of word, phrase, and rhythm. The poems that he liked sought to capture moods and impressions, often tenuous moods and elusive impressions, by means of a verbal witchery that magnetizes the mind like a spell, and imparts a wonder and grace, which Marlowe thought no virtue could digest into words. His own poems were songs without thoughts, the most difficult kind, in which it takes the labour of years to attain distinction.

His favourite poem in Dowland's Songs was 'Weep you no more, sad fountains', a poem which, in spite of its simplicity, it would be difficult to paraphrase in prose. In fact if the thought of a poem can be adequately paraphrased in prose, there seems to be little reason for writing it in verse.

Weep you no more, sad fountains!
What need you flow so fast?
Look how the snowy mountains
Heaven's sun doth gently waste!
But my Sun's heavenly eyes
View not your weeping,
That now lies sleeping
Softly, now softly lies
    Sleeping.

Sleep is a reconciling,
A rest that peace begets.
Doth not the sun rise smiling

When fair at even he sets?
Rest you, then, rest, sad eyes!
Melt not in weeping,
While she lies sleeping
Softly, now softly lies
Sleeping!

The poem being attributed to Dowland, my brother sought out whatever Elizabethan song-books he could find in the National Library and copied out many of Dowland's songs and also one or two by Henry VIII; Cosgrave ('Lynch'), who had some knowledge of music, helped him with enthusiasm. His interest in Elizabethan composers was extended to English folk-songs, which he found principally in a collection by Cecil Sharp. The happy lilting airs of 'Dolly, Dolly, ah', 'The Leather Bottèl', and 'Spanish Ladies' suited his mood then better than the puling Irish traditional music, too often heard, even in the excellent arrangements of Moffat and Villiers Stanford. Surfeited with the tawdry melancholy of patriotic Irish poets, he used to say that Ireland had contributed nothing but a whine to the literature of Europe. I think, however, that he had in mind rather Irish music than Anglo-Irish literature, in which satire and comedy predominate. Nevertheless, the next paper that he read before the Literary and Historical Society was on an Irish poet all of whose work remembers wrong and suffering, a poet who was straitly shackled to the bitterness of history and had inherited the worst part of the tradition of his race. James Clarence Mangan, who invented part of his name and part of his life-story, had been badly served by those who had written about him before my brother, both by Mitchell's patronizing memoir and by Duffy's uncritical labours. Even Yeats found only 'a certain arid force' in 'The Nameless One' and 'Siberia'. My brother was the first, I think, to claim for

Mangan the highest place among the Anglo-Irish poets of an elder day, and to try to justify that claim in a pondered essay. He held that some of Mangan's poetry was of a higher order than anything written in English by Irish poets before Yeats, but there is little in the essay of the unmeasured enthusiasm of youth. My brother harnessed his enthusiasms, which were deep, strong, and vital. The air of maturity that marked him out among his coevals in spite of the meagreness of his output may be attributed partly to this, and partly to the fact that with him there was no scission between life and thought. Work and career were not synonymous for him as they are for most young writers; his work was something above his personal success or happiness and conceivably even inimical to them.

The essay on Mangan, which was published in *St. Stephen's* in May 1902, is ornate, involved, highly stylized, and sometimes deliberately obscure. It bore witness to a determined struggle to impose an elegance of thought on the hopeless distortion of the life that surrounded him, but it announced, too, certain purposes from which he never receded, and certain ideas that were to guide the course of his life through much waywardness and error.

The essay was no mere literary exercise, nor yet simply an appreciation of Mangan; my brother was clearly feeling his way in it towards the literary tenets that were to dominate his work. A little before my brother read his paper on Mangan, Yeats had written that 'Poetry is the utterance of desires that can be satisfied only in dreams', and that, wherever civilization has not ploughed up to the roots of religion and romance, poetry lives with passionate incoherence in the hearts of the pure and simple peasantry. This poetry, he asserted, is the imperfect form of what in the perfect form is genius.

My brother's outlook was very different. He cast aside 'the

passionate incoherence in the hearts of the pure and simple peasantry' together with the 'desires that can be satisfied only in dreams'. His first paper had been called 'The Drama and Life'; the paper on Mangan could have been called 'Poetry and Life'.

He recognizes the classical and the romantic school as representative of two constant states of mind, the one beset by materialism, the other by incoherence. He accuses the romantic temper of being impatient (for him the literary 'sin against the Holy Ghost'), and of creating symbols of ideals that obscure the light. The classical temper, he declares, accepts the place in nature that is given us without doing violence to the gift and so fashions the events of life that the quick intelligence can go beyond them to their meaning which is still unuttered. This intuition of the deeper meaning of life and the elevation of the mind that goes with it are what he understands by poetry; for the highest poetry and philosophy deal with the laws that do not take holiday. Poetry is a revolt against artifice and in a sense against actuality. It is the poet's simple intuitions which are the tests of reality, and every age must look for its sanction to its poetry and its philosophy, for in these the human mind as it looks backward or forward attains to an eternal state. This ecstatic contemplation is the aim of the highest poetry.

'Beauty, the splendour of truth', he wrote, 'is a gracious presence when the imagination contemplates intensely the truth of its own being or the visible world, and the spirit which proceeds out of truth and beauty is the holy spirit of joy. These are realities and these alone give and sustain life'.

The ecstatic contemplation is identifiable with the 'radiance' of which Dedalus in *A Portrait of the Artist* speaks to his friend Lynch, when expounding his aesthetics based on his study of Thomas Aquinas. He has manifestly transferred his homage to a new Trinity, or perhaps in his view to a new understanding of the other. In the essay on Mangan he declares for the classical school, for its serener spirit, and (quoting Ibsen) for the beautiful, alluring, mysterious life of earth. How far we are here from Yeats's phrase, adapting Pope, 'the rag-and-bone-shop of the heart'.

I had suggested that in view of certain odes and laments Mangan might be considered a survival of the old tribal bards, and Jim had at first intended to include the idea in his paper, but then he rejected it. The paper and the debate that followed it were as notable and successful as his first paper had been. The student from Magherafelt, to whom I have already alluded, Walsh* by name, made it the occasion for a personal attack upon my brother, based not on the paper but on 'The Day of the Rabblement'. And perhaps not altogether on that either. Walsh had published in instalments in some North of Ireland country paper a novel or long story, which had been shown to my brother by some admirer of Walsh's budding genius. I also read it. From one of his poems my brother quotes the stanza in *Stephen Hero*,

> *Art thou real, my Ideal?*
> *Wilt thou ever come to me*
> *In the soft and gentle twilight*
> *With your baby on your knee?*

Stephen Dedalus hands back the poem without a word of blame or praise; my brother's comments on both productions, instead, were extremely caustic. Walsh had good reason to be nettled. At the end of the debate, my brother in his turn replied to all

---

* Louis Walsh (1880-1942) was District Justice in Donegal from 1923 till his death. Known in youth as 'the boy orator', he wrote several books of no consequence.

his critics in a politely controversial tone, but he ignored Walsh's onslaught. In any case, that rabid and wrathful patriot had already had his answer in a sentence in the paper. He was the archetype of those 'who hurl their anger against tyrants, and yet would establish upon the future an intimate and far more cruel tyranny'.

I fancy it must have been his success in arousing interest in 'the Nolan' that tempted my brother to use the same technique of curiosity twice again in the essay on Mangan; in one case to set his listeners guessing who 'the most enlightened of western poets' might be, in the other to dissociate himself from the worship of broadcloth (respectability) into which the cult of another poet had degenerated. The deliberate obscurity overshoots the mark: it affords no clue to his admiration for Blake and mild antipathy for Browning. My derisive protests were of no avail. There is, however, an evident and more interesting hint of self-revelation when he describes Mangan, who because of some 'matchless passages' merited the high title of poet, as being 'driven inward by surrounding brutality' and as 'doubting his dreams', and when he assigns a low station to 'literature', that 'domain between ephemeral writing and poetry'. For my brother the man of letters, who indulges in literature as an intellectual pastime, is a man of little faith.

The self-assertiveness and hankering after fine writing reveal another influence that was strong with my brother just at that time, the influence of D'Annunzio. In the course of his reading in Italian he had come across *Le Vergini delle Rocce*, and had been deeply interested in the imaginary portrait of Socrates in the first chapter. The exaltation of an ardour of life, manifested in a diversity of forms by the development of each one's native energies, appealed strongly to him at this early stage of his own development. The thought expounded in those pages is that the elect are those few spirits who, conscious of their gifts, endeavour by a self-imposed discipline to become the deliberate artificers of their own style of life; and that they owe obedience only to the laws of that style, to which they have willingly bent their free natures in pursuit of a personal ideal of order and beauty.

He held style, good or bad, to be the most intimate revelation of character, and slovenly writing invariably provoked his angry contempt. When I had read W. H. Mallock's *Is Life Worth Living?*—that forerunner of many modern conversions to Anglo-Catholicism—some remarks on it in my diary induced Jim to begin reading it. After ploughing through about a third of the book, he threw it aside with a contemptuous question, 'Is prose of that kind worth writing?'

I was glad that he had turned from verse to prose, and full of admiration for his striking phrases such as that about 'the faith that in the Middle Ages sent the spires singing up to Heaven', but in discussion with him I admitted to a liking for a different style which I attempted to define as the style the man in the street would use if the stress of emotion urged him to express himself in the words he knew best. I liked also original effects of the same kind, and drew his attention to instances in Turgenev's *Diary of a Superfluous Man*. When the Superfluous Man went to call on friends, he observed that they would come to meet him, eagerly expecting someone else, and, concealing their disappointment, say with an uneasy smile, 'Ah, how d'ye do, Tchulkaturin?' I said that the funny Russian name must surely correspond to Higginbotham in English. The conclusion of the *Diary*, with the man's face drawn on the blank space at the foot of the last page, and the aimless scribbling by someone who had found and read the diary after the unfortunate Tchulkaturin's death, seemed to me a masterstroke in the expression of futility. Jim was interested; he said he would read it again.

Although the Irish national question is barely glanced at in the article, it is evident that the young writer of it is already 'struggling to awake from that nightmare' which is history. In his childhood, the vaguely understood drama of Parnell had not stirred any feelings of patriotism or nationalism in his heart; rather, under his father's influence, it had implanted there an early spirit of revolt against hypocrisy and clerical authority and popular servility to it. When Parnell's name became the symbol of a national struggle, he stood aloof from it because there was something else he understood so clearly and keenly that its presentation in the art for which he had a vocation became imperative above all other things. When he attended the University and listened to its groups of talkative students, Parnell's story had become a memory of the dead and, though rancours still remained, time had begun to mellow the harshness of opinions that had been so violently agitated. My brother was always of opinion that a dramatist could understand only one or two of life's tragedies, and that he always presented different aspects of the few he understood. One of the tragedies that obsessed my brother's imagination, beginning from the time when he first understood the Mass as drama, was the tragedy of dedication and betrayal. In later life, the story of Parnell became for him another aspect of that tragedy.

The question of his time was the movement founded by Arthur Griffith in the *United Irishman* and afterwards called Sinn Fein. It advocated a new economic plan of campaign which was unparliamentary but pacific. Besides the absenteeism from Westminster of Irish members, he proposed a nation-wide agitation to be based, I think I remember, on an Irish trade mark, to buy only Irish goods. Griffith frequently quoted Dean

Swift's advice 'to burn everything English except their coal'.*
He was a rather insignificant-looking man, with none of Parnell's glamour. I never heard him speak at any public meeting,
but my brother was quick to grasp the importance of the movement. He said that the *United Irishman* was the only paper in
Dublin worth reading, and in fact, he used to read it every
week until a priest took an action for libel against the meagrely
financed paper and killed it. In spite of its perfervid nationalism,
the paper had found very little favour with the students of
University College or with their masters. Its tone was too independent, its line too unusual; it was suspected of lukewarm
Catholicism, of disrespect for priests (Griffith had been a Par-
nellite); and it did not seem to be hostile to intellectual movements in Ireland and on the continent. Yeats and AE, and others
who contributed to it gratuitously, were of Protestant stock and
on the Catholic blacklist. In my last year at Belvedere, the
Jesuits there, whenever they mentioned it, spoke openly against
it. A former classmate of mine at Belvedere, whose father was
on terms of close friendship with a prominent Jesuit, Father
Finlay, and who probably thought I shared his animosity to
the paper because I had listened in silence to the strictures of
our Jesuit masters, told me in great secrecy of the coming publication of a paper with Jesuit backing. Some months later another
weekly paper called the *Leader*, which had clerical support,
was started under the editorship of a blatant nullity, D. P.
Moran by name.

My brother did not belong to the Sinn Fein movement,
though he afterwards wrote about it in Trieste, but he favoured
it rather than the 'ineffectual parliamentary struggle' in which
I believed. His political leanings were towards socialism, and

---

* 'Burn only what's Irish, accepting their coals.' *Finnegans Wake*, p. 447.

he had frequented meetings of socialist groups in back rooms in the manner ascribed to Mr. Duffy in 'A Painful Case'. I sometimes accompanied him to these dimly illuminated, melancholy haunts and listened to unconvincing arguments. My brother thought that fanned nationalisms, which he loathed, were to blame for wars and world troubles. Mr. Duffy's disillusionment with socialism, however, does not reflect my brother's ideas but mine. At Trieste he still called himself a socialist. This political attitude of his I considered inconsequent in an artist, who abhorred the multitude and who cared, or should care, only about the quality of his work, whereas socialism seemed to me a discussion about hours of work and wages to the exclusion of every other interest. I asked him what difference socialism would make to his admired Ibsen? What hours of work and wages should he have in a socialist state? Nor did I follow him in his approval of Sinn Fein. I maintained that 'Speak Irish' and 'Buy Irish' would soon become 'Read only Irish' and 'Think only of Ireland' and generally tend to make—as I phrased it at the time—'another Tibet of the country'.

It is clear from phrases in the paper on Mangan that he already looked upon histories as chronicles riddled with falsehoods, and that he did not believe in the guiltlessness of the oppressed. Above all, he did not find that the yoke of the oppressor becomes any lighter or sweeter for being imposed by one's own people.

At the University he formed some friendships, and found amongst the students some admirers, who took over my job of listener and became the critics of his theories as well as the more congenial recipients of his confidences. First among them was George Clancy ('Davin'), who became a teacher of Irish, and while still a young man was elected mayor of his native Limerick. He was murdered by Black and Tan ruffians in the

hall of his house at Limerick under the eyes of his wife in 1921.
As a student, Clancy was an Irish-language enthusiast and a
sportsman, so that he and my brother had very little in common except the mutual attraction of brilliance on one side and
of plain honest intelligence on the other, of city-bred and
country-bred. It was under his influence that my brother
studied Irish for a year or two. Clancy was an ingenuous admirer of the first volumes of poems, and once when he was
going home to the country Jim lent him one or both. I have
seen it suggested that these poems, which my brother rejected
and which in any case would have only a curiosity value, may
still exist among Clancy's papers. Clancy brought them back;
he was not the sort of man to be careless in matters of that
kind. I remember seeing in the margin of a poem on the Valkyrie pencil markings apparently of approval, not by Clancy,
but perhaps by some younger brother. Jim lent the poems also
to John Francis Byrne ('Cranly') with whom he had now
formed a close friendship. When some days later Byrne brought
the two copy-books containing the poems with him to University College intending to give them back to Jim, Father
Darlington, 'the dean of studies', noticed them in Byrne's hand
and asked to see them. Byrne told him that they were verses
by my brother. The dean showed still livelier interest, and, as
Byrne made no objection, began to skim through them.

—Ha, no raptures here! he exclaimed in feigned admiration
as he turned the pages and read here and there.

The Jesuit snooper had no doubt expected to find turbulent
dithyrambic atheism after the manner of Swinburne. He asked
Byrne to lend them to him, and Byrne let him have them. I
damned Byrne's and the dean's impudence, but Jim, though he
was not pleased, said nothing. He narrated the incident without comment. When the dean returned the poems, he dispar-

ality, the deficiency of his example is such that it weakens his teaching.

Vincent Cosgrave ('Lynch'), another friend, was the eternal student. He was inscribed in the faculty of medicine, but, so long as I knew him, never sat for any examinations. He was chiefly the companion of my brother's dissipations, but he also shared his interest in Gregorian chant and choral music. Whenever the Palestrina choir of the Pro-Cathedral in Marlborough Street sang the music of Palestrina or Victoria, conducted by Vincent O'Brien, they used to go together to hear it as other people go to the opera. Cosgrave had a good bass voice and sang in some choir or other, and sometimes he used to copy out chants or other music for my brother.

Far more important in its consequences was my brother's friendship with Oliver St. John Gogarty. A chance conversation about Yeats at the counter of the National Library, as my brother told me, was the beginning of this acquaintance, which soon became a close friendship. My brother discovered with some surprise that the prosperous-looking youth, whom he at first took to be a sporting character, was a poet. Gogarty used at that time to write his poems, mostly lyrics of a few verses, in the centre of large separate folio sheets of paper. The idea took my brother's fancy and he, too, copied out his poems in the same fashion, a few neatly written verses in the middle of a large page. Gogarty protested that what my brother admired about other fellows' poems was the blanks, not the words. About then Gogarty was writing a poem for the vice-chancellor's poetry prize at Trinity, which he won. He was frank enough to tell my brother that Edward Dowden had singled out for approval the last line of the poem, 'Shines on thee, soldier of song, Leonidas', which my brother had suggested for a full close.* When his poem was printed, he made my brother a present of a copy of it. As for Jim, he had not yet found a title for his little collection of verses, and as usual, he asked me for suggestions. One of these, *Chamber Music*, he adopted. It had seemed to me suitable to the passionless love themes and studious grace of the songs.

At first Gogarty and my brother hit it off very well together. Oliver St. John (St. Jesus to his friends) Gogarty was then a stoutly built young fellow, a student of medicine at Trinity College, who had been a racing cyclist and twice jumped into the filthy waters of the Liffey to save men from drowning. He was full of bustling energy, wit, and profanity, and had a seemingly inexhaustible supply of bawdy rhymes, some original and some collected from unedited English folklore. He affected a naturalism he supposed to be Greek; and he and my brother went whoring together. Yet my brother noted that the most casual scenes appeared to his mind as the theatres of so many violent sexual episodes, and casual objects as gross sexual symbols.

He was, moreover, in loquacious revolt against the drabness and smugness of Dublin life; but in the background there was always 'the Mother', a widow with a house in town and a villa in the surroundings of the city, who was usually able to prevent any too open breach with time-honoured custom and authority. Gogarty used to go to confession and Communion at Easter to please 'the Mother', and to show, after the manner recommended and practised by Samuel Butler, that he did not take religion seriously one way or the other. In fact he frisked and laughed at 'the mockery of it'.

---

* The subject set for the prize in 1903 was 'The Death of Shelley'.

It may have been through Gogarty that my brother first met Russell. It was not difficult to get acquainted with Russell, for he was always looking for recruits for his and Yeats's literary movement. A very friendly but undated letter of Russell's seems to refer, in spite of its informality, to their first meeting.

Dear Joyce,
   Could you come on Monday evening next to see me? I think it would be better than Sunday. No one will disturb us and I want to have a good talk with you. Please let me know if you can come then. I am threatened with an invasion of other folk on Sunday evening and it is impossible to talk while there is a general gathering of odds and ends of acquaintances.
                                        Yours sincerely,
                                        Geo. W. Russell

At that first meeting, whenever it was, Russell and my brother remained talking about the spirit world until the small hours of the morning. Knowing my brother's satirical humour, his friends, foremost amongst them Gogarty, were sure that it was a glorious leg-pull, and my brother preferred to let them think so. In fact, however, he had been even then as much in earnest as Russell himself.

For my part, I hung on the borders of these friendships, dubiously accepted by the students as my brother's rather taciturn henchman. My father, Thersites-like, called me my brother's jackal,* and when his tongue tired of that, he would explain to me scientifically that I gave no light of my own, but that I shone with borrowed light like the moon. On this simile he harped lovingly, until I retorted that, instead of worrying about the moon, he had better do something about

---

* 'What are you laughing at? said his father. Everyone knows you're only this fellow's jackal.' *Stephen Hero*, p. 204 (228).

his nose, which was beginning to shine with its own light. He was still strangely vain and vulnerable to remarks on his personal appearance.

A comic incident, however, showed me that he was not alone in entertaining such an opinion. One evening when I was accompanying Jim across town to the National Library, we stopped to look in at the window of a bookseller's in Nassau Street. To attract attention to his wares and foster the love of art among his customers, the bookseller had arranged a modest picture-show in his window. It consisted of about a dozen prints, all representing beautiful models with nude busts. After looking at the display for a minute or two, I said to Jim:

—Come along, for God's sake. With all those briskets hanging around, it's like a butcher's shop.

Jim turned away and walked on without replying. The following evening I again accompanied Jim across town, as was my custom, but this time Cosgrave was with us. When we came to the bookseller's Jim went in to inquire whether a book he had ordered had come, and Cosgrave and I remained outside standing in front of the window. After surveying it for a few minutes Cosgrave began to laugh silently, and, repeating my unappreciated witticism of the evening before, I said:

—Isn't it dreadful? It's like a butcher's shop.

Cosgrave laughed more heartily but still without saying anything. Just at that moment Jim came out of the shop.

—What are you laughing at? he asked.

—Irish art, said Cosgrave with a nod of his head in the direction of the window. His hands were in his trousers pockets as usual.

Jim glanced at it and said lightly:

—Yes, it's like a butcher's shop.

Cosgrave turned full round and looked at me, laughing de-

lightedly and slapping me gleefully on the back. He obviously
thought that I was found out, properly caught in the act. But
as Jim said nothing, neither did I.

Yet the only real pleasure I ever got from pictures belongs,
if not to that year, to that period. The Hone collection of
pictures of modern French schools, chiefly of the Impressionists,
was being offered for sale to the city of Dublin, and was on
view in the gallery around the entrance hall of the Museum
opposite the National Library. As admission was free, I used
to go in there almost every time I was in that neighbourhood
and wander around the gallery for an hour or so, hardly noticing the names of the artists—there were Corots, Manets, Monets
—without any cultural purpose or critical effect, just imbibing
intense pleasure. I recollect a house amid snow, into which it
seemed I could plunge my fingers, and a Ganymede—only the
head and one shoulder of Ganymede and one bronze wing of
the eagle—which gave me a sinking sensation in the pit of my
stomach, as great heights do.

The opinion of the eminent intellectuals of the capital as to
whether the offer should be accepted or rejected was canvassed
in the Dublin papers. George Moore took part in the public
discussion. He said in a letter to a newspaper that the collection
was worth far more than the thirty thousand pounds (if I am
not mistaken) that Hone asked for it; but he criticized one of
the pictures attributed to Corot. He called it 'a pretty picture
of the tea-tray pattern', and asserted confidently that it was
not by Corot. It certainly was very different from his acknowl-
edged works in the collection. Padraic Colum's opinion was also
taken. In view of the economic situation in Ireland etc. etc.,
with great regret etc. etc., he was against the purchase. Cursing
is evidently sheer waste of energy. If even one of the curses I
sent him had struck home, it would have broken his neck.

When Edward Martyn presented a like sum to the Pro-Cathedral for the foundation of the Palestrina Choir, the *United Irishman* had censured the gift because, it opined, such a large sum could have been more usefully employed. Many years later I found the same spirit rampant in communism, fascism, and nazism. Everything was to be sacrificed to the narrow ideals of fanatical and mainly dishonest leaders. For the moment Jim was disgusted with the *United Irishman*. Although the money came under the control of priests, who were the people in Ireland that least needed it, it was for a specific artistic purpose. If that art was religious, that did not condemn it out of hand in my brother's opinion, and certainly not if it was a question of Palestrina's music or that of his school. Moreover, we had seen together a wonderfully good performance by the amateurs of the Elizabethan Stage Society of *Everyman*, that masterpiece among English medieval morality plays, and it had been something of a revelation. Even I had been deeply impressed by its simple but powerful dramatic sincerity. During the Second World War, I translated it into Italian for 'Il Teatro Medioevale', published by the Italian firm of Bompiani. But on the whole I think that my brother's interest in sacred art was very slight.

The manner of his first meeting with Yeats, of which Gogarty, of course, gives a wrong account, has been much discussed, and Yeats himself has given an account of it 'fabled by the daughters of memory'. My brother introduced himself to Yeats, accosting him in the vicinity of the National Library. It is reported that at their first meeting my brother said to Yeats, 'I regret that you are too old to be influenced by me'; and it seems that my brother always denied the story. To the best of my recollection it is at least substantially correct, though perhaps Jim may have phrased it somewhat differently. As it stands, it sounds rather like one of Yeats's good stories; what is certain is that at that meeting my brother told Yeats how much he admired two stories of his, 'The Tables of the Law' and 'The Adoration of the Magi', and urged him to reprint them. In 'The Day of the Rabblement' my brother had already spoken of them as 'stories which one of the great Russians might have written'. Yeats did reprint them a couple of years later, and in the few lines of preface to the reprint, he said that he had met a young man in Ireland 'the other day', who admired these stories very much and nothing else that he (Yeats) had written. That young man was my brother, unless some other young man told him exactly the same thing, which is improbable, for in that case there would have been at least two 'young men in Ireland' who told him so. The words 'and nothing else that he had written' have been added for dramatic effect. I believe that the other phrase has been similarly edited. I do not think that Yeats ever cared much about pointing a moral, but he undoubtedly liked to adorn a tale.

Already at that time when Yeats was regarded in Dublin as a minor poet and a poseur, and even his friends, except Moore, treated him as an eccentric, whose poetry was likely to find favour only with literary cliques, my brother had claimed for him that his poetry was of the highest order. He considered him to be the greatest poet Ireland had produced, with only Mangan worthy to be his predecessor, and the greatest of contemporary English poets. I have no doubt that he said so to Yeats. He was not the kind of youth to stint his praise of work he admired, and more than once (in the case of Italo Svevo, for example, and to some extent of Dujardin) he astonished writers by the claims he made for their work, claims which at the time seemed even to the writers themselves to be wildly extravagant. But he regarded with disdain Yeats's attempt to write popular drama and to win the favour of an Irish mob and its leaders, who derided him openly. He could not understand Yeats's avowed intention of singing 'to lighten Ireland's woe'.

A couple of years later Yeats wrote *The King's Threshold*, in which he magnified the poet and his importance in the state. It is among the least of his works, a weak and unconvincing play, because words alone are not certain good.* My brother, too, believed in words (that, at least, was common ground) but not *pour s'en payer*. He regarded psychology, which he was then studying, as the basis of philosophy, and words in the hands of an artist as the medium of paramount importance for a right understanding of the inmost life of the soul. The revelation of that inmost life was, my brother firmly believed, the poet's high office, spurning recognition by the state, and to traffic in words was a kind of literary simony.

In fact my brother's opinion of Yeats then was not very unlike Yeats's own judgment of himself when, as an aging poet, he regarded himself in retrospect. When he died on the Riviera, the wreath my brother sent for the funeral was a token of sincere homage. What my brother said, or meant to say, at their first meeting was in plain words that Yeats did not hold his head high enough for a poet of his stature, that he made himself too cheap with people who were not worthy to dust his boots. But he was aware of the futility of trying to ingraft into the elder man any of his own pride or arrogance as a poet—the choice of the words matters little. Jim had written this criticism in 'The Day of the Rabblement', and said it to me a dozen times, and to the best of my recollection that is what he told me after the meeting that he had said to Yeats.

---

* 'Words alone are not certain good'. Yeats, 'The Song of the Happy Shepherd'.

Yeats may have had some inkling of the real respect underlying the crude phrases, for he took no offence and always remained willing to help Jim practically and with advice. He was
about to start for London when my brother introduced himself; when he returned, my brother brought him his poems and
epiphanies. Yeats read them carefully and then wrote him a
long, four-page letter, urging him to devote himself to literature. In that letter he said among other things, 'You have a very
delicate talent, I cannot yet say whether for prose or verse'.

It was Yeats, too, who introduced my brother to Lady
Gregory, one of the founders of the Irish Literary Theatre and
one of the principal figures in the literary movement, in which
the theatre was the dominant factor. Eglinton tells a different
story, describing, as if he had been an eye-witness, how my
brother gate-crashed his way into a reception given by Lady
Gregory, who did not want to invite him. I was not present,
but I have two letters which are hardly reconcilable with
Eglinton's story. One is from Russell and seems to have been
written after Yeats's return to Dublin. It is undated.

My dear Joyce,
    Yeats will be in Dublin all this week and will be at the An-
tient Concert Rooms every night. He would like to meet you,
and if you could come here on Tuesday at 5 o'c. I will bring
you to his hotel. I told him I would try to get you to come at
that hour if possible. If this will not suit you you could call
some other time on him yourself with this letter. He is staying
at Nassau Hotel, South Frederic Street. He will be glad to see
you.
                                                      Geo. W. Russell

The other is from Yeats and is also undated.

Dear Mr. Joyce,

Lady Gregory begs me to ask you to come and dine with her at the Nassau Hotel to-morrow (Monday) at 6.45 to meet my father.

Yours sincerely,
W. B. Yeats
Nassau Hotel
South Frederic St.
Dublin

However unconventional his way of introducing himself may have been, it is plain that he had aroused no little curiosity amongst the leaders of the Irish literary movement.

If newspaper reports can be trusted at least in such indifferent matters as the last wills and testaments of prominent people, Mrs. G. B. Shaw left her private fortune, which seems to have been by no means inconsiderable, for the purpose of founding a school to teach Irishmen the social graces. It was a resounding, public, posthumous rap over the knuckles for her surviving partner; but the implied accusation of a certain provincialism in Irish manners can hardly be denied to have some justification. When Irishmen are well-mannered, there is a kindliness in their civility which many people find charming. But kindliness, we are told, has little to do with good manners, which should not be a matter of personal sympathy but be like justice equal for all. This impartial courtesy was one of the social graces that my brother lacked. With those few people who, he felt, were his friends, he was open and frank even to excess, but with acquaintances whom he knew but little or whom he thought he saw reason to distrust, there was a coldness and aloofness in his manner that frequently aroused hostility. Moreover, social intercourse is based on falsities of all kinds, which my brother could not stand. When literature was in question my brother considered even a European, or rather a world, war to be just literally a bloody nuisance interfering with his work; he was not likely then to allow good manners to obscure an issue he deemed important—as little likely as a religious reformer would be when his vital beliefs are threatened. His distant manner was not a pose prompted by arrogance: it was, as in many less sensitive people, a form of self-protection. Yet not merely that. It came inevitably from an awareness, not always flattering for his self-esteem, of the gulf fixed between the thoughts and aspirations that tormented him and the apparent preoccupations of more normally constituted people. But it is easy to exaggerate both his aloofness and his discourtesy. Gogarty called him 'the scorner of mediocrity and scourge of the multitude'. His compassion was not facile or Dickensian; yet even then his sympathies were wider and went deeper than those of people who judged him to be callous to all common human interests.

In 1902 Yeats's *Cathleen ni Houlihan* was produced in the Molesworth Hall by Frank Fay with Maud Gonne in the title role. The Poor Old Woman (one of the symbolical names for Ireland, like the title of the play) arrives in 1798, the year of the rebellion, at the cottage of a young peasant, Michael Gillane, on the eve of his wedding. She keens over Ireland's wrongs; a peasant rushes in to announce that the French have landed at Killala. The Poor Old Woman goes out with 'the walk of a queen', and Michael Gillane leaves bride and family to follow her. The one-act play was received with rapturous applause. My brother was scornful and indignant that Yeats should write such political and dramatic claptrap. If my brother's personality is at all interesting, it must be remembered that the attitude of this supposedly callous youth towards common and higher

human interests was exactly the contrary of the rest of the
audience save me.

In *A Portrait of the Artist*, Dedalus speaks of a certain disadvantage at which Irish writers find themselves in using the
English language. The very slight differences in the shades of
meaning which English words may have for Englishmen can
give pause, I fancy, only to Irishmen like Yeats or my brother,
whose sensibility to words applies extreme tests. To me it seems
that the real disadvantage of Irishmen is of quite a different
nature. In Ireland, a country which has seen revolutions in
every generation, there is properly speaking no national tradition. Nothing is stable in the country; nothing is stable in the
minds of the people. When the Irish artist begins to write, he
has to create his moral world from chaos by himself, for himself.
Yet, though this is an enormous disadvantage for a host of
writers of good average talent, it proves to be an enormous advantage for men of original genius, such as Shaw, Yeats, or my
brother.

My brother had the further advantage of being unhappy in
an unhappy country. Unhappiness was like a vice which forced
him either to look experience in the eye or to take refuge in
dreams. No comfortable compromise was possible. When an
English writer—Wells or Galsworthy or Huxley or Aldington
—deals with social, religious, or intellectual problems, one has
the impression that even though the problems are real and the
writer is striving to be sincere, the life that produced him is
in general stable and balanced. It has been lived for centuries
against a Constable background. And if he poses as an extremist,
it is mainly a picturesque attitude like Count Tolstoy's donning
of his Russian smock-frock, over trousers cut by the most ex-
pensive tailor in Petersburg, to play at being a peasant saint.

The characters whom these writers create to voice conflicts of opinions are people of ease and culture. They discuss problems instead of playing golf. It does them great honour that they prefer dialectic to golf, but those pastimes are both on the same level of importance. Their brilliant chatter gives the impression of purely academic after-dinner discussions. In Ireland, on the other hand, the dinner itself is often lacking, and in consequence the discussions assume a different tone. The bread-and-butter test is not irrelevant. For my brother life was not an interesting subject for discussion; it was a passion.

There had been a further visit to London to see Duse in D'Annunzio's *La Gioconda* and *La Città Morta*. On this trip he met William Archer, who invited him to lunch, and appropriately they had 'wild duck'! I remember little or nothing of their conversation as retailed to me by my brother, except that Archer in comparing Duse with Bernhardt in Sudermann's *Magda* (I think) gave it as his opinion that 'Duse could act Sarah off the stage', though for Archer Italian was a stumbling-block. My brother, who had not seen Duse act in any of Ibsen's plays, thought that she would be an ideal actress for Ibsen parts. In an interview reported in some London paper of the day, she was quoted as speaking rather slightingly of Ibsen's minute drab realism. 'What does it matter to me', she was reported to have said, 'how many links you have on your watch-chain?' My brother, with his usual self-confidence, declared, 'If I could have had half an hour's conversation with her, I would have converted her'.

Before returning to Dublin, Jim procured a photograph of Duse which for a long time stood on his desk. He translated 'Eravamo sette sorelle' into verse with a different rhythm beginning

> *Seven sisters beautiful*
> *By a mirror pool reclining.*

He also addressed some adulatory verses to her, of which I did not think much, and which probably enriched a waste-paper basket in some hotel, for he never received any acknowledgement of the poem. Duse already had one poet on her hands, and that was more than enough. The poem was among those my brother burnt.

On October 31, 1902, my brother took a degree with honours of bachelor of arts in modern languages (English, French, Italian) in the Royal University of Ireland, and at his father's wish had himself photographed in cap and gown. He did not come out well in the photograph. He had a far-away look in his eyes because he posed for it, and it never suited him to pose. If the Dedalus of *Ulysses* were intended to be a self-portrait, it would be a very unflattering one. In temperament he was as unlike that figure, mourning under the incubus of remorse, as he could well be. He had a lively sense of humour and a ready laugh. Uncompromising in his new-found faith in the life of earth and in everything that concerned his artistic integrity, he was in all other things even-tempered and with friends unreserved. He was never eager, like Yeats, to blurt out clever opinions at each new moon, but he meant what he said, and there was no pose. And far from being depressing, he inspired confidence, like one who, conscious of his growing powers, feels in himself a cheerful boldness and is resolute.

Through Skeffington, the registrar, he was offered a few evening classes for French at University College, with more to come, no doubt, if he proved tractable. My brother considered it an attempt to buy him or in some way put him in debt to the Jesuits. He called upon the dean, Father Darlington, however, to thank him and decline the offer with the excuse that he did not feel competent to teach French. The dean was surprised. As for the alleged incompetence, he said that my brother would only have to teach 'little bits of clerks'. He asked my brother what career he intended to take up. Jim said that he intended to try the career of letters.

—Isn't there some danger of perishing of inanition in the meantime? asked the astonished dean.

—Of course, said my brother, smiling, that is by tradition one of the ever-present perils of the career, but it has its prizes, too.

The conversation turned on literature, my brother expounding a theory of 'the literary tradition' to an inattentive dean, in much the same way as Dedalus does in *A Portrait of the Artist*. Not altogether inattentive, however, to my brother's case, for while holidaying in the west of Ireland, he wrote Jim a letter, telling him how he had been gazing down from the Cliffs of Moher and wondering how many of those who dared to go down into those depths could ever come up again. Only the trained diver could do so. The parable was monitory, the tone friendly, but the depths were still regarded as a priest's preserves for exploration.

The dean urged upon him the practical necessity of following some less hazardous occupation, and instanced one of the leading lights of the Dublin bar, named in 'Eolus', who, while studying law, had maintained himself at the University by doing journalism. As it was generally rumoured in Dublin that the young law student had given early proof of his cleverness by writing leading articles contemporaneously for two newspapers of opposite politics, my brother said dryly:

—I may not have that gentleman's talents.

But the sarcasm was lost on the dean.

—You never know, he said encouragingly; you never know till you try.

My brother came away from the interview pleased with himself at having escaped another of the minor 'snares that were spread about his feet', and tripped nimbly down the steps of University College lilting 'Solvejg's Lied'.*

I was inclined to think that my brother had been foolish. I couldn't see that giving a few lessons would establish any obligations and I said that I thought the offer might have been made in good faith; but Jim flouted the idea so confidently that in the end I, too, was convinced that he was right.

But Jim was not wholly deaf to the dean's advice, and after some hesitation he chose medicine as an interim career and was inscribed in that faculty. I can hardly believe that he did more than dally with the idea, though he took some real interest in medicine and attended lectures for a while. My father was more or less satisfied with the decision (in his youth he himself had made a pretence of studying medicine, and really he deserves a monument for all the lives he saved by abandoning that study), and, moreover, the choice of medicine rather than letters seemed to betoken a nascent sense of practical values.

Meanwhile my other brother Charlie had discovered, after about a year in a seminary, that he had no vocation; and had come back home. 'Hat and gloves and hymn-book, too'. His return was a godsend for my father; it was like a freshet to swell his constant stream of abuse. It appeared that the last time my father had gone to the seminary to pay the fee, the rector, while still playing with the sovereigns in the palm of his hand, had told him that Charlie was 'a parti-cularly stupid boy'. The phrase was too good to be wasted. We had it at meal-times and fasting, in all weather, Sundays, holidays, and cavil-

---

* From *Peer Gynt*.

ling days not excepted. It became Charlie's theme song—'A parti-cularly stupid boy'—like some of the leit-motifs in the 'Sirens' episode of *Ulysses*.

—A parti-cularly stupid boy, I repeated, who has a parti-cularly foolish father to pay his gold, as you call it, to a parti-cularly cunning cunning priest.

—Begad, you're right there anyhow, said my father.

Priests were included in the broad charter of his vituperation. But my efforts succeeded only temporarily in stemming the current.

My mother had not recovered from the loss of her youngest son. I found her more than once in the kitchen cooking, or sitting alone in a room sewing, with the tears coursing down her cheeks. Her confessor, as is usual with those religious snoopers, tried to turn the weak and broken woman's grief to his own purpose. He advised her to put my brother and me out of the house 'before they corrupt the other children'. When in a moment of bitterness she told us of this pretty piece of advice from her spiritual counsellor, Jim and I reversed our roles. I laughed at the impudent lout and called him choice names culled from my father's vocabulary, but Jim was indignant.

In the late autumn of 1902 my brother suddenly decided to go to Paris to continue at the Sorbonne the study of medicine which he had barely begun. I do not remember that anybody questioned whether such a degree, if he ever took it, would be of any practical use to him in the United Kingdom, or whether his intention was to practise in France. His avowed purpose was to study medicine and meanwhile to keep himself and pay his fees by contributing articles to various newspapers and periodi-cals and by teaching English; and to this end he set about canvassing people who might be useful to him with a thoroughness that secretly dismayed me. In my brother business lost to poetry a 'go-getter' on the American model, and as for the dean, he suffered the just fate of the givers of unsolicited counsel, which is to see their advice taken and misapplied.

Through Lady Gregory's influence Jim obtained a promise from E. V. Longworth of the *Daily Express* of books to review for the paper's literary page. The fee was very small, more frequently a matter of shillings than of pounds, but the work was fairly regular and I was to act as intermediary while my brother was in Paris, fetching the books and sending them on to him. The *Daily Express* was conservative and pro-English, but my brother gave no thought to the politics of the newspaper, because knowing himself he knew that he would never alter a comma in what he wanted to say either to suit the editor's views or flatter his patroness.*

Russell, too, bestirred himself actively in my brother's behalf as the following very friendly and informal letter shows. The four words referring to George Moore are unconsciously epitaphic.

[No address; no date]

Dear Joyce,

I have written Miss Gonne and Lady Gregory, and will let you know anything further I may hear from them. George Moore is useless. I saw him today and he was in one of his bad moods, irritable about everything, and as I expected before I went, he said his friends in Paris would wonder why the devil he sent anybody to see them who was not in their craft. I think Miss Gonne is more hopeful as an acquaintance there. Yeats may know more people in Paris than I and I think you

---

* This is the newspaper for which Gabriel Conroy in 'The Dead' also writes reviews.

should write to him now and give him time to meet people
before you go to London. If I can think of anybody or anything likely to help you then I will write you, and hope to see
you again before you go.

Yours sincerely
Geo. W. Russell

P.S. There was a M. Dubois who wrote an article in "Revue
des 2 Mondes" (I think) about Irish literature modern writers,
who is a professor in some College. Could you get a letter to
him?

William Archer, laid under contribution for advice and
introductions to people in Paris, was not unwilling to help, but
he strongly advised my brother against his purpose to try to
work and study in Paris at the same time:

71 Alleyn Park
West Dulwich, S.E.
25 Nov. 1902

Dear Mr. Joyce,

I am going to Italy on Friday, so cannot see you as you pass
through London. If you carry out your intention of going to
Paris, and care to call upon Miss Blanche Taylor at 28 Avenue
Friedland, I will write to her asking her to give you any information she can. But I am sure she will only tell you that
you are on a hopeless quest. Indeed I cannot dissuade you too
strongly from making this attempt, if you are really dependent
on earning money by teaching English. The market for such
teaching is, I believe, extravagantly overstocked in Paris, and
even if you did ultimately get a little teaching you could not
possibly combine it with medical studies. It is hard enough by
giving lessons all day to keep body and soul together in Paris;
and how you can expect to do that, and at the same time qual-
ify as a doctor, passes my comprehension.

Forgive my frankness. It is of course, no business of mine; but I am sure you are making a mistake.

Yours faithfully,
William Archer

The answer to the last sentence came after the mature reflection of twenty years and was as gallant as any gasconade in *The Three Musketeers* or as Scott's 'Time and I against any other two': 'Bosh! A man of genius makes no mistakes. His errors are volitional and are the portals of discovery'. Archer was also mistaken, from too much caution, about the market for teaching being 'extravagantly overstocked'. Shortly after his arrival in Paris, my brother was offered a position in the Berlitz School there. For some reason that I have never been able to fathom, he refused it, but he bore the offer in mind; at a turning-point in his career, the Berlitz School saved him from disaster.

The most successful in his efforts to be of assistance was Yeats. My brother had him to thank for Lady Gregory's interest, and in London Yeats mentioned my brother's name to editors and literary people with whom he had some influence. He asked my brother to call on him on his way to Paris.

18 Woburn Buildings,
Euston Road
[No date]

My dear Joyce,

Come about 11 on Wednesday morning and I will send you straight to the manager of a big new weekly who may be able to help you to your new ambition. I cannot ask you to come before 11 as I shall be out late on Tuesday night and must sleep late.

Yours sincerely,
W. B. Yeats

Late in November or at the beginning of December 1902, he set out for Paris, scantily provided with clothes and with little more than his fare in his pocket, to realize his new ambition. But I cannot imagine that his intentions were any more serious than those with which Oliver Goldsmith, another improvident Irish believer in providence and his own genius, had gone with like intent about a century and a half before to Leiden.

V · *First Blossom*

My BROTHER STOPPED OVER IN London for a day or so, and Yeats introduced him to many people, including Arthur Symons. In every way Yeats was most encouraging; he seemed to enter into the spirit of the adventure. Not only did he praise highly the slight things in prose and verse which were all my brother had to show so far, but he also told him that he had never met anybody, except William Morris, in whom he felt the joy of life to be so keen as in my brother. He described Morris as a man of robust physique.

—I am afraid, said my brother laughing, that my physique cannot by any stretch of the imagination be described as robust.

Yeats, too, though very tall, was of the willowy sort.

The editor to whom Yeats sent him, C. Lewis Hind of the *Academy*, proved to be something of a wet blanket. When my brother suggested books for review, the editor said that he had only to put his head out the window and he could get a hundred young men to do reviewing. My brother fortunately checked, out of consideration for Yeats, the question that came to the tip of his tongue, whether the editor meant that he could get a hundred young men to review his head, and then suggested articles instead. No, the editor wanted 'moments of his spiritual life'. In the end some kind of agreement was reached that my brother should send him articles from Paris, but I don't think he ever did. He had chanced upon a vulgarity equal to that he was leaving behind him but with the added vice of a sated air of property. The smug, pretentious phrase had displeased him. Too gross to be an epiphany of the editor and of London literary life, the comfortable distinction it implied between the physical and the spiritual life, the former reserved for after-dinner stories, the latter for sale to high-class literary reviews, illuminated certain differences which he held to be insuperable between English editors and himself, and revealed just that attitude of English literature against which, more than against English dominion in his country, he was in revolt. His own physical and spiritual life were all one or nothing; there were not two watertight compartments in his soul.

My brother's contempt for the editor's complacency became a generalization, and generalizations are always hazardous; but the fact is that while our antipathies for people of our own race remain purely personal matters, our antipathies for those foreign to us in blood and culture tend to become generalizations and include the race that produced them. An artist, however, must follow his own lights wherever they lead or mislead him.

London at that time was just coming to the end of the most prosperous period in its history, but my brother never liked the city. It was reeling in a kind of hangover from Mafeking Night and the end of the Boer War; but besides the uneasy psychological environment which marked the break-up of the old social order and which he could only sense in passing, the smoke-laden atmosphere, the silent hurrying crowds in the streets, bent on making money for others, the endless rows of houses all the same that harboured lives he could not understand, depressed his busy-ant spirit. The Continent, where he was to spend the greater part of his life, was calling him away from all that and away from his own belated race to another climate and another people, whose shouts in the street would not touch him or cause him to turn aside from the work in hand, which, for the moment, was that of tempering the keen blade of his spirit.

Yeats had evidently been speaking to Symons about my brother. When they called on Symons at his flat, furnished with studiously decadent elegance, he was hospitable and sympathetic. He offered to submit some of my brother's poems to various editors, and said that as soon as my brother had a volume of poems ready, he would try to find a publisher for it. Then and later he kept both promises. It was Symons who, in the end, persuaded Elkin Mathews to publish *Chamber Music* and, when it came out, wrote the first criticism (and a very good one) of my brother's work to appear in any paper. During this meeting, the only one my brother had with him, I think, Symons told stories of the poets and artists he had known, of Verlaine and Dowson, of Lionel Johnson and Beardsley, and, hearing that my brother was interested in music, he sat down at the piano and played the Good Friday music from *Parsifal*.

—When I play Wagner, he murmured, closing the piano and standing up, I am in another world.

Meanwhile Yeats, who, like Russell, was almost tone-deaf, listened patiently, but when he was coming away with my brother, he said wittily:

—Symons has always had a longing to commit great sin, but he has never been able to get beyond ballet girls.

My brother's sojourn in Paris was a failure. He set out with a flourish of trumpets, a great many good wishes, and some assistance willingly given; but his stay in Paris represents an episode of *défaillance* in his life, such as many strong-willed men have known in youth, Napoleon at the Tuileries, Wellington in the wood of Sultanpettah. In the mythology of our

times it is figured both in the temptation in the desert and in
the passion in Gethsemane.

He found a room in the Grand Hôtel Corneille, rue Corneille, and soon learned to dodge the dark-visaged landlady
whom he called 'Baa-baa Black Sheep'. He was informed at the
École de Médicine that his Dublin degree was of no validity in
France, and that in any case fees had to be paid in advance, both
things which he could have ascertained without going to Paris.
He straightaway dropped the idea of studying medicine, but
remained in Paris with some undefined purpose, vaguely literary.
He studied Aristotle in French and Aquinas in Latin, wrote
a few poems, and planned an essay or short treatise on aesthetics; he also read systematically all the works of Ben Jonson,
a curious choice when one bears in mind that my brother read
only when moved by interest in a writer or a subject and never
for purely cultural reasons. These were all studies, however,
which he could have pursued with equal facility in the Kildare
Street Library, had the mental and moral atmosphere of the city
not been an impediment to reflection.

The letters of introduction which my brother had procured
proved to be of little use to him. Maud Gonne, who was then
in Paris, was eager to meet him and might have been able to
assist him, but my brother did not follow up her invitation because of some very unusual qualms regarding his shabby appearance.

                                        7 Avenue d'Eylau, Paris
My dear Mr. Joyce,

I was very sorry not to see you when you called last evening. The polite lie about my being in bed was diplomacy on
the part of my concierge as at such an early hour I never re-
tire to rest. The truth is that my little cousin who is staying
with me took ill with diphtheria last Sunday, and I have been

and still am nursing her and consequently am in quarantine on account of the danger of infection.

I shall be in quarantine for the usual 10 days or so. I do not like to invite you to the house till after the doctor tells me there is no danger for anyone coming here. There would of course be no possible danger seeing me out of doors, and if I can be of any use to you, come up any day at about 2 o'clock and I will come out and see you in the Trocadero Gardens.

This is a cold, inhospitable welcome. I am very sorry for Mr. Russell and Mr. Yeats have both spoken and written to me so much about you that I have been looking forward to making your acquaintance. However as I hear you are thinking of staying in Paris for some time, it is only a pleasure deferred.

With kind regards,
Sincerely yours,
Maud Gonne

The welcome could hardly have been warmer or more friendly, but I was glad that circumstances had prevented him from responding. I should have liked him to go to Paris without his viaticum of introductions of dubious utility, and I believe he would have succeeded in his adventure if he had not relied on them. It was a rare moral weakness in him to do so, and I felt obscurely that not only was he not cut out for social relations even on a literary footing, but that nothing he would write would ever be an ornament for a drawing-room table.

In Paris my brother made quite casually a few bohemian friends of assorted nationalities and no consequence except that he had somebody to discuss things with. Some of them he introduced into 'After the Race', one of the first stories in *Dubliners*. Jim did not like the story but would not rewrite it owing to a fixed objection to altering anything he had published. To publish was to assume responsibility and he would

not disavow it. The discussions of the bohemian group must
sometimes have been very lively, for my brother was informed
by one of the group, the Englishman Routh, that the Austrian
poet Däubler, born in Trieste, who seems to have been a Nazi
ante litteram, was thinking of challenging my brother to a duel
to avenge some hard home thrust in controversy. When my
brother told me the story, I asked him:

—What would you have done if he had challenged you?

—Started for Dublin by the first train leaving Paris, Jim
answered promptly.

However, Herr Däubler continued to think of challenging
without actually doing so, and my brother's real reaction to this
special form of continental stupidity was never put to the test.

The first two of the book reviews, which, as had been arranged, he sent to the *Daily Express*, appeared on December
11, 1902. He had sent them to me and I had brought them to
Longworth, the editor, to whom they served me as a kind of
introduction. Longworth was a young man—young, I mean,
to be the editor of a daily paper—with a quiet, considerate
manner. He might have been, perhaps he was, a young lawyer.
That, at least, was the impression he made on me. His interest
in my brother seemed genuine. It is worth quoting from the
first of the articles because in it my brother declares his attitude
towards patriotic poetry in a country where patriotism is considered the paramount civic virtue. The second, too, throws
an interesting sidelight on his own work, and both show the
firm grip he had even then on his own unwavering ideas.

The first article bore the title 'An Irish Poet', and was a review of the collected poems of William Rooney, a poet and
political journalist, who was one of the founders of the movement afterwards called Sinn Fein. He had died recently while

still quite young. At the beginning of the review my brother writes:

> These are verses of a writer lately dead, whom many consider the Davis of the latest national movement. They are issued from headquarters, and are preceded by two introductions wherein there is much said concerning the working-man, mutual improvement, . . . etc. They are illustrative of the national temper, and because they are so the writers of the introductions do not hesitate to claim for them the highest honours. But the claim cannot be allowed, unless it is supported by certain evidences of literary sincerity. For a man who writes a book cannot be excused by his good intentions, or by his moral character; he enters into a region where there is question of the written word, and it is well that this should be borne in mind, now that the region of literature is assailed so fiercely by the enthusiast and the doctrinaire.

The theme of the poems, he says, is consistently and uncompromisingly national. Perhaps 'patriotic' would have been nearer to what my brother meant, that is, characterized by the exploitation of national and racial themes for a political purpose. Patriotism was for my brother as for Johnson 'the last refuge of a scoundrel'. He sees in Rooney's poems uninteresting imitations of other poets, who sometimes achieved distinction 'though not driven along by any poetic impulse', and comments:

> So much can careful writing achieve, and there can be no doubt that little is achieved in these verses, because the writing is so careless and is yet so studiously mean. For, if carelessness is carried very far, it is like to become a positive virtue, but an ordinary carelessness is nothing but a false and mean expression of a false and mean idea.

After quoting a sample of Rooney's literary sins, he concluded:

They were written, it seems, for papers and societies week
after week, and bear witness to some desperate and weary
energy. But they have no spiritual and living energy, because
they come from one in whom the spirit is in a manner dead,
or at least in its own hell, a weary and foolish spirit, speaking
of redemption and revenge, blaspheming against tyrants, and
going forth, full of tears and curses, upon its infernal labours.
Religion and all that is allied thereto can manifestly persuade
men to great evil, and by writing these verses, even though
they should, as the writers of the prefaces think, enkindle the
young men of Ireland to hope and activity, Mr. Rooney has
been persuaded to great evil. And yet he might have written
well if he had not suffered from one of those big words which
make us so unhappy. There is no piece in the book which has
even the first quality of beauty, the quality of integrity, the
quality of being separate and whole, but there is one piece in
the book which seems to have come out of a conscious personal life. It is a translation of some verses by Dr. Douglas
Hyde, and is called 'A Request', and yet I cannot believe that
it owes more than its subject to its original. It begins:

> *In that last dark hour when my bed I lie on,*
> *My narrow bed of the deal board bare,*
> *My kin and neighbours around me standing,*
> *And Death's broad wings on the thickening air.*

It proceeds to gather desolation about itself and does so in lines
of living verse, as in the lines that follow. The third line is
feeble, perhaps, but the fourth line is so astonishingly good
that it cannot be overpraised.

> *When night shall fall and my day is over,*
> *And Death's pale symbol shall chill my face,*
> *When heart and hand thrill no more responsive,*
> *O Lord and Saviour, regard my case!*

And when it has gathered about itself all the imagery of desolation, it remembers the Divine temptation, and puts up its
prayer to the Divine mercy. It seems to come out of a personal
life which has begun to realize itself, but to which death and
that realization have come together. And in this manner, with
the gravity of one who remembers all the errors of his members and his sins of speech, it goes into silence.

In saying that the poems were issued from headquarters, my
brother was alluding to the fact that William Rooney had been
one of the founders of the *United Irishman*. The review in the
Daily Express displeased Rooney's remaining associates, principally Arthur Griffith, the editor, and the advertisement for
the volume of poems, which appeared in a subsequent number
of the *United Irishman*, quoted ironically that part of the review which ends with the phrase 'the big words that make us
so unhappy'.* Russell thought it a very clever reply on the part
of Griffith. The review offends against the main tenet of Anglo-
Irish poetry, which is that patriotism covers all literary sins.
The scathing contempt of the adolescent critic seems to have
got under Griffith's skin, and perhaps the phrase was clever
enough to get under Russell's skin, too, for he was the outstanding dealer in big words in Dublin at that time.

Yet my brother had a stronger stomach for patriotic poetry
than I. He could read through the collected poems of those
insignificant poets with high-sounding names, Thomas D'Arcy
McGee, Denis Florence MacCarthy, with cold patient scorn,
when a very few pages of them left me helpless and speechless
with devastating boredom. At one point of the review my
brother's ideas seem to be confused. It is hard to see how care-

---

* 'I fear those big words, Stephen said, which make us so unhappy.' *Ulysses*,
p. 28 (32).

lessness can ever become 'a positive virtue' except by some fortunate chance. What he meant to say was that these poems of Rooney's are the false and mean expression of a false and mean idea, but that studious (that is, careful) meanness can become a positive virtue. Writing to my brother at the time I raised this objection, and in a letter to Grant Richards from Trieste some years later he spoke, returning to the phrase, of the 'scrupulous meanness' of the style of his own *Dubliners*.

It is evident from the last paragraph that while the business of saying adieu to the Catholic Church was still continuing, he had transferred his allegiance with diminished intransigence from the Word of God to the written word, about which at least we can know something, and further that in this new religion the paramount virtue was literary sincerity.

The other article is a review of an essay on George Meredith by Walter Jerrold. The tone is flippant and the review rather unsatisfactory, because the reviewer apparently does not see any reason why he should break a lance for Meredith, who had long since been recognized as one of the most original and most powerful forces in the English novel. He considers Meredith 'a true man of letters' who had at last come into his own in spite of the obtuseness of public opinion, and he comments ironically on the strange company in which Meredith found himself in the series of English Writers Today which included Pinero and Hall Caine. He declares, however, that though Meredith has occasionally the 'power of direct compelling speech', as a poet, he lacks the irreplaceable 'fluid quality, the lyrical impulse, which it seems, has been often taken from the wise and given unto the foolish'. The novels, he says, are unique, but have no value as epical art. For the reviewer they are the essays of 'a philosopher at work with much cheerfulness upon a very stubborn problem'.

There is a spice of malice in the phrase 'a true man of letters'. Shortly after the publication of his article on *When We Dead Awaken* in the *Fortnightly Review*, Mr. Lyster, 'the Quaker librarian' of the National Library, in congratulating his youthful reader effusively, had said:

—I see, Mr. Joyce, that you are a true man of letters.

It was exactly what my brother was striving heroically not to be. The review is a strange appreciation of a novelist whose influence, after all, was predominant in the first draft of *A Portrait of the Artist*. There is no mention of Meredith's wit or humour, or of those passionate glowing passages of a poet writing prose, which are Meredith's most characteristic contribution to the novel. Yet I know that my brother liked them and imitated them in various places—for example, at the end of the fourth chapter of *A Portrait*. In Trieste, when making a pupil a present of *The Ordeal of Richard Feverel*, he accompanied the gift with a letter advancing many reservations as to the author's merits, but he would not have chosen that book if he had not liked it. He was altogether out of sympathy with the class of people Meredith wrote about.

Meanwhile I had left Belvedere, and after a couple of months found by recommendation a position in an accountant's office. My expectation was to be of some assistance at home and to save enough for university fees, but I received no salary. The firm, consisting of a prominent Catholic accountant and his son in partnership, regarded it as an apprenticeship, though no articles had been drawn up. I went around with the fully fledged accountants or with the principal's son to the various shops and firms that were our clients in order to check long tots and cross-tots and vouchers, and to listen to the smutty stories of the clerks—their only unconstrained interest in life. I do not know whether my work for ten months was worth tenpence to that firm of accountants, but if it was they defrauded me, for they never paid me even that sum.

Before I entered the accountant's office, my father was temporarily engaged as election agent and canvasser for a candidate in the municipal elections in Dublin, and I as his clerk. Writing to Jim in Paris, I described the committee-room and the people who frequented it just as they appeared in 'Ivy Day in the Committee Room'. The old caretaker and his family woes, Mr. Henchy (a sketch of my father toned down to the surroundings), the other canvassers, the unfrocked priest, the wastrel who recites the poem—everything, in fact, except the poem, he got from my letter or from my verbal description when he came home at Christmas. My brother was never in a committee-room in his life. I unwittingly supplied all the material for the story except, as I have said, the poem, which strikes a faint note of pathos and saves the story from being cynical. It is introduced in such a way that, as Padraic Colum observes in his preface to the American edition, despite the hackneyed phrases and the tawdry literary graces, one feels in it a loyalty to the departed chief and a real sorrow.

Of all the stories in *Dubliners*, 'Ivy Day' was the one my brother said he preferred. As for my part in it, I had written and spoken of the committee-room and its canvassers and callers in a mood of sour disgust. It had never entered my mind that there might be material for a story in all that many-faceted squalor. I thought that not only were those Dubliners below literary interest but even below human interest except for hardened philanthropic societies. Still less had it occurred to me that by making a story of it in a spirit of detachment and in a style of 'scrupulous meanness', one could liberate one's soul from the contagion of that experience and contemplate it from above with tolerance, even with compassion.

Yeats found time to correspond with my brother in Paris, an honour which alone would have flattered any other young unpublished and unknown poet; and besides busying himself in my brother's behalf, Yeats encouraged him with praise and sage advice. Clearly, he believed that he had gained a remarkable recruit for his movement, and he did not underrate him. He alone seems to have recognized then and later that if my brother's talent developed in a manner that disappointed his hopes, there was no reason to take offence; there was reason rather to welcome an artistic individuality so marked and so self-confident. When my brother wrote to him, informing him of the failure of his project to study medicine in Paris and enclosing a poem, or rather a song, Yeats replied with a long letter urging him to take up literature as a profession. He liked the delicacy of the song, though he could remember that several of the other poems of my brother's collection 'had more subject, more marginal phrases, more passion'.

'I would strongly recommend you', he continued, 'to write some little essays. Impressions of books, or better still, of artistic events about you in Paris, bringing your point of view in as much as possible, but taking your text from some existing interest or current event. You could send some of these at once to the "Academy" or later on to the "Speaker". It is always a little troublesome getting one's first start in literature; but after the first start, one can make a pittance if one is industrious, without a great deal of trouble'.

Yeats gave proof of his perspicacity, the sensitivity of a poet rather than that of a critic, in divining that prose and not verse would be my brother's medium, but I take a personal satisfaction in recording that I was the first and perhaps the only one to understand then that ruthlessness, not delicacy, would be the keynote of my brother's work.

Shortly before my brother left Paris to return to Dublin for the Christmas holidays, he received a further letter from Yeats in which he tempered his praise with certain doubts:

> 41, Montague Mansions
> Portman Square, London
> Dec. 18th 1902

My dear Joyce,

The last time I went to the 'Speaker', and I think I have been twice since I wrote you, I succeeded in finding somebody in. But when I spoke of my business, the man asked me to see the editor, as he alone could act in such a matter, and told me that the editor would not be in town till after Xmas. I am sorry, but for the present you can send some prose to the 'Academy', if you feel an impulse to write. You had better mention my name so as to remind the editor of what I told him. I won't give him your little poem, for I gathered from his conversation that he does not like publishing verse, unless it has an obvious look of importance. He told me for instance, that he would prefer two columns of verse, if it were good, to a little lyric. If I had all your MS I might have picked a little bundle of lyrics, but I think you had really better keep such things for the 'Speaker', which makes rather a practice of publishing quite short scraps of verse. I think that the poem that you have sent me has a charming rhythm in the second stanza, but I think it is not one of the best of your lyrics as a whole. I think that the thought is a little thin. Perhaps I will make you angry when I say that it is the poetry of a young man, of a young man who is practising his instrument, taking pleasure in the mere handling of the stops. It went very nicely in its place with the others, getting a certain richness from the general impression of all taken together and from your own beautiful reading. Taken apart by itself it would please a reader who had got to know your work, but it would not in itself draw attention to the work. It has distinction but I cannot say more than this. Remember what Dr. Johnson said about somebody: 'Let us wait until we find out whether he is a fountain or a cistern'. The work which you have actually done is very remarkable for a man of your age who has lived away from vital intellectual centres. Your technique in verse is very much better than the technique of any young Dublin man I have met during my time. It might have been the work of a young man who had lived in an Oxford literary set. However, men have started with as good promise as yours and have failed, and men have started with less and have succeeded. The qualities that make a man succeed do not show in his work, often, for quite a long time. They are much less qualities of talent than qualities of character—faith (of this you have probably enough), patience, adaptability (without this one learns nothing), and a gift for growing by experience, and this is perhaps rarest of all.

I will do anything for you I can, but I am afraid that it will not be a great deal. The chief use I can be, though perhaps you will not believe this, will be by introducing you to some other writers, who are starting like yourself, one always learns one's business from one's fellow-workers, especially from those who are near enough one's own age to understand one's own difficulties.

Yours sincerely,
W. B. Yeats

The little song in question was either 'O Sweetheart, hear you' or 'I would in that sweet bosom be', probably the former. In both the thought is 'thin', and both were subsequently printed in the *Speaker*. The analogy with musical composition in these little songs, and with a piping poet practising his instrument, which Yeats dwells on in his letter, was another little personal triumph for me. I had already suggested and Jim had accepted

the title *Chamber Music* for the collection. Another version of
the origin of the title is given in Herbert Gorman's biography
of my brother, but the story there told, which seems to have
tickled the fancy of some American critics and been the occasion of at least one book, is false, whatever its source.

One of the letters my brother wrote me from Paris during
the first part of his stay there contained a pound note which
he asked me to give Byrne. It was the repayment of a small
loan, and as my brother was not habitually prompt in settling
his debts, I was surprised. I was puzzled that Jim did not write
to Byrne direct, but I went, as I was asked to do, one evening
to Byrne's house in Essex Street and found him at home. He
received me on his doorstep, and seemed to be considerably put
out when I told him why I had come. He asked me a few times
whether I was sure my brother intended me to repay him the
loan, and when I replied that there could be no mistake about
it, he stood there on the doorstep, gazing over my head into
the gathering dusk and tapping the banknote against his finger-
nails in tight-lipped meditation.

Since I thought, wrongly, that he was aware of my hostility
to him and was trying to disconcert me, I stood my ground and
began ostentatiously to whistle softly to myself. After several
minutes of grossly over-acted ponderation, it seemed to strike
Byrne at last that an envoy is personably inviolable, for he
accompanied me part of the way home, talking about my
brother in a not unfriendly tone.

When I met Cosgrave perhaps on the following night and
told him about Byrne's strange behaviour his amusement from
the moment I mentioned Byrne's name was so irrepressible that
I knew something must have happened between them. At length
he said:

—I know what's the matter with him.

It appeared that several nights before, when he and Byrne were strolling about together, Byrne had shown him a post card which he had just received from Paris. On one half of it was the photograph, reproduced in Gorman's biography, representing Jim in a long overcoat that makes him look much taller than he was and rather like an anarchist who is thinking of emulating Orsini, and on the other half in neat small handwriting the poem which begins:

> *All day I hear the noise of waters*
> *Making moan.*

I have placed it last but one in *Chamber Music* because of the sense of loss to which it gives lyrical expression, but it was in fact one of the last Jim wrote for many years. Byrne was evidently flattered at having been chosen to be the recipient of what the English editor had called 'a moment of my brother's spiritual life'. He talked about him enthusiastically, possessively, boastfully.

—I'll take my dyin' Bible, said he, that there's not a man in Dublin knows more about Joyce than I do.

—Do you know this? asked Cosgrave, taking an exactly similar post card out of his pocket.

It was written in the dog Latin they often used, and concerned the 'scorta' of Paris. It was, as Cosgrave suspected, something Byrne did not know. He was too stunned to reply at once. The implication of like unto like did not appease him. He could find no words strong enough to express his anger.

—Here, take this, said he, handing the post card with the poem to Cosgrave. You can have this, too. I don't want it.*

---

* Mr. Byrne, now living in New York, denies that he gave the card to Cosgrave.

At that moment they happened to be passing an underground lavatory.

—It's like a thing, d'ye know, said he savagely, alluding to the poem my brother had sent him, that a fellow would write down in there, by God.

Cosgrave gave me Byrne's post card. He was still whinnying with laughter, like Lynch, at his triumph.

Byrne's anger was not based on moral disapproval. He took it as a personal offence to him that there should be something concerning my brother that others knew and he did not know. My brother, too, had humoured his friend's possessiveness so far that Byrne began to think he had established rights of control over my brother's private life. Yet, in spite of his outburst, my sympathy, for the moment, was with him. Manifestly, some kind of idol had fallen and was shattered.

When my brother returned to Dublin at Christmas and while the breach still lasted, he broke his silence when we were walking together to tell me in his usual halting fashion, 'I think I have been mistaken in Byrne'. Stopping in the street I took off my hat and began to recite the '*Te Deum*'. My brother smiled wryly. The breach was soon mended but they were never quite so friendly again. The warmth had gone from their friendship, and it was not really renewed until years later when my brother returned from Trieste to visit Dublin. And then it was renewed on a very different footing.*

The incident may easily seem trivial and insignificant and from one point of view my brother may not appear in it in

---

* While Joyce was on a visit to Dublin in 1909, Cosgrave told him that, at the time that Joyce was courting Nora Barnacle in 1904, he (Cosgrave) was secretly courting her too. In consternation at this unwelcome news, Joyce went to consult Byrne, who was then living at 7 Eccles Street, and was relieved to have Byrne denounce Cosgrave for telling a nasty lie out of malice. The event proved Byrne to be correct.

too favourable a light, but I wish to emphasize here as clearly as possible that all his life till the day he died, my brother never cared a rap what people thought, said, or wrote about him. His indifference to obloquy surpassed belief. In friendship, there-fore, he was not likely to allow himself, with quite superfluous deference, to be influenced by the false, even if better, image of himself which he saw reflected in a friend's eyes. That is, in fact, the higher morality of an artist: not to believe the cleverly untrue things he thinks and others tell him about himself.

My brother came home for Christmas, but stayed only a couple of weeks and went about little. He was still at home on New Year's Eve, for I remember him throwing a loaf of bread in at the front door at midnight, a rite which was supposed to bring peace and plenty in the coming year. He hurled it in vigorously because he liked complying with that sort of pic-turesque superstition, but I fancy that for our house one loaf was insufficient. He should have pitched in the rest of the batch.

I remember, too, a visit to the Sheehys during which he was invited to sing French songs. He obliged with 'Cadet Rousselle' and 'Viens, poupoule', and amused himself by omitting perfectly innocent lines and humming and nodding significantly to the company instead in order to see them smile their cultured smiles, shocked but complacent, as who should say, 'We, too, have been in Arcadia'. At other times, though he didn't often in-dulge in such mischievous tricks, he would sing 'Sally in Our Alley' and come out strongly with the lines

> And then we'll wed
> And then we'll bed,

in order to observe their really embarrassed silence.

In January he was back again in Paris, with what purpose I am at a loss to say. My brother had a hard time of it during that winter in Paris. He suffered so severely from toothache that he could hardly eat. It is needless to say that he had no money to pay a dentist. Even at the best of times, he lived miserably, sometimes going without food for almost two days. Poverty-stricken artists in an attic, famished and perished with cold, can be amusing on the stage; on nearer approach in my brother's letters home, *La Bohème* is less amusing. My mother was greatly upset by them. Unfortunately I, too, was ill with a bronchial cold that I could not shake off, and, as I was very thin, my mother got it into her head that I was in decline. It passed with time and without doctor's care, leaving no trace, but my mother's excessive anxieties were a sign that she herself was not well. It was about this time, I think, that my brother received an offer of a teaching job in the Berlitz School. He refused it, as I have said. It would have interfered with his liberty, but surely not more with his work or reading than hunger and suffering did.

In Paris my brother met Synge, who was living there almost as poor as my brother himself, and he had many quarrelsome discussions with him about language, style, poetry, the drama, and literature in general. Synge was ribald only in his comedies, and occasionally in his language; his habits were puritanical. At heart a pessimist, like all puritans, he held that our real life is in the imagination, which offers us a rich rainbow-land, whither by the aid of 'a power of talk' we can escape from reality. He was inclined to take the Irish-language revival seriously, and when he was at a loss for an argument was inclined to lose his temper, too. When that happened Synge's angry face and wagging beard used to send my brother into kinks of laughter that made Synge still angrier. In all matters of opinion and in manner of life Synge was the antithesis of my brother, and yet he showed him the manuscript of *Riders to the Sea*, which he had just finished. My brother may have been the first to see it. He objected that, owing to the lack of action, it could not be called a tragedy. It did not fit in with the Aristotelian definition of tragedy, and that for my brother then was final. He called *Riders to the Sea* a tragic poem. Synge did not agree, but he listened and countered my brother's arguments calmly. Perhaps he was mollified by the fact that the rhythm of certain phrases had stuck in my brother's memory—he already knew Maurya's final speeches almost by heart—and he repeated them with such a keen sense of their beauty that it must have tempered his strictures. Shortly after I joined him in Trieste, I remember his quoting the lamentation of Maurya to his Florentine friend Francini, who knew no word of English, when they were discussing the musicality of language. Those speeches, and the passage from Yeats's story 'The Tables of the Law' which ends with the words, 'Why do you fly from our torches that were made out of sweet wood, after it had perished from the world and come to us who made it of old times with our breath?' as he recited them, almost chanting, certainly sounded like incantations woven out of magic words.

In Trieste many years before the First World War, my brother translated *Riders to the Sea* into Italian for the actor-manager Sainati, who would have liked to produce it, but the project fell through owing to difficulties that arose with Synge's heirs. His translation, revised by a pupil of his, the lawyer Nicolò Vidacovich, was published after the war in *Solaria*. I have read that the play attracted the attention of the great Duse, who began to study the part of the tragic mother, but I do not know whether in my brother's version or in Carlo Linati's.

Meanwhile my brother continued to contribute from Paris occasional reviews, which were often short articles, to the *Daily Express*, a review of Stephen Gwynn's *To-day and To-morrow in Ireland* being accorded a prominent place in its literary columns on January 29, 1903. Some phrases in it are interesting because they reflect my brother's almost neutral attitude in Irish politics. Stephen Gwynn was the eldest of four brainy sons of a family that had been closely connected with Trinity College for two generations. He was well known in Dublin. He had been a classical tutor, and besides doing journalistic work had tried his hand at poetry, biography, and the novel without ever achieving distinction. The book under review was a collection of essays dealing with the Celtic literary and industrial revival, and, although the author's alma mater, Trinity College, was the stronghold of English culture in Ireland, the book was, according to the reviewer, 'a distinct accusation of English civilisation and English modes of thought'. The review, which is generally favourable, notes Mr. Gwynn's 'sense of the humorous', which 'it is pleasing to find . . . in a revivalist'. Deadly serious revivalists aroused the reviewer's sardonic contempt. When he came to write 'The Dead', he introduced one, a woman of course, Molly Ivors, who annoys Gabriel Conroy by heavy-hoofed attempts at quizzing and by her tactless familiarity. The references to Mr. Gwynn's nationalistic leanings, though noncommittal, are interesting pointers to my brother's own political attitude at the time. He writes, 'Mr. Gwynn, too, is a convert to the prevailing national movement, and professes himself a Nationalist, though his nationalism, as he says, has nothing irreconcilable about it. Give Ireland the status of Canada and Mr. Gwynn becomes an Imperialist at once. It is hard to say into what political party Mr. Gwynn should go, for he is too consistently Gaelic for the Parliamentarians, and too mild for the true patriots, who are beginning to speak a little vaguely about their friends the French'.

The reviewer could have found nearer home one whose political thought ran more or less in the same direction as Gwynn's, and in himself one whose political attitude was equally indefinable. My brother was not favourable to an English government in Ireland, but he would have disliked with equal intensity any foreign government, had it been Spanish, French, or German, as it might well have become at various moments of his country's history. Industrial and commercial efficiency and the wealth that goes with them were nothing to him, mere dust and ashes. He preferred people whom the world rated as failures. The supercilious airs which the possessors of wealth gave themselves seemed to him ludicrous. He felt a closer kinship of spirit with continental peoples, which he attributed to the greater importance of art in their types of civilization, yet he thought that art might very well be a form of decay and accompany a decline in the fortunes of a nation. But English, not Irish, was his mother tongue, and moreover he could not imagine any form of Irish government that would not be still more uncongenial to him than anything to be found in England or abroad. He did not try to solve the problem of nationality. He flouted it to save his soul. It was, as he understood later, Ulysses deriding Polyphemus and proclaiming his name and rank.

A week later on February 6, 1903, a group of three reviews appeared in the same paper, the *Daily Express*. In one of them the contempt for violence that was characteristic of him, a contempt deeper and stronger than hatred, finds expression for the first time as far as I am aware. The article bears the title, taken from the text but probably not my brother's, 'A Suave Philosophy', and is a review of a book about Burma called *The*

Soul of a People by H. Fielding Hall. The book, which I, too, read and liked and remember fairly well, gets a very sympathetic notice, which says among other things:

> He [Fielding Hall] states at some length the philosophy (if that is the proper name for it) of Buddhism. The Burmese people seem naturally adapted to follow such a wise passive philosophy. Five things are the five supreme evils for them— fire, water, storms, robbers, and rulers. All things that are inimical to human peace are evil. Though Buddhism is essentially a philosophy built against the evils of existence, a philosophy which places its end in the annihilation of the personal life and the personal will, the Burmese people have known how to transform it into a rule of life at once simple and wise. Our civilisation, bequeathed to us by fierce adventurers, eaters of meat and hunters, is so full of hurry and combat, so busy about many things which are perhaps of no importance, that it cannot but see something feeble in a civilisation which smiles as it refuses to make the battlefield the test of excellence.

Here we have in germ the weariness of the immeasurable stupidity of violence of an author who was to speak of the 'bluddle filth' of Waterloo* and who in his last days, when moving southwards before the invading German hordes in France, wondered only whether it was possible for him to procure a book which he had forgotten in his flat in Paris. When a sufficient number of men and women have attained his attitude of calm, supreme contempt for violence, even when violence is doing its damnedest, there will be no more fear on earth that civilization may be wiped out by A-bombs or H-bombs or some other alphabetical, scientific monstrosity. Men can begin to cultivate that attitude in peacetime by quietly

---

* *Finnegans Wake*, p. 10.

breaking wind from behind, as Mr. Bloom does, when they listen to patriotic speeches, when flags are waved, military bands, led by band-masters crooked with straightness, blare, and rational beings convert themselves into funny, goose-stepping, uniformed robots—things that never failed to provoke my brother's derisive comments.

An article which he contributed to the *Speaker* of March 21 of that year, although it is a review of an unimportant work of Ibsen's, shows more than his previous article in the *Fortnightly Review* that there was no taint of idolatry in his admiration for Ibsen; it points out just what qualities he admired in the Norwegian dramatist, and, one may suppose, was determined to cultivate in his own work. The article is a review of a French translation of *Cataline*, a romantic drama written when Ibsen, then twenty years of age, was 'a poor student, working all day in a druggist's shop, and studying during the night as best he could'. The reviewer does not hesitate to say that 'by the time the last act is reached, the characters . . . in the acted play would be related to life only by the bodies of the performers'. The phrase is as devastating as some of Shaw's contemporary dramatic criticism in the *Saturday Review*, and is astonishing when one bears in mind the high claims my brother made for Ibsen, and the profound influence the old Norwegian had upon his life and work. But my brother judged his own work with the same severity and objectivity, and in later years used to speak of the first draft of *A Portrait of the Artist* as a 'puerile production'.

'The imagination', says the review, 'has the quality of a fluid and it must be held firmly lest it become vague, and delicately, that it may lose none of its magical powers. And Ibsen has united with his strong, ample, imaginative faculty a pre-occupation with the things present to him.' When he points out the

unflinching courage with which Ibsen pursued his purpose so
calmly and ironically amid the cries of hysteria raised against
him and other confused voices of war, statecraft, and religion,
the words are almost prophetical of my brother's own struggle
and triumph that were to come. 'But Boötes', concludes the
review, 'we may be sure, thinks nothing of such cries, eager as
ever at that ancient business of leading his hunting dogs across
the zenith "in their leash of sidereal fire" '. It is clear that the
qualities in Ibsen's work that stir my brother's admiration are
patience and self-control, a vigilant acceptance of the visible
world of the imagination, and the serenity for which Boötes
stands—qualities that may well seem strange in their appeal to
a youth living in such harassing circumstances as was my brother
then.

A few days later, on March 27, an article appeared in the
Daily Express which provided further proof of my brother's
almost quixotic intransigence in literary questions, even when
it spoiled his good relations with those who had been and could
still have been useful to him. It was an adverse review of *Poets
and Dreamers* by Lady Gregory and was published, unlike the
other reviews, over my brother's initials, the editor wishing by
this signature to disclaim any personal responsibility for the
article. Lady Gregory was much annoyed by it. She had procured the work on the *Daily Express* for my brother, and seems
to have expected in return the log-rolling common in literary
movements. As my brother did not like the book, it might have
been wiser for him, since he could not speak well of it, to return it unreviewed or at least to censure it more mildly. My
brother cut through these knotty difficulties very simply. He
had been given a book to review and he had reviewed it on its
merits, which were scarce. He was aware of other aspects of
the matter but they did not seem important to him. Good or

bad literature was in question, not good or bad manners. He held most firmly that artists, poets, and writers mould the conscience of their race by expressing it and that they betray their high office when they give less than their best or stoop to curry favour in the market-place, and perhaps he was not altogether unwilling to approve his belief when the occasion offered.

As the article represents his first breach with the tutelary spirits of the Celtic Renaissance, I shall quote it at length, though the matter may not justify quotation, to show once more how tetchy such divinities are apt to be. The article begins, as one rather expects, with a reference to Aristotle, and bears the title 'The Soul of Ireland', which practically repeats the title of a previous article and is surely not my brother's.

Aristotle finds at the beginning of all speculation the feeling of wonder, a feeling proper to childhood, and if speculation be proper to the middle period of life it is natural that one should look to the crowning period of life for the fruit of speculation, wisdom itself. But nowadays people have greatly confused childhood and middle life and old age; those who succeed in spite of civilisation in reaching old age seem to have less and less wisdom, and children who are usually put to some business as soon as they can walk and talk, seem to have more and more 'common sense'; and perhaps, in the future little boys with long beards will stand aside and applaud, while old men in short trousers play handball against the side of a house.

This may even happen in Ireland, if Lady Gregory has truly set forth the old age of her country. In her new book she has left legends and heroic youth far behind, and has explored in a land almost fabulous in its sorrow and senility. Half of her book is an account of old men and old women in the West of Ireland. These old people are full of stories about giants and witches, and logs and black-handled knives, and they tell their stories one after another at great length and with many repetitions (for they are people of leisure) by the fire or in the yard of a workhouse. It is difficult to judge well of their charms and herb-healing, for that is the province of those who are learned in these matters and can compare the customs of countries, and indeed, it is well not to know these magical-sciences, for if the wind changes while you are cutting wild camomile you will lose your mind.

But one can judge more easily of their stories. These stories appeal to some feeling which is certainly not that feeling of wonder which is the beginning of all speculation. The story-tellers are old, and their imagination is not the imagination of childhood. The story-teller preserves the strange machinery of fairyland, but his mind is feeble and sleepy. He begins one story and wanders from it into another story, and none of the stories has any satisfactory imaginative wholeness, none of them is like Sir John Daw's poem that cried tink in the close. Lady Gregory is conscious of this, for she often tries to lead the speaker back to his story by questions, and when the story has become hopelessly involved, she tries to establish some wholeness by keeping only the less involved part: sometimes she listens 'half-interested and half-impatient'. In fine, her book, wherever it treats of the 'folk', sets forth in the fulness of its senility a class of mind which Mr. Yeats has set forth with such delicate scepticism in his happiest book, 'The Celtic Twilight'.

Something of health and naturalness, however, enters with Raftery, the poet. He had a terrible tongue, it seems, and would make a satirical poem for a very small offence. He could make love poems, too (though Lady Gregory finds a certain falseness in the western love poems), and repentant poems. Raftery, though he be the last of the great bardic procession, has much of the bardic tradition about him. He took shelter one day from the rain under a bush: at first the bush kept out the rain, and he made verses praising it, but after a while it let the rain through, and he made verses dispraising it.

Lady Gregory translates some of his verses, and she also translates . . . four one-act plays by Dr. Douglas Hyde, three of which have for their central figure that legendary person, who is vagabond and poet, and even saint at times, while the fourth play is called a 'nativity' play. The dwarf-drama (if one may use that term) is a form of art which is improper and ineffectual, but it is easy to understand why it finds favour with an age which has pictures that are 'nocturnes', and writers like Mallarmé and the composer of 'Récapitulation'.* The dwarf-drama is accordingly to be judged as an entertainment, and Dr. Douglas Hyde is certainly entertaining in *The Twisting of the Rope*, and Lady Gregory has succeeded better with her verse-translations here than elsewhere, as these four lines may show:

> *I have heard the melodious harp*
> *On the streets of Cork playing to us;*
> *More melodious by far I thought your voice,*
> *More melodious by far your mouth than that.*

This book, like so many other books of our time, is in part picturesque and in part indirect or direct utterance of the central belief of Ireland. Out of the material and spiritual battle which has gone so hardly with her, Ireland has emerged with many memories of beliefs, and with one belief—a belief in the incurable ignobility of the forces that have overcome her—and Lady Gregory, whose old men and women seem almost their own judges when they tell their wandering stories, might add to the passage from Whitman which forms her dedication, Whitman's ambiguous word for the vanquished— 'Battles are lost in the spirit in which they are won'.

---

* Catulle Mendès.

Lady Gregory had little reason, it seems to me, to take offence at the review, for there is no direct criticism in it of her part in the traditional Irish droolery; on the contrary, the reviewer, as far as his literary conscience allows him, seems to be disposed to praise slight merits and even to be hampered by the wish, in spite of his principles, to shift the blame from the writer to her subject. What is noteworthy in the review is that when he mentions Raftery's vituperative verses it is to make them seem half-witted. Apparently he had no suspicion at the time of his own gift for lampoon. But when he speaks of the one belief that survives in Ireland, it is plain that his own heart goes with it, though not unchecked.

How soon Lady Gregory began to manifest her displeasure at the article I do not know. I had never met or even seen Lady Gregory, yet in spite of what she had done for Jim, I conceived an unreasoning antipathy for her. I imagined her to have been one of those awfully clever girls who in late middle age become awfully tiresome women. Jim had told me that she was the widow of a man who had held important positions under the English government, and, enlarging fancifully on these bare facts, I pictured to myself that he may have governed some province or colony, but that she governed him. Disrespectfully, I called his ghost 'poor dear Gregory', and then extended the designation to his widow, in an attempt, I suppose, to counteract any influence she or her flattering group might have. I was also secretly happy that Jim had not met Maud Gonne in Paris. I took Maud Gonne to be the youth of Lady Gregory.

My brother wrote a few poems while he was in Paris, the last four in *Chamber Music*, which I placed at the end of it because of their sombre tone. He tried his hand, too, at dialogue in the style of Ben Jonson, not seriously but merely as an exercise. I never saw these efforts but he told me that though they were just nonsense he had caught the style. They had, he said, the true Jonsonian ring.

His last contribution to Irish newspapers from Paris was an interview for the *Irish Times* of April 7, 1903, with a French motorist, Henri Fournier, who was to take part in the race for the Gordon Bennett Cup to be run in Ireland in the following July. The interview is ingenuous. My brother did not know what car M. Fournier would drive, or whether a big race in Madrid was before or after the 'Motor Derby', and considered a top speed of eighty-six miles an hour 'an appalling pace'. It is evident from the interview that he knows nothing about motoring and cares, if possible, less.

The cup was won by a Belgian driving a Mercedes. When speed trials, in which Fournier probably took part, were held in the Phoenix Park after the Motor Derby, my brother did not go to see them or to renew his acquaintance with Fournier, although 'all Dublin' was in the Phoenix Park that day. He did, however, make the Motor Derby in Ireland the background for 'After the Race', the third story of his to appear in the *Irish Homestead*.

Before my brother left Paris an absurd incident at home supplied him, through my letters and diaries, with the materials for another story, 'Grace', which some years later he wrote at Trieste. A retreat for businessmen was to be conducted by a Jesuit father in Gardiner Street Church, and one of my father's friends ('Mr. Cunningham' in the story) persuaded his broogy cronies, including my father, to attend it, 'all together, my boys'. Matt Kane, for such was 'Mr. Cunningham's' name, was a squat, black-bearded man. He was ignorant but shrewd, and his energy and self-confidence caused him to be regarded by his friends as very reliable and level-headed, a solid man. He had a good position as chief clerk in the solicitor general's office, but was burdened with a wife who was an incorrigible drunkard. He had set up house for her two or three times during her periods of reformation, but she sold the furniture and neglected her young children, so that at the time I speak of he had put his wife in a home for inebriates and his children in a school.

Out of sarcastic curiosity I followed them to the church on the last evening of the retreat to listen to the sermon and watch my father fumbling shamfacedly with his lighted candle. The sermon was a man-to-man talk in a chatty tone. I came out into the fresh air before the end. On Saturday they went to confession, and on Sunday morning in a group they approached the altar. On Sunday evening after an outing with his friends, my father came home only moderately drunk with the aforesaid 'Mr. Cunningham', to whom he explained many times over that in confession the priest had told him that 'he wasn't such a bad fellow after all', which authoritative and consoling information caused him both to laugh and weep.

My brother has used this thin material, transforming it in his own way. The accident with which the story begins happened to my father, but as model for the recalcitrant convert my brother substituted an acquaintance of my father's, a plump, rubicund commercial traveller and tea-taster. He was a competent man in his line, and in England would probably have earned a comfortable income. He could distinguish blindfold fifteen or twenty different kinds and blends of tea, prepared in little bowl-like cups on a table in his office. Besides this, he cultivated a taste for Scott's novels and an interest in cricket. His name was Dick Thornton—he always voiced the 'th' distinctly in pronouncing it—and when asserting something confidently, he called the friend to whom he happened to be speaking 'my buck'. He was known to his boozing companions as 'the Dicky Bird', a nickname my mother had given him. There was in fact something bouncing and bird-like about the drunken little man. But he could sing—that was the common interest. He loved Italian opera, and, like my father, swore by Sims Reeves. His vocal chords were whisky-frayed, but he could sing semi-traditional English ballads, sentimental and humorous, very well, not in the plaintive Irish manner, but with rollicking swing and humour. He had been a Protestant, but, though his wife and children, whom he maltreated, had unaccountably turned Catholic, I think he was still a Freemason. He did not take part in the retreat. As for the amusing argument about the candles in 'Grace', it is reproduced very closely from an entry in my diary.

The strange doctrine of actual and sanctifying grace and its relation to original sin, which last was to be the subject of *Finnegans Wake*, had puzzled and fascinated my brother, as he found it in the teaching of the Church, and in his reading of St. Augustine, and even viewed from outside the Church it held his interest. He had, in fact, gone to listen to a sermon on the subject preached in Gardiner Street Church or University College Chapel, and had come away angry and disgusted at the inadequacy of the exposition. He said the preacher had not even tried to know what he was talking about, but assumed that anything was good enough for his listeners. It angered him that such shoddy stuff should pass for spiritual guidance. In 'Grace', in which the preacher also chooses a difficult text and deals with it like a self-confident charlatan, he has used as model for the preacher of the sermon, 'Father Purdon', the figure of Father Bernard Vaughan, a very popular evangelist in those days, whose name was frequently in the newspapers and who had appeared to crowded congregations also in Dublin. He was a Jesuit, a member of an old English family, and a vulgarian priest in search of publicity. Besides preaching from his legitimate stage, the pulpit, he used to deliver short breezy talks from inappropriate places, such as the boxing ring before a championship match.* My brother's contempt for him is evident in the choice of the name with which he has adorned him, Father Purdon. The old name for the street of the brothels in Dublin was Purdon Street.

Since the order of the songs in *Chamber Music*, which follows the coming and passing of love, is my arrangement of them, not my brother's, 'Grace' is, so far as I am aware, the first instance of the use of a pattern in my brother's work. It is a simple pattern not new and not requiring any great hermeneutical acumen to discover—inferno, purgatorio, paradiso. Mr. Kernan's fall down the steps of the lavatory is his descent into hell, the sickroom is purgatory, and the Church in which he and his friends listen to the sermon is paradise at last. In 'Grace' the pattern is ironical with a touch of suppressed anger, but my brother used patterns in his later work because he found a pattern even in the disorder of his own life; being an artist and not a philosopher, in spite of his interest in philosophy, he made this personal experience the informing spirit of his later work. That notion was the actual grace the story conferred on its author.

Late on the Good Friday night of 1903 my brother returned, hungry and tired, to his room in the Hôtel Corneille to find a telegram that had been pushed under his door. It ran, 'Mother dying. Come home. Father'. He was penniless, and the money for his fare was not enclosed with the order to come home. Among his friends in Paris there was none whom he thought

---

* 'Yes, it was very probable that Father Bernard Vaughan would come again to preach. O, yes: a very great success. A wonderful man really.' *Ulysses*, p. 207 (216).

able or likely to lend him the few pounds he required for the journey. At his wit's end he decided to try a pupil of his, a certain M. Douce, a bluff, middle-aged champagne-merchant, with whom my brother had found a common interest in socialism. Without waiting for the morning, he went straight to him that night. As Douce's flat was at some distance from the Hôtel Corneille, my brother had a long and anxious walk through the almost deserted streets of Paris. He succeeded with great difficulty in arousing the concierge of the big house, made his way upstairs in the pitch dark, and rang at the door of Douce's flat. Douce himself got up and opened the door. In spite of the unearthly hour of the visit, the Frenchman was courteous and sympathetic, and without hesitation he lent my brother the money he asked for. I wonder what would have happened if a penniless French student in Dublin had awakened a respectable wine-merchant after midnight in the same way. On his return to Dublin my brother saw to it that the money was repaid, my father accompanying his cheque with a letter of thanks adorned with those flowers of eloquence that were so dear to the heart of Mr. Wilkins Micawber.

Alone in Paris my brother had felt the black shadow of the priest that had fallen between him and his mother fade away into a vague, troubled memory. She had come to him in a dream confused in his sleeping brain with the image of the Virgin Mother.

She comes at night when the city is still, invisible, inaudible, all unsummoned. She comes from her ancient seat to visit the least of her children, mother most venerable, as though he had never been alien to her. She knows the inmost heart; therefore, she is gentle, nothing exacting, saying, I am susceptible of change, an imaginative influence in the hearts of my children. Who has pity for you when you are sad among the strangers? Years and years I loved you when you lay in my womb.*

The epiphany may have been suggested by a letter of my mother. In answering one of my brother's more desperate and disheartened outpourings she had spoken comfortingly of her love for him when he was a child. The sudden summons home had come like the rude shock of reality to the softening influence of Newman's prose, revealed in the epiphany, and, weakened as he was by the manner of his life in Paris, it left indelible traces on his soul.

He had a bad crossing on the cheaper route from Dieppe to Newhaven. Another epiphany describes how, as he lay along the deck, against the engine-room from which the smell of grease exhaled, he watched the gigantic mists marching under the French cliffs and enveloping the coast from headland to headland. 'The sea moved with the sound of many scales.' Weak and sick, he dozed where he lay, gazing towards where a church stood on top of a cliff, and beyond the misty walls in the dark cathedral church of Our Lady, he seemed to hear 'the bright even voices of boys singing before the altar there'.

An unwilling unbeliever like Renan, my brother regretted parting with many things in Catholic services that still appealed to him emotionally and artistically; but there was also, perhaps, in his unhappiness a pang of remorse that he, the eldest of the family, of whom so much was expected, had left it to its fate. That was one of the accusations by which my mother's confessor had tried to embitter her relation with her eldest son; he had told her that Jim was 'very cowardly'. My brother did not react to such imputation with violent and bitter curses as

---

* 'Years and years I loved you, O my son, my firstborn, when you lay in my womb.' *Ulysses*, p. 548 (566).

I did; he said nothing. It was I that spoke. But the fact that my mother listened with docility to her clerical counsellors sank into his soul and gradually estranged him from her. In that her confessors succeeded. If my brother had abandoned his family to enter the Jesuit order, that would not have been cowardly; that would have been obedience to a higher call to a spiritual life—the spiritual life of the Jesuits! My brother had hearkened to a spiritual call, inaudible to their dull ears, and he followed it to the end with an unflinching courage unique in his generation in Ireland, but not without being assailed on occasion by sharp pangs of doubt.

Paris, I have said, was for my brother that season of fasting and meditation in the desert, which, it would seem, men who are born under the dominance of ideas that cause them to run counter to their fellow men must endure before setting out on their journey. The fruits of that season may be briefly reckoned up. He had learned in Paris that the world was not waiting for him, at least not just yet. He had learned there to look at Dublin with travelled eyes, and to regard continental life, which he experienced in the most unfavourable conditions, as the only life for him. Above all, he had learned that extreme hunger and physical suffering and anxiety are less inimical to the growth of the soul than the invisible pressure of religion and nationalism. As a by-product of that sojourn in Bohème there must be noted an attitude towards money that to me, with my middle-class ideas on the subject, was like a hair-shirt during all our life together.

So, possibly, his stay in Paris must be written off as a failure. He failed in his plan to live there by giving a few lessons and publishing occasional articles and poems. It can never have been a serious plan, really, but perhaps subconsciously there had been another purpose. He told me that often when he had no money and had had nothing to eat he used to walk about reciting to himself for consolation, like 'Little Chandler' in *Dubliners*, his own poems or others he knew by heart or things he happened to be writing then. Poets have their personal superstitions. Perhaps he felt the need to put his faith in himself as an artist, as a poet, as a believer in the vivifying grace of the imagination by which the soul lives—to put all that to the test of hunger, cold, and suffering in a foreign country. If such was his purpose, his stay was not a failure. He found his spirit proof against any of the shocks that the common life of men might reserve for it, and, no longer fearing it in his heart, he found himself in consequence less hostile to that life which he had till then despised.

He had been reading eagerly in Paris—he told me he used to spend the greater part of the day in the Bibliothèque Nationale—but his creative work had been very meagre, just a few poems, his last for many years. But he had begun taking notes for an essay on aesthetics. That essay, if he had completed it, would have been the manifesto of his faith as an artist. His paper on 'The Drama and Life' had been a kind of preface to it, and only his change of life when he came back to Dublin and fell in with a hard-drinking group of students, chiefly medical, who made a dead set at him with the privily announced intention of leading him to ruin himself, prevented him from finishing it.

My mother did not die immediately after my brother's return. She had a partial recovery, and the doctor even allowed her to get up for a few hours each day, but then she was obliged to take to her bed again. In order to make sure that the diagnosis and treatment were right my father called in a specialist for a consultation, a Professor Little, who had a considerable reputation. The consultant confirmed the diagnosis and approved of the treatment, but my mother did not recover. She lingered on for several months, and began to wander in her mind. The doctor who was treating her was a short, spare man with a rather elegant figure and carriage. My mother used to call him 'Sir Peter Teazle',* and was annoyed if my Aunt Josephine Murray, who nursed her through her long illness, did not at first understand whom she meant.

My father was on his good behaviour for the first few weeks, but as the illness dragged on he became unreliable and had to be watched. One evening towards the end, my father came home 'screwed', as Aunt Josephine called it, after having drowned his sorrow copiously with various friends, and went into my mother's room. Besides my aunt, my brother and I were both there. My father asked some perfunctory question, but it was evident that he was in vile humour and itching to say something. He walked about the room muttering and then, coming to the foot of the bed, he blurted out:

—I'm finished. I can't do any more. If you can't get well, die. Die and be damned to you!

Forgetting everything, I shouted 'You swine!' and made a swift movement towards him. Then to my horror I saw that my mother was struggling to get out of the bed. I hurried to her at once, while Jim led my father out of the room.

—You mustn't do that, my mother panted. You must promise me never to do that, you know that when he is that way he doesn't know what he is saying.

A few days later, however, she said something to me that I am happy to remember. My mother died on August 13, 1903 at the early age of forty-four. She had thrown her wasted body

---

* 'She calls the doctor Sir Peter Teazle and picks buttercups off the quilt. Humour her till it's over.' *Ulysses*, p. 6 (10). Sir Peter Teazle is a character in Sheridan's *The School for Scandal*.

between her husband and her family, and succumbed only in death in her struggle to preserve it from the ravages of his drunkenness.

Amongst those around her death-bed at the end, besides her husband, the elder members of her large family, and the sister-in-law who had nursed her untiringly and unselfishly for long months, there was also an elder brother of my mother's, whom my father hated so intensely that only events of this kind could induce him to tolerate his presence. John Murray was a re-formed atheist and drunkard (what a tiresome generation it was!) whose reformation, though liable to occasional relapses, had won him the favour of his uncle, Canon Murray, and a position on the management staff of the *Freeman's Journal*, the principal Catholic newspaper in Ireland. When my mother lapsed into unconsciousness and it became apparent that her last moments had come, Uncle John knelt down with all the others and began to pray in a loud voice. Then seeing that neither my brother nor I was praying, he made an angry, per-emptory gesture to us to kneel down. Neither of us paid any attention to him; yet even so the scene seems to have burnt itself into my brother's soul. Not into mine. Religion, either as consolation or remorse, was so completely eliminated from my system that the refusal to pray had no part in the confused pain of loss then or later. At the moment I thought of nothing; I was only aware of something brutal, inevitable, final, and damnably unfair. Later, believing that we have only one life and that all talk of another is just a priestly swindle, I saw that my mother's life, which had begun happily, had been made as unhappy as it could well be for the last fifteen years or so by circumstances that were far from inevitable. She ought to have rebelled. That was my insistent thought. And I saw clearly against whom, near and far, and against what she ought to have rebelled. But in the hateful country and hateful times in which she lived it would have required very considerable strength of character, which she did not possess.

Two or three months after my mother's death I found the following piece added to my brother's series of epiphanies:

> Two mourners push on through the crowd. The girl, one hand catching the woman's skirt, runs in advance. The girl's face is the face of a fish, discoloured and oblique-eyed; the woman's face is small and square, the face of a bargainer. The girl, her mouth distorted, looks up at the woman to see if it is time to cry; the woman, settling a flat bonnet, hurries on towards the mortuary chapel.

When I read it, I remembered that I too, had noticed the pair. They were in a little group at the gate of Glasnevin Cemetery in a funeral preceding my mother's. As Jim disliked funerals and avoided going to them, his impressions for the 'Hades' episode of *Ulysses* must have been gathered either at my mother's funeral or at my younger brother Georgie's. He was never in the cemetery again. That does not mean, however, that he was vigilant, still less that it was his habit to take notes, as Gogarty and Eglinton both assert with misleading assurance. The only note he took was the one I have quoted; it was taken in the way I have described. The epiphany means rather that his mind was in that raw state when scenes make indelible impressions, and that false sentiment was his bugbear, all the more repugnant when he was expected to share it.

My mother's death brought about a reconciliation, lasting perhaps a fortnight, between my father and her elder brother, John. There was no intelligible reason for any quarrel, but that did not matter. There was personal antipathy on my father's side and that was enough, though the other party was willing to be friendly. The antipathy was intensified by my father into a bitter, life-long family feud, which was his *raison d'être*. With the younger of her brothers my father's relations were precarious. William Murray, Aunt Josephine's husband and also a heavy drinker, was a good-natured, impulsive man of quite unreliable temper, who was boisterous and often witty when he was tipsy, and generally suffering from a hang-over when he was not. He was proud of the strength of his arm and of his very even white teeth. From time to time my father and he ran into each other in some bar in town and agreed to a truce, but with the elder brother the cold war was permanent.

After the funeral, Uncle Willie accompanied my father home and in the afternoon went with us for a short walk in the country. The weather was dismal but did not preclude a visit to a country pub. When the visit seemed likely to be a lengthy session, my brother cut it short and we returned home. After my uncle had gone, I found my father sitting alone in the parlour whining. Uncontrollable anger seized me. I vented all my seething bitterness on him, forgetting very little. He listened in silence, and when I had done, said without resentment:

—You don't understand, boy.

The one who was most inconsolable was the youngest of the family, Mabel, but called, of course, Baby, a clever and gentle child of about nine whom everybody liked. She died when she was about fourteen, the last victim of our family life. Her childish grief for her mother's death knew no bounds; she could not be quieted. She would steal upstairs and hide in some corner or throw herself on a bed to cry her heart out until she was missed and the others ran up to look for her. It was Jim who succeeded in calming her. He caught her as she was creeping upstairs in tears and made her listen to him. I remember him sitting on the top step of the first flight of stairs with his arm round her, talking to her in a very matter-of-fact voice.

—You must not cry like that, he said, because there is no reason to cry. Mother is in heaven. She is far happier now than she has ever been on earth, but if she sees you crying it will spoil her happiness. You must remember that when you feel like crying. You can pray for her, if you wish. Mother would like that. But you mustn't cry any more.

In the end he succeeded in imposing a calmer grief on the child's mind, for he always had an ascendancy over the girls of the family because of his cleverness, his talents, his good looks, and that even temper which was in striking contrast to mine though we were always together.

A more dramatic version of the death-bed scene is used in *Ulysses* but it is attributed to Malachi Mulligan and is one of his well-aimed stabs. There was never any real hostility between my mother and my brother. I should rather say that every man who has known the torment of thought attaches himself spiritually to one or the other of his parents, when he has left youth behind him and attained maturity, and that in the case of an author the elective affinity strongly influences his artistic production. Those in whom their mother's influence is stronger, are, for the most part, inclined to the narrow-minded wisdom of inflexible judgment; whereas those in whom their father's influence prevails generally show a broader humanity. We know that Shakespeare obtained for his father the title of 'gentleman'. Some commentators insinuate that it was a sly way of inheriting the title himself. Although honouring one's father, when one has little reason to do so, may be a subtle way of honouring oneself, it would not seem outlandish to maintain that Shakespeare was able to set its proper value upon the title he had bought, that he wished to restore to his aging father at Stratford the honour and moderate wealth that he had lost in bankruptcy—and that, in treating the theme of fathers and children, the author of *Hamlet* and *King Lear* could draw upon deep personal feeling. The elective affinities of Sterne, Goldsmith, and Dickens, and on the other hand of Carlyle, Ruskin, Shaw, and Lawrence are well known and bear out the assumption, while Milton must be reckoned an exception.

My mother had become for my brother the type of the woman who fears and, with weak insistence and disapproval, tries to hinder the adventures of the spirit. Above all, she became for him the Irishwoman, the accomplice of the Irish Catholic Church, which he called the scullery-maid of Christendom, the accomplice, that is to say, of a hybrid form of religion produced by the most unenlightened features of Catholicism under the inevitable influence of English Puritanism, the accomplice, in fine, of the vigilant and ruthless enemy of free thought and the joy of living.

The two dominant passions of my brother's life were to be love of father and of fatherland. The latter was not the love of a patriot, which is an emotion for the market-place, part hatred of some other country, part falsehood. It was the comprehending love of an artist for his subject. Both passions stemmed, I believe, from his ancient love of God, and were already at that time spreading tough roots underground in a most unpropitious climate: love of his country, or rather of his city, that was to reject him and his work; love of his father, who was like a mill-stone round his neck. The roots of feeling in some men sink all the deeper for the difficulties that surround and frustrate them; and I wonder that people do not see how much higher than the divine love, which is the preacher's theme, is

that human passion which can love an unworthy object utterly
without return and forgive without waiting to be supplicated.

A week or so after my mother's death, my brother discovered
a packet of letters. They were the letters written to her by my
father before they were married. My brother took a little table
and a chair out into our back garden, and remained there all
the afternoon reading them with as little compunction as that
of a doctor or a lawyer who wants to get at the truth of a
matter and puts questions. When he had finished, I asked:

—Well?

—Nothing, he answered curtly and with some contempt.

Nothing for the young poet with a mission, who applied the
acid test inexorably to the written word; but evidently something for the woman who had kept them through all those
years of squalor and neglect. I burnt them unread.

How necessary my mother's ceaseless efforts had been in
order to keep the family together became apparent soon after
her death. Within two years we were scattered. The eldest
sister, who was nineteen, took over a task that would have taxed
the strength of any woman, and was certainly too difficult for
her to cope with. My mother, when dying, had recommended
the young members of her family to the aunt who had nursed
her, and although Aunt Josephine had six children of her own,
her house was open to us at all times and on all occasions as if
it were our own. There was no limit to her patience. My sister's
main difficulty was to get any money from my father when
he drew his meagre pension. On the twenty-seventh of the
month, when he was paid, he was usually up early and in a
state of high agitation at the thought of all the whisky in view
for that day. As he brushed his hat in the hall, he would keep
humming in a very fair imitation of suppressed anger and

muttering curses against his family, whom he divided roughly into two categories, 'wastrels' and 'little bastards'.

—I'll show you a little trick.

The threat was addressed probably to two or three of the latter category, children of from nine to twelve years of age, who were going out to school; and they, prematurely cynical in self-defence, would answer:

—We know that little trick by heart, Father.

The 'Father' was of course, ironical. In more jovial moments he would tell the fable, culled from Aesop or who knows what medieval bestiary, of how a fox gets rid of its fleas. When the fox is plagued with fleas, he explained, it jumps into the river and swims about until all the fleas collect on its nose. Then it gives one good whiff and blows them all into the water. That's what he would do with the whole bloody lot of us, with the help of God and His Holy Mother, and go back to Cork. He would quote Goldsmith's lines,

> And as a hare, whom hounds and horns pursue,
> Pants at the place from whence at first he flew,
> I still had hopes, my long vexations past,
> There to return—and die at home at last.

—I'll get rid of you all, and go back to Cork. But I will break your hearts before I go. Oh yes, by God! See if I don't. I'll break your hearts, but I'll break your stomachs first.

When in the end he was rid of his family and finally unencumbered, with still twenty-six or twenty-seven years to live, he went about his usual haunts telling anybody that cared to listen to him that his unnatural family had deserted him.

Two of the older girls were admitted to a convent school, and I, despairing of ever getting paid in the accountant's office, left it and found a poorly paid job as a clerk in the Apothe-

caries' Hall. This was an old Protestant institution, the Apothecaries' Hall of Ireland, which had the right to confer degrees
in medicine, and my undeclared intention was to find out
whether I could take a degree in it as a chemist. The work was
easy but uninteresting. It was not difficult to memorize the
abbreviations in use for the commonest drugs and medicines
as well as the few Latin terms that cropped up in prescriptions,
so that when the manager, an Englishman, asked me if I had
ever worked in a chemist's before, and I replied that I had not,
he looked at me suspiciously. I gave my miserable wages to
my sister, but that did not make our situation any easier, for
my father, with the cunning of drunkards, gave proportionately
less.

My brother knew, in a detached way, of my activities as
a clerk. Gogarty, with whom phrase-making was a pastime,
had called my brother 'the scorner of mediocrity and scourge
of the multitude', and, in fact, his attitude towards that lower-
middle-class life which forms the bulk of city life and which
he was to portray with 'scrupulous meanness', was at that time
observant but contemptuous. The detailed acquaintance with
office life which some of the stories show, as well as the end
of one of them, 'Counterparts', he got from my diary and
more fully from me in conversation. When some years later
he was English and French correspondent in a bank in Rome,
he was too outraged by the prevailing servility there to gather
anything to his purpose from that experience. It was not a
'portal of discovery'. In any case, all but the last two stories of
Dubliners were already written.

My brother's friendship with Gogarty was then in its earliest
and best phase. It was frank and spontaneous on both sides.
My brother had found, or thought he had found, another of
his own age in whom the poet's outlook was not a timorous,

cultural attitude, not a thing apart, but an inherent part of life itself for which no apologies were due. He was attracted by Gogarty's talent and freedom of spirit, and amused by his inexhaustible vitality and witty obscenity. Gogarty could be witty on other subjects, too, though less consistently. As for my brother, he was rarely brilliant or lively in conversation. He used to say what he had to say simply, but often it was unexpected and profound. He was not affected with that national itch of Irishmen which produces a kind of wit that is too cerebral and artificial in substance and too mechanical in form. His wit, when it does crop up in his work, as it frequently does, is sardonic. It comes from the heart and seems to be forced out of it by the impact of circumstances. However, liveliness attracted him in others, and in the drab streets of Dublin, the stolid masks of secret and disappointed lives, he and Gogarty made a vital pair.

Jim was, as usual, far less depressed by our conditions at home than I was. He took things as they came with good-humoured, almost gay indifference. When he was paid for his book reviews by the *Daily Express*, he gave part of that small sum towards the upkeep of the house, but said bluntly that it was not his business to support it, and that in any case he had already done enough. He was alluding to the prize money he had won at school, twenty and then thirty pounds each year, most of which he had given freely without its making any appreciable difference in our comfort. As regards work he was at a loose end, and, probably acting on Yeats's suggestion, asked me to give him some titles for essays. I made out a list of half a dozen or so, of which I remember 'Revellers', 'Athletic Beauty', 'A Portrait of the Artist' (I was then reading *The Portrait of a Lady* with boundless admiration), '*Contra Gentiles*' (Jim was reading the *Summa*; I knew only the title, but it struck me as a good one for a modern essay), and 'World-troubling Semen' (the last was intended as a pun on a phrase in Yeats's ballad 'The Madness of King Goll'—'world-troubling seamen', a pun which seemed to me more significant than the original phrase). Nothing came of it for the moment; he wrote no essay then, but he spoke to Gogarty of his intention to write an essay and call it *'Contra Gentiles'*. A short time afterwards Gogarty produced an essay with that title, and showed it to my brother. Jim read the essay, and then turned down and creased and neatly tore off the top of the page that bore the title. Gogarty pooh-poohed the gesture, and made some rambling statement about 'all of us using the same alphabet'.

I asked Jim why he had torn the title off.

—After all, said I, if Gogarty borrowed the title it wasn't yours either.

—I did not tear it off because he borrowed it, said Jim, I tore it off because he wasted it. What he had written was all nonsense.

Two very brief notices of books, rather than reviews, from his pen appeared in the *Daily Express* of September third, 1903. They were written a couple of weeks after my mother's death and are hurried and careless, and yet the shorter one—no more than a few lines—is interesting because it throws a side-light on his choice of a name for the principal character in *A Portrait of the Artist*. It dismisses cursorily a novel in a Pseudonym Library series issued by Fisher Unwin. The title of the novel was *A Ne'er-Do-Well* by Valentine Caryl. My brother wrote, 'After all a pseudonym library has its advantages; to acknowledge bad literature by signature is, in a manner, to persevere in evil'. When a year later his own first stories were published, he yielded to a suggestion (not mine) and used a pseudonym, 'Stephen Daedalus', but then bitterly regretted the self-conceal-ment. He did not feel that he had perpetrated bad literature of which he ought to be ashamed. He had taken the name from the central figure in the novel *Stephen Hero*, which he had already begun to write. Against that name I had protested in vain; but it was, perhaps, his use of the name as a pseudonym that decided him finally on its adoption. He wished to make up for a momentary weakness; in fact, in order further to identify himself with his hero, he announced his intention of appending to the end of the novel the signature, *Stephanus Daedalus Pinxit*.

A few weeks later, on September 17, 1903, another group of reviews by my brother appeared in the *Daily Express*. The regularity of his work for this newspaper shows that the editor bore him no ill-will, in spite of his having slated a book by Lady Gregory. In the discussion in the library, which forms the fifth episode of *Ulysses*, Malachi Mulligan informs Stephen that Longworth, the editor, is 'awfully sick about it'. It is a falsehood or an exaggeration thrown off with an air of irresponsibility but really in the hope of intimidating Stephen, who will thus see that slender source of income threatened. The reader of *Ulysses* who has grasped the character of Malachi Mulligan should be able, I think, to suspect this for himself without knowing it for a fact, and so be in the same position as Stephen.

Some of the reviews are of very slight interest except for certain incidental revelations of personal opinions and antipathies. In a review of a collection of stories (*The Adventures of Prince Aga Mirra*, by Aquila Kempster), some of which are tales of Indian magic while others treat of camp life, he says of the latter that they 'are soundly seasoned with that immature brutality which is always so anxious to be mistaken for virility. But the people who regulate the demand for fiction are being day by day so restricted by the civilisation they have helped to build up that they are not unlike the men of Mandeville's time, for whom enchantments and monsters, and deeds of prowess were so liberally purveyed'.

Shortly after my mother's death in August, my brother began to drink riotously. Until then he had not been a teetotaller, but he had always been abstemious, and none of his friends had been drinkers. Once when he and George Clancy were undergraduates, Clancy had confided to him with no little mortification that he was upset because the evening before he had 'made a night of it' with a group of friends. My brother had listened to him and then said with ironical approval:

—If it is your intention to go to the devil I think you have chosen the shortest and straightest road.

Yet Clancy was by no means a drinker. He studied regularly; besides, he was a sportsman and usually in training for some match or other. In the excitement of a victory, however, he might join his team-mates in a spree. Now my brother had need of his own advice. Gogarty, who was now his closest friend, was a drinker and wanted to have my brother as a companion in his drinking bouts. But whereas Gogarty was robust, my brother had not the *physique du rôle*, nor had he a substantial basis of square meals to help him to carry his liquor. It seems also that Gogarty was beginning to resent my brother's intransigence and air of superiority. He had confided to Elwood (the gypsy-like student in *A Portrait of the Artist*) that he wanted 'to make Joyce drink in order to break his spirit', and Elwood, who was more foolish in manner than in reality, had broken the secret to my brother and to me. Gogarty did not relish my company (he said there was only one freak in the family), but I was so often with my brother that he could not help meeting me.

It so happened that I was with them one day when they were quoting one against another songs from Shakespeare's plays. I believe I can even localize the memory. They were in Berkeley Street, going towards the centre of the city. When trudging after my brother in his reading, I had sometimes attempted to spell out the Latin books he was studying—at Belvedere, Ovid's *Metamorphoses* and Horace in the thick brown second-hand volume with abundant notes, formerly belonging to John Calverly Inverarity, and later, at the University, Virgil. In this last I had found lines which seemed to me applicable to him and Gogarty:

> *Ambo florentes aetatibus, Arcades ambo,*
> *et cantare pares et respondere parati.*

Though I was doubtful now, still the illusion persisted. My brother was reciting Autolycus's song, when at the words

> *The white sheet bleaching on the hedge,*
> *With heigh! the sweet birds, O, how they sing!*
> *Doth set my pugging tooth on edge,*
> *For a quart of ale is a dish for a King*

Gogarty broke in with:

—A quart of ale! A quart of milk is more in your line!

My brother defended his right to appreciation of the song with arguments based on sympathetic understanding. To me the plea sounded rather lame. Gogarty would not listen. He started forward petulantly, waving his arms as if to rid himself of such irrelevant sophisms.

—Oh, I know all about that sort of thing, he exclaimed, Aquinas and the rest of them.

In emulation of Falstaff and the poets of the Mermaid Inn, my brother began drinking sack, which to my astonishment he found in the *Bodega* in Dame Street, but soon he declined upon

Guinness's porter. He was talkative in his cups, and his natural speaking voice, a pleasant tenor, seemed to be keyed up a few tones higher. I hated to see him glossy-eyed and slobbery-mouthed, and I usually told him so heatedly, either on the spot or the morning after.

—It makes me sick, said I, just to look at you.

—Try Bile Beans, advised my brother with soothing sarcasm. I'm sure they'd be the proper diet for you.

—Last night when Byrne brought you home, you were scarcely able to stand. Don't you know that you are disgusting?

—You're a tiresome Puritan.

—Rubbish.

—What's the matter with you is that you're afraid to live. You and people like you. This city is suffering from hemiplegia of the will. I'm not afraid to live.

—Do you call that kind of thing life?

—Yes, I do. What's your favourite definition?

—You thought differently when you were in Paris.

—Perhaps I was different then.

—Do you remember the advice you once gave Clancy? Have you changed your mind on that, too?

—Do I contradict myself? said my brother smiling and quoting Whitman. Very well, then, I contradict myself.

—The fact remains, said I, that except for those reviews, you haven't written anything for months.

—You would like me to put on a nice clean collar and take the tram at nine o'clock down to some office, like a second-division clerk, and then come home in the evening and be a 'pote' and write 'pomes'.

He almost always pronounced these words disparagingly, adopting them in that form from his father's constant gibes.

—Then you don't want to be a writer?

—I don't care if I never write another line. I want to live.
As for writing, he added ironically, I may perhaps employ my
sober moments in correcting the grammatical errors of the more
illiterate among the rugged geniuses.

—That's all nonsense, I replied. You just can't give up writing. This kind of life won't stop you writing; it can only interfere with what you write. It leads nowhere.

—The road of excess, quoted my brother again, leads to the
palace of wisdom.

—Why the hell do you quote that bloody lunatic to me? I
retorted, angrily alluding to Blake. In any case I know the
name of the palace. It's called Bedlam.

—Seeing that you're so full of wise advice for others, said
my brother, again ironical, you ought to start writing yourself,
now that I've 'gone on the beer'.

—I have no talent, said I, dismissing the gibe and then returning to the main topic. But for the life of me I can't imagine
what you have to say to those drunken yahoos of medical students. That stumps me.

—At least, they don't bore me as you do, said my brother.

So began the long struggle between us, in which I lost the
first tussle, won the second, and retired, declining the third.*
My brother, who never did things by halves, was soon career-
ing along the road of excess at full gallop. He became the hero
of a rowdy group of students, chiefly medical, whose own excesses, however, were still tempered by some invisible control.
They recounted his wild exploits and mishaps amid abundant
laughter. His odd manner of dressing suited the part he was

---

* Professor Joyce refers to his first attempt to stop his brother's drinking in
Trieste, which ended when James Joyce went to Rome in 1906; to his second
and more successful attempt after his brother's return to Trieste in 1907; and
to his refusal to try again to stop him after the World War, when James was
in Trieste in 1919-1920.

now to play. In a conventional city such as Dublin was, even
slight deviations from the normal are noticed at once. My
brother's tall, slender figure and bohemian garb were bound to
catch the eye: the flowing butterfly bow, the inevitable ash-
plant, and the round wide-brimmed soft felt hat, which in that
Dublin of the past was much in favour with Protestant ministers. The echoes of his drinking bouts generally reached my
ears at once, and I could hear, as the latest and greatest jest,
how after swilling all night he sank insensible under the table
and was borne by his boon companions on their shoulders to
some neighbouring park or garden to sleep on the grass there
and digest his drunkenness in the open air. It seems that one of
the group walked in front, intoning and carrying my brother's
hat hoisted on his ash-plant after the manner of a processional
cross. Some little ragamuffins who were still in the street at
that late hour began to run and cut capers around the mock
funeral, and, seeing the hat, shouted to one another:

—Yurah, come and look at the drunken Protestan' minister.
Did ye ever see the like? He's blind to Jaysus.*

A poet, whether great or minor there is little basis for judg-
ing, was drowned in those carousals. If my memory is correct
my brother wrote no more poems until many, perhaps ten,
years later, and then they were those few incidental songs of a
very personal character that are included in *Pomes Penyeach*.
Frustration was, perhaps, inevitable. High-spirited ambitions
and poetic feeling could not run in harness with the base, or
even the jog-along, emotions his surroundings afforded. Disaster must overtake the charioteer. And yet, in the economy of
nature, the drinking revels may have served some purpose in

---

* 'Jay, look at the drunken minister coming out of the maternity hospital?
Benedicat vos omnipotens Deus, Pater et Filius. A make, mister. The Denzille
lane boys. . . . Parson Steve, apostates' creed.' *Ulysses*, pp. 405-406 (417).

the formation of the disillusioned realist who was to be the interpreter of that sottish capital.

If I did not choose to follow my brother's example, he nevertheless found at home a substitute disciple in intemperance. The youngest surviving brother, Charlie, the one who had been in a seminary, began to drink rather heavily for a youth of his age, so that I sometimes had to cope with three drunken men at the same time. Another, perhaps, might have been able to distil low comedy out of a situation in which a drunken father rails at two drunken sons for being drunk, but I fancy that to do so one must know the situation only at second hand. The hobbledehoy Charlie had found a job in the office of a wine-merchant in a small way, where, though there was only one other clerk, he had little to do. Unluckily for him the wine-merchant was a careless man in his forties, who was as fond of women as of wine, and sometimes on Saturday afternoons he took his young clerk about with him from public house to public house, amused to see how much drink he could stand.

Charlie, though not a 'particularly stupid boy' as the rector of his seminary had called him, was not clever, but he was not without talent. He had had a very pure soprano as a boy, and when his voice developed, which it did slowly, it was fuller in tone and stronger than Jim's. There were facilities for gratuitous voice training in Dublin, as Jim frequently pointed out, but for any study a minimum of regularity is requisite, and in our house one had always the impression of being in an open boat on a choppy sea. Charlie got it into his head, however, that he would like to be an actor, and, after a summary test, was accepted by a little company which was to go on tour to country towns and give patriotic plays such as *Lord Edward, or Ninety-eight*, or comedies like *Con the Shagraun*. As well as I can remember, he was expected to pay his own fare. I foolishly interfered. I could foresee nothing but starvation for him. I imagined him thrown out of the company for turning up drunk at the theatre and being left stranded in some out-of-the-way place without a penny in his pocket. I did not reflect that the manager would soon have discovered that his voice could be an asset to the company, and would have turned it to good use, and that in any case to interfere in other people's lives is generally to assume an unwarrantable risk. In fact, we were living like gipsies, so it did not really make much difference if he got stranded somewhere. Charlie might have learned something on the road, for besides his voice he had a good presence. At the worst he could have tramped home. Moreover, his life could hardly have taken a more unfortunate course than it did eventually. At any rate, I went to the actor-manager's poor lodgings and made some excuse for breaking off the engagement.

Charlie was as tall as Jim but a good deal stronger. As a boy he had been the strongest of us four in spite of his clumsiness. He was good-looking in a small-featured way, with dark hair inclining to curl, and had in abundance that silly vanity which stands actors and singers in such good stead in their careers. Girls liked him. When he walked along the street with his head in the air, it was like a procession of one. Charlie now conceived that he was a poet, and, not venturing to show his efforts to Jim, he confided them to me, and I relayed them to Jim for his amusement. One prose poem which Charlie had recited to me in a far-away chaunt described an amorous adventure, and ended dramatically with the words, 'In the silvery moonlight that flooded the room, I took off her drawers'. I also quoted one of his poems, containing the lines

> *Her milky breast, so full of woe,*
> *Doth rise beneath a fall of lace.*

The fluctuations of the milk situation in this sad Amazon, together with my sour way of repeating the lines, were too much
for Jim. He screeched with laughter.

My brother's own lyrical vein had dried up in the mood
closely akin to disgust that now possessed him. The sensual
romantic attitude towards love no longer satisfied him and his
own part as singer of it had come to seem to him a poor kind of
comedy. The scrolls on which he had transcribed his poems
lay neglected and unopened in his desk in their shiny black
wrapper of limp glacé leather. The only poems which he still
added to the collection were 'He who hath glory lost' and 'I
hear an army charging upon the land'—an actual dream which
for some reason had troubled him—and I do not remember
whether they had the honour of being inscribed in the centre
of the usual folio sheet. He did not openly declare any change,
except in the defiant and half-ironical declaration that I have
quoted, but he was no longer willing to lend his poems to anybody. He had shown or recited poems to various people from
time to time as he wrote them, but he had lent the whole collection only to Gogarty, Yeats, Russell, and one or two others.
While Russell had them in his keeping, he showed them to
George Moore. Moore read some of them languidly and then
handed them back to Russell with one weary word of criticism.

—Symons!

They were, he opined, mere imitations of Arthur Symons.
There was some talk about my brother's wild life, in which
John Eglinton, who was present, and Gogarty, the source of my
information, took part. Eglinton had heard that my brother
'was going the way of Maginn and Burns to ruin'; Gogarty
mentioned his keenness on women. That, too, Moore waved
aside.

—We have all kissed women, he pronounced. If we have not kissed them on the mouth, we have kissed them otherwhere.

Then up spoke stout John Eglinton, and

—I never did it, said he.

His words became a catch phrase with Gogarty's medical friends to be used in various contingencies by that group of ribalds. My brother laughed at Gogarty's story, and said that Eglinton was a sad example of horrible virginity. He nicknamed him 'the horrible virgin'.

And yet the idea of sin and virginity—two obsessions with things of no moment that astonished me—had not altogether lost their hold on his imagination, as if the memory of the keener zest they had given to the enjoyment of women still lingered on. An epiphany which he wrote at this time marks the end of his brief appearance in the garb of a 'piping poet':

Here are we come together, wayfarers; here are we housed, amid intricate streets, by night and silence closely covered. In amity we rest together, well content, no more remembering the deviousness of the ways that we have come. What moves upon me from the darkness subtle and murmurous as a flood, passionate and fierce with an indecent movement of the loins? What leaps, crying in answer, out of me, as eagle to eagle in mid air, crying to overcome, crying for an iniquitous abandonment? *

---

* 'Together, folded by the night, they lay on earth. I hear
From far her low word breathe on my breaking brain.
Come! I yield. Bend deeper upon me! I am here.
Subduer, do not leave me! Only joy, only anguish,
Take me, save me, soothe me, O spare me!'
'A Prayer' in *Pomes Penyeach.*

That he disliked prostitutes though he had recourse to them—
and especially disliked the more successful ones—appears from
this fleeting memory of a Parisian scene:

> They pass in twos and threes amid the life of the boulevard,
> walking like people who have leisure in a place lit up for them.
> They are in the pastry-cook's, chattering, crushing little fabrics
> of pastry, or seated silently at tables by the café door, or
> descending from carriages with a busy stir of garments, soft as
> the voice of the adulterer. They pass in an air of perfumes:
> under the perfumes their bodies have a warm humid smell. . . .
> No man has loved them, and they have not loved themselves:
> they have given nothing for all that has been given them.

'Indecent', 'iniquitous', 'adulterer'—my brother, I am afraid,
never quite rid himself of that Iago complex towards women,
radix malorum, which he imbibed in youth and which is distinctive of the medieval Catholic Church, and perhaps of all the
Christian churches. In these, striving to wean men from the love
of women to the love of God, it is logical, however absurd; in
my brother, it was just illogical and residuary.

This period marks a change not only in his life but in his
outlook of life; with him the two things were inseparable. Two
foreseeable results of his manner of life were that it attracted
more attention among the many that knew him than if the
change had not been sudden, and that many wild escapades
were mischievously attributed to him or invented for him only
because they seemed to be in character. Gogarty playfully spread
a few, as Malachi Mulligan does about Dedalus, and Gorman in
his life of my brother has fallen for many of them. One story,
which had at least the merit of being funny, will serve as typical
of many. Something brought Gogarty and my brother one afternoon to the room or rooms of the Hermetic Society. I think

they were looking for Russell, for the Hermetic Society was a place where young would-be mystics met under the brooding wings of 'their master dear' * to read esoteric poetry, hear discourse of the Father, Son, and 'Holy Breath' and generally to discuss the dreamy and visionary short-cut to the solution of the riddle of the Universe. For me, of course, it was the 'Emetic Society'.

The room was empty at that hour, but in a corner the two ribalds found George Roberts' travelling-bag. George Roberts, afterwards manager for Maunsel and Company, was a member or frequenter of the Society and had addressed poems to his 'master dear', but in the flesh he was then a commercial traveller for women's underwear. Gogarty found a pair of open drawers in the bag, stretched them out by tying the strings to two chairs, and by means of another chair fixed the handle of the Hermetic broom between the legs of the drawers, while on the hoisted head of it he hung a placard bearing the legend 'I never did it' and signed 'John Eglinton'.

The first to arrive that evening were Russell and Miss Mitchell together, and when later other members arrived, Russell told them in high disdain that on entering the room he had discovered 'an obscene effigy set up there by Joyce'. He should have verified his facts. I have read somewhere that Gogarty and my brother took the rest of the 'swag from Maunsel's manager's travelling-bag' † and distributed it joyously among their delighted female friends. That seems to me improbable. Commercial houses have scant sympathy with bohemianism. Roberts would have had to answer for his samples and would certainly have protested. He did not do so.

Rumours of my brother's wild dissipation reached the Sheehys

---

* Professor Joyce is quoting his brother's broadside, 'The Holy Office'.
† The quotation is from another broadside, 'Gas from a Burner'.

almost overnight, one may suppose, and very probably in the form of stories, curiously illuminated with ancient traditional Irish art, to which

All who told them added something new,
And all who heard them made enlargements, too.

At any rate, one Sunday night coming away from the Sheehys' house in a group, my brother suggested taking a stroll as it was a very fine starlit night. A certain member of the little group, however, an undistinguished dullard at school and at the University and a comically self-satisfied blockhead ever after, said he was going home because he was tired. He had been up at seven that morning, he said, to go to early Mass and he had to get up early the following morning, too.

—I withdraw the motion, said my brother amiably. It must have been close on eleven when I got up this morning; but I know you are a man of regular habits.

—And I don't drink, added the rude blockhead pointedly.

—*La riposte courtoise*, commented my brother.

I was not present at the brief passage at arms, but when my brother came home, he related it to me as an example of the way in which 'people' (not specified) were making his supposed dissipation a byword in the town. He made the same complaint in Trieste, where it was certainly unfounded, and, I have been told, also in Zurich, for young rakes who paint the town red always expect the inhabitants to be colour-blind.

His 'supposed dissipation' did not prevent him from being invited to a dance at the Sheehys' to celebrate, I think, an engagement. They were a religious but not a narrow-minded family. I had been omitted from the last invitations without

regret on either side. To be able to go to the dance, Jim had
to borrow a dress-suit from Gogarty, and although Gogarty
was bulkier and there was some slight difference in height, Jim
looked well in his borrowed finery. The dance was at least
the occasion for an epiphany in which the girl in whose honour
the dance was given figures anonymously.

She is engaged. She dances with them in the round—a white
dress lightly lifted as she dances, a white spray in her hair; eyes
a little averted, a faint glow on her cheek. Her hand is in mine
for a moment, softest of merchandise.
—You very seldom come here now.
—Yes, I am becoming something of a recluse.
—I saw your brother the other day. . . . He is very like
you.
—Really?
She dances with them in the round—evenly, discreetly, giving
herself to none. The white spray is ruffled as she dances, and
when she is in shadow the glow is deeper on her cheek.

I cannot be certain who the subject of this epiphany was but
I surmise that it was the same girl that prompted the following
epiphany, which, however, he had written before the one
already quoted:

Her arm is laid for a moment on my knees and then withdrawn and her eyes have revealed her—secret, vigilant, an
enclosed garden—in a moment. I remember a harmony of red
and white that was made for one like her, telling her names
and glories, bidding her arise, as for espousal, and come away,
bidding her look forth, a spouse, from Amana and from the
mountains of the leopards. And I remember that response

whereto the perfect tenderness of the body and the soul with
all its mystery have gone: Inter ubera mea commorabitur.*

Whoever the girl was, she awoke in his heart memories of
the Song of Solomon, which are traceable in *Chamber Music*.

> *Wind of spices whose song is ever*
> *Epithalamium.*
>
>   .   .   .   .
>
> *Now, wind, of your good courtesy*
> *I pray you go,*
> *And come into her little garden*
> *And sing at her window . . .*
>
>   .   .   .   .
>
> *My dove, my beautiful one,*
> *Arise, arise!*
>
>   .   .   .   .
>
> *I wait by the cedar tree,*
> *My sister, my love.*

At Trieste we went together to see *Il Cantico dei Cantici* by
Giacosa.† It is a short comedy in which Giacosa, to be in the
anti-clerical fashion of this time, derides the Song of Solomon
in the tone and manner that best appeal to the top-gallery. His
anti-clericalism was misplaced. The Song of Solomon is not,

---

* 'The book which he used for these visits was an old neglected book written
by Saint Alphonsus Liguori, with fading characters and sere foxpapered leaves.
A faded world of fervent love and virginal responses seemed to be evoked
for his soul by the reading of its pages in which the imagery of the canticles
was interwoven with the communicant's prayers. An inaudible voice seemed
to caress the soul, telling her names and glories, bidding her arise as for
espousal and come away, bidding her look forth, a spouse, from Amana and
from the mountains of the leopards; and the soul seemed to answer with
the same inaudible voice, surrendering herself: *Inter ubera mea commorabitur.*'
A Portrait of the Artist, p. 173 (176).
† Giuseppe Giacosa (1847-1906), Italian dramatist and librettist.

in origin at least, a religious poem. It is quite plainly a nuptial ballad for two voices and a chorus, and may well be the greatest ever written. My brother was violently angry and would have come away from the theatre but that he wanted to see the piece that followed it. In the interval, he told Francini, who was with us, that Giacosa 'is a paunchy vulgarian whose highest ideal in life is a bellyful of *pasta asciutta*'. Francini agreed, and when we went home, they revenged themselves by reading *Canticum Canticorum Solomonis* in the Latin Vulgate in order to take the taste of *Il Cantico dei Cantici* off their mouths.

I surmise, however, that these fugitive literary *études*, which seem to be attempts at lyrical poems in prose, were the only expression that the attraction which the girl had for him ever received. If the two had spoken, I should have heard of it. He was not secretive, and if he had been deeply moved, something would have happened. He would not have allowed any sincere emotion to peter out, as here, in words, but neither was he the kind of youth that dupes himself into belief in the grand passion. He was dissatisfied with both of these trivial fond records and rejected them. I have kept them because I felt then that they were straws in the wind, and that they would form a graceful exit of the all-for-love theme. He was dissatisfied with them not only as literary exercises, but more significantly with the mood that prompted them.

[The manuscript ends here.]

Index